I0096003

Praise for Jack Roney

'Fast and furious! No, this is not some rev head Vin Diesel movie, it's *The Demons Woke*, the second novel in Jack Roney's series of Jarrod O'Connor detective novels. Jack was a cop in real life: better yet, a detective – and not only does he know his stuff when it comes to police action, detection and forensics, he can write! The action in *The Demons Woke* makes it unputdownable. Don't read this one if you want a good night's sleep.'
Gary Crew, Professor Emeritus Creative Writing UniSC/Author.

'Jack Roney draws on his 30-plus years of policing experience to take you on a highly charged, suspenseful and authentic crime story. He exposes the raw underbelly of society's darkest secrets and disturbing behaviours towards the most vulnerable. *The Demons Woke* is another page-turning thriller you won't put down until its riveting conclusion.'
Darryl Elliott Green, Twiceshot.com.

'Gripping. Terrifying. Had me on the edge of my seat cover to cover.'
Bryn Smith, Author.

'Jack Roney takes you on one hell of a ride in this explosive sequel to *The Angels Wept*. Likeable characters, murder, intrigue and a game of cat and mouse. It's been a long time since I've read a book I couldn't put down. *The Demons Woke* is a fantastic read.'
J.A. Bryden, Author.

'Jack Roney has given us another gripping police procedural with twists and turns that keep the reader guessing. A complex web of murders, revenge and the hunt for a dangerous predator. Detective Jarrod O'Connor is a flawed hero who must battle his own demons while trying to solve the case.'
Richard Evans, Author.

Praise for Jack Roney

'This gritty crime novel is infused with tender moments, setting it apart from other police procedurals. I warmed to Jarrod O'Connor, a tough and compassionate cop who breaks the stereotype of the hard-boiled detective. The Australian small-town setting was relatable, the characters authentic and action scenes realistic and compelling. The story was gripping and heart wrenching with a powerful and emotive ending.'
Vicky Stevens, Author.

'One of the best crime novels I've ever read, a thrilling mystery from start to finish. Detective Jarrod has to be one of the most heartfelt cop characters in fiction and the criminals range from horribly human to truly tragic.'
Nita Delgado, Editor.

'Jack Roney masterfully takes us on a string of strange cases that test the fortitude of Detective Jarrod O'Connor. Roney brings us through the intense, fast-paced world of a criminal investigation, while also showing us how difficult life is for people within the police force. My heart ached for O'Connor so many times. There were times when I laughed out loud, many more when I was moved to tears, and a few times when I was on the edge of my seat! If you are looking for a fast-paced crime tale that will absolutely leave you wanting for more, then this is it!'
S.Faxon, Author/ Creative Director of No Bad Books Press.

A DETECTIVE JARROD O'CONNOR STORY

JACK RONEY

THE DEMONS WOKE

BOOK TWO IN THE SERIES

Published in Australia in 2023 by Hawkeye Publishing.

Cover Design by Alex Jay MacDonald

A catalogue record of this book is available from the National Library of Australia.

ISBN 9780645714920

Proudly printed in Australia.

www.hawkeyepublishing.com.au
www.hawkeyebooks.com.au

PROLOGUE

THE darkened room was his temporary refuge. Alone in the gloom, he hid from prying eyes, free from scorn. There were no mirrors down there, no reflections. He peered through a gap in the drawn curtains, the window ajar and glass distorted with age. Dwindling rays of sunlight caught dust particles and fell to the floor. Background shapes were monochrome shadows.

The world had abandoned him, discarded him as trash – a forgotten footnote. But soon *they* would fear him. His hunger for revenge intensified with each passing day. Hate drove him. He knew what had to be done. They didn't know the suffering coming for them. As they drew their final breaths, he would make them understand. Then they would beg for mercy, for forgiveness they didn't deserve.

He waited as the setting sun kissed the peak of the roof across the street. His heart raced when *she* walked by. He squinted, his eyes following her as she meandered along the footpath. She didn't notice him. She never did. For a fleeting moment, she consumed his entire world. He blinked and she was gone.

He sniffed the air, searching for her lingering fragrance. Every day he watched her walk by, his gaze burning through her clothing, caressing her skin. He longed to touch her, to savour the warmth of her body against his. His urges grew stronger. He craved her. She would be the first kill. He imagined her eyes dimming as life drained away. She had sealed her own fate the day their paths crossed, the inexplicable moment their destinies entwined. His plans were set in motion, the momentum unstoppable.

He focused on his breathing and the rhythm of his beating heart. Outside, the dusk sky bled into night. The street took on the look of an old photograph, everything a shade of grey. The stars and moon cowered behind a curtain of cloud. He reached over, grimacing. A sharp pain shot through his temple. He flicked on a lamp, shrouding him in a sepia glow. His muscular frame cast a long shadow up the wall. His fingers traced the ridges of scar tissue smeared down one side of his face, hardened like cooled lava.

The searing pain had never left him, not since *that* day. He'd learned to live with the endless burning, the torture. Sleep eluded him. His fingertips stroked the coarse skin where his eyebrow used to be. He caressed the melted flesh on the side of his face and top lip as he swallowed more painkillers with a chug of whiskey.

He turned off the lamp and lay on the bed, his stare carving through the blackness towards the ceiling. The booze and pills took hold, and he became lost in his fantasies. His mind swirled and his thoughts returned to her. She didn't know it yet, but she was already dead.

ONE

A Monday morning in early November. The trial was adjourned the previous Friday afternoon for the judge to consider legal argument. The jury had been stood down, a bad sign. Detective Sergeant Jarrod O'Connor faced the front of the old courtroom. He shot a furtive glance towards Daniel Barkley, the smug little shit seated beside his defence counsel. Daniel's eyes skipped around the courtroom, basking in the attention. He looked over his shoulder to Jarrod, the corners of his mouth rising to an unsettling grin. When Jarrod had earlier given his evidence, the sixteen-year-old delinquent stared him down with scheming eyes. Jarrod had fought the urge to jump out of the witness box and backhand the smirk off his face. The boy's father had spawned a clone. Eric Barkley sat behind Jarrod, eyes boring into the back of his head.

Mid-morning sunlight breached the blinds of semi-circular windows, breaking up the monotony of freshly painted walls. The room was a time capsule from the heritage days but smelled of new carpet.

Judge Boyne folded chubby arms across a round belly, grey tufts of hair poking out from under the curls of his wig. 'The court has considered the evidence, or lack thereof,' he began, addressing the bar table in a condescending tone. He cast a sceptical eye at the Crown Prosecutor over the rim of his bifocals, a plump roll forming under his lowered chin.

The judge continued. 'I need not remind counsel that it is up to the Crown to prove the defendant child's guilt. There is no onus on the defendant child to prove his innocence. I am of the view the Crown has not met the required standard of proof. The defendant child has no case to answer and is dismissed of all charges. He is free to leave the custody of the court.'

He slammed his gavel on the bench. 'This court is adjourned.' He stood with a groan.

The bailiff fumbled with a folder of paperwork and shot to his feet. 'Silence, all stand,' he bellowed like a town crier.

The creaks of nineteenth-century furniture and murmurs filled the room as the public gallery rose to its feet. Judge Boyne nodded and disappeared into his chambers.

Jarrod felt numb. His stomach turned into a clenched fist that punched up into his throat. His entire case had unravelled before his eyes. Daniel Barkley had gotten off. He'd assaulted an elderly woman and robbed her in broad daylight. The evidence spoke for itself, but the court declared the victim's identification of her assailant unreliable. The judge also deemed Barkley's partial admissions during the record of interview inadmissible because, in his view, the boy may not have understood his right to silence. What a joke.

Daniel Barkley rose from his seat with a triumphant fist pump. With the other hand, he formed a heavy metal sign of horns with his index and little fingers. Turning to meet his father, awkward embraces and backslapping followed. The Barkleys celebrated their victory, joined by their gloating defence counsel, Winston Sheffield, fees paid courtesy of taxpayer funded legal aid.

Jarrod watched the pompous barrister tilt his pointy chin and pout his lips, thin nose prominent. Sheffield wore a cocksure grin, basking in self-importance. His lanky arms appeared from beneath his black gown as he reached up and removed his wig. He shook his client's hand. Jarrod didn't catch what Eric Barkley said, but Sheffield patted his back like old chums, his hyena laugh filling the room. They chatted briefly before parting company. Daniel Barkley swaggered towards the exit, swaying one arm across his torso like a gangster. His father followed, giving Jarrod one last death stare for good measure. As the courtroom emptied, Jarrod seethed.

He dreaded telling Mrs Richardson. She'd suffered a broken hip when Daniel Barkley shoved her onto the pavement as he yanked her handbag from her frail grasp. *Bloody little mongrel.*

Mrs Richardson had endured her time in the witness box, badgered by Sheffield until she didn't know up from down. So flustered by his rapid-fire questioning, her evidence became a confused muddle. Sheffield seemed to revel in her suffering, a little too much even for a lawyer. It sickened Jarrod to watch. He had forced himself to look away as the poor woman squirmed in the witness box. The ordeal traumatised her more than the assault itself. He promised he'd take care of her, support her through the court process. The justice system had let her down. No, he'd let her down.

Jarrod swallowed hard against the bitter tang in his mouth, his throat closing. His muscles ached from sitting rigid and clenching his jaw. He left through the side entrance onto the veranda, making his way down the stairs to the courthouse lawns. He passed between parallel rows of agapanthus gardens in early bloom, their tubular purple flowers clinging to long stems, indifferent to the dramas unfolding in the adjacent courthouse.

The court precinct hugged the Kings Park botanical gardens. He stopped under the cool shade of a Bunya Pine, gazing out at the lace-trimmed rotunda and war memorial, piecing together his broken case. He wondered how it all went wrong. How could he have done things differently? From the corner of his eye, he caught Eric and Daniel Barkley sauntering by. Heat came from Eric Barkley's stare. The spring inside Jarrod coiled even tighter.

'Suck shit, copper. Ha ha!' chuckled Daniel as he gave Jarrod the bird.

His father muttered through one side of his mouth. 'You and your family better watch ya back, pig.'

Red mist clouded Jarrod's vision. He bounded towards Eric Barkley, grabbing him by the scruff of his shirt. He slammed the man's back hard against the rough bark of a tree. Jarrod caught himself and glanced around the park. Deserted, no witnesses.

'Threaten my family again. Let's see what happens,' Jarrod whispered in his ear, words even and low as he wedged Barkley against the old oak. Stale alcohol leached from the man's pores. 'Come on then, you smart-mouthed piece of shit, have a go. Go on.' Jarrod held his grip firm, hands clenched into balls against Barkley's throat.

He applied even more pressure as Barkley grimaced. 'Come on, arsehole! I'm all yours. Let's finish this right here, right now. Whaddya say?'

Barkley stared back, wide-eyed and startled. He stood frozen, hands clutching at Jarrod's fists. Jarrod pulled Barkley away from the tree and released his grip, allowing him to drop to his knees, gagging.

'Yeah, I thought as much. Gutless cowards, both of you.' Jarrod fought to control his rage, angrier with himself for letting the Barkleys get to him.

Daniel had nothing to say, his eyes bulging and mouth gaping. Jarrod glared at him and then walked away.

Daniel's bravado returned, firing one last shot over his shoulder. 'See ya around, *Jarrod*.'

The way he said his name made Jarrod's skin crawl. He stopped without turning around. He inhaled through his nose, releasing the air through gritted teeth, and kept on walking.

Screw them.

TWO

JARROD walked along the footpath of the main street through the business centre to the Lockyer police station, his second home. Lately, he'd spent more time there than he did with his family. Drained of energy, he trudged up the stairs. The court case had taken its toll. Detective Senior Constable Brad Harding, busy on the phone, gave Jarrod a wave as he walked in. Together, they formed the two-man Youth Crime Unit.

Jarrod hung his suit jacket on the back of his chair and dropped his briefcase on the floor. He tugged at his necktie and undid the top button. He sat at his desk and sighed at the pile of paperwork. He needed a coffee and signalled to Brad if he wanted one. Brad scrunched his face and shook his head.

Jarrod went to the tea-room and concocted a potent brew of caterer's blend instant coffee. Back in the office, he slumped in his chair and blew steam off his "best dad ever" mug. He sipped. The bitterness reminded him of a scene from the first Austin Powers movie. '*This coffee tastes like shit. It's a bit nutty.*' Picturing the international man of mystery's teeth and lips smeared with liquid poo made Jarrod smile, despite himself. Katie had loved that movie from the time she could stand, propping herself against the coffee table, jiggling her bottom to the beat of the goofy theme song. 'Yeah, Baby,' were among her first words. She belly-laughed at the zany antics and colourful characters, oblivious to the one-liners and risqué gags. In hindsight, probably not the best parenting.

Happy memories emerged, of clippy-cloppy high-heeled plastic shoes, tiaras, pink tutus, onesie pyjamas and a Dorothy the Dinosaur tail strapped around his little girl's waist. A time before lost innocence. Disturbing images clouded his thoughts, like black ink swirling in milk. He wished he could turn back time and return to those simple days before darkness had crept into their lives.

Brad got off the phone. 'Back so soon? What happened?'

Jarrod snapped out of his daze and swivelled his chair to face Brad. 'Huh?'

'How did court go?'

'Oh, um. Let me put it this way. What's the difference between a catfish and a lawyer?'

Brad leaned back and folded his arms with a grin. His expression said he knew the punchline. 'One's a cold-blooded bottom feeder and the other is a fish.'

Jarrod put his coffee down and rubbed his stiff neck. 'Court sucked if you really want to know. Barkley walked.'

'You shitting me? That case was watertight. You had Sheffield defending, right?'

Jarrod nodded. 'And Judge Boyne.'

Brad shook his head. 'Say no more.'

Jarrod motioned to Brad's desk phone. 'What was that about?'

'Children's Services. They've made a court application for a child protection order. They're taking a baby into care and need our help. Expecting trouble from the parents, especially the old man. Emergency briefing at their office as soon as we can get there.'

Jarrod sighed. 'Bloody hell. I hate those jobs.' He closed his eyes and rubbed his temples. 'Righto. Give me a minute. I have to call Mrs Richardson.' Jarrod's gut churned.

The call didn't go well.

No time to reflect on old jobs. He placed the Daniel Barkley folder in his filing cabinet and slammed the heavy metal drawer closed, filed for good. Ancient history. More jobs waited, as usual.

He didn't expect things to change.

THREE

JARROD and Brad approached the front counter of the Children's Services office. Maureen, the administration assistant, poked her head up behind the glass security panel. Her guarded look softened, her eyes smiling over a pair of bifocals. She buzzed them through an internal security door, apparently expecting them.

'Hello, detectives. Right this way.' She motioned for Jarrod and Brad to follow, guiding them through a maze of workstations divided by partitions.

Each workstation reflected the personality of their owners. Candid photographs, crayon drawings and child protection posters were pinned to corkboards. Framed pictures of loved ones on desks, buried behind piles of paperwork and case folders. Knick-knacks and caricatures were blu-tacked to the top of computer screens.

The open plan office hummed with voices talking on phones and fingers tapping on keyboards. Other phones rang unanswered as case workers held discussions with team leaders in private huddles. Some juggled two phone calls at once, while others flicked through case files and entered reports onto their computer terminals. A case worker recognised Jarrod and waved, rolling her eyes while feigning sincerity to an irate client on the phone.

Maureen led them down a corridor to a cramped conference room. An oval-shaped meeting table and tan chairs from the seventies were crammed into the room, a whiteboard up front.

'Take a seat, gentlemen. Somebody will be with you soon.'

'Thanks, Maureen.' Brad gave her a wink and a smile.

She blushed and dabbed at the bobby pin holding her fringe in place.

'Lady's man,' Jarrod said after Maureen scurried from the room.

'Hey, I'm just keeping my options open. You know what they say about the older ladies.' Brad nudged Jarrod in the stomach with his elbow as he sat down.

'Yeah, well, I wouldn't know. You can keep the details of your love life to yourself. How is Cindy, by the way? You've been back together for what, two months?'

Brad chuckled. 'Cindy's great. My pad has never been so tidy.'

'I might just tell her you said that.'

They both jumped as the door swung open and banged against a chair.

'Hello, Jarrod. Brad. Sorry. I didn't mean to startle you.' Stony-faced, Cassie Turnbull strode into the room with an armful of case files. A young social worker hovered behind, flashing an apprehensive smile that didn't reach her eyes.

'Ah, don't worry about it, Cas. Nerves of steel us detectives have,' said Brad.

'Good to hear, you'll need them for this job.'

Cassie, a tall woman in her mid-forties with a frightful mauve rinse in her boyish hairstyle, wore enormous hoop earrings, green eyeshadow and bright red lipstick. She rocked cargo pants, boots and a denim shirt beneath a leather vest with tassels, a hint of hippie. The scent of cigarette smoke mingled with her perfume. Jarrod and Cassie had been on countless joint child protection jobs together. He respected her competence and take-no-shit attitude.

The rookie, short and plump, looked early twenties and fresh out of university. Dressed plainly with flat shoes, she wore no make-up, her mousey hair styled in a bob. She nibbled the fingernails of one hand and fumbled with a notepad and pen in the other. Jarrod guessed she was the new replacement for Sarah Morgan who'd been charged with official misconduct.

They sat and Cassie placed the case files on the table. 'Jarrod, Brad, this is Natalie. Thanks for coming so soon. Here's the profile of the family. It's a sad history.'

She shuffled the files and selected a folder. 'Karl Mundy and Kimberley Hewitt blew into town five days ago. Both are in their early thirties. The information we have is they travelled up in their combi-van from Sydney, passing through Lockyer on their way north looking for fruit picking work. Kimberley was thirty-six weeks pregnant. They stopped at a rest stop on the highway where she went into labour and gave birth on the floor of a public toilet. Karl dropped mum and bub off at the base hospital. Kimberley discharged herself the next day, but the baby, a little girl they called Zalia, remained in hospital with respiratory issues, most likely caused by neonatal abstinence syndrome.'

Jarrod caught Brad's look of confusion.

'Illicit drug withdrawals,' said Cassie, pausing to make sure they were still on the same page.

Brad scribbled notes. Jarrod gave Cassie a nod. 'Go on.'

'This morning, they came and took the baby. The hospital staff couldn't stop them. Karl was aggressive. The hospital called us, but it was too late. They had given their address as site sixteen, Riverside Caravan Park.'

Brad cut in. 'That bloody caravan park is a disgrace. I don't know why the Council hasn't done something about it. It's full of ferals. That poor little baby.'

'We prefer to call them clients, that's the politically correct term.' Cassie lowered her voice, as though the walls had hidden microphones. 'But yes, it *is* full of ferals.'

She referred to the file again and continued. 'But it gets a lot worse, I'm afraid. Before they snatched the baby, Karl and Kimberley would come to the hospital to visit her, high as kites. Kimberley had a black eye and bruises to her upper arms. The hospital staff noted Karl showed no affection towards the baby. Kimberley presented as having an intellectual impairment. The paediatrician is concerned she doesn't have the skills to care for a newborn. Karl dominated over Kimberley, making all the decisions. We've received the file from our Sydney office and these people have an alarming history. Kimberley has two other children, fathers unknown, who were taken into care because of physical abuse and neglect. Karl and Kimberley both have a history of drug abuse. We believe Karl has an extensive criminal history. Of most concern, we believe he spent time in prison in Western Australia for the manslaughter of a three-year-old boy, the child of his former girlfriend.'

'This is a real shit sandwich,' said Brad.

'Yep, that it is,' said Cassie. 'Can you guys confirm his criminal history records?'

Jarrod turned to Brad and opened his mouth to speak.

Brad returned a knowing nod. 'On it. I'll call the station. Give me a minute.' He squeezed out of the conference room as he dialled and spoke into his mobile phone out in the corridor.

'It sounds like we're dealing with a nasty piece of work,' said Jarrod.

Cassie gave Jarrod a sharp look and sucked in a mouthful of air. 'You could say that.' She slid a document across the table. 'Here's a copy of the Emergency Child Protection Order the magistrate issued today. We need to take this baby into care so we can have her medically assessed. The mother refused to breastfeed, and we're concerned their money is being spent on alcohol rather than baby formula. The risk of harm is just too high.'

'They're also a flight risk,' said Jarrod. 'It sounds like they've got no ties here and if they hit the road again with that baby, God knows how long she'll survive.'

Cassie frowned, lines of concern appearing across her forehead. 'Exactly, that's why we had to get the court order now.'

She pushed the entire case file across to Jarrod and he flicked through it. The history was appalling. Brad soon reappeared in the doorway, scrolling through an email on his phone.

'Here's the summary of the crim history. I'll forward it to you, Cassie.' He squinted as he read the information on his phone screen. 'Mundy's been arrested in Queensland, New South Wales and Victoria for offences ranging from assault, weapons, robbery, drugs and fraud. He was convicted of manslaughter in the Perth Supreme Court and served seven years. He has warnings on the system for resisting arrest. Oh, just for good measure, he has hepatitis C. Apparently, he's got form for spitting at police.'

Jarrod cringed. 'Perfect.'

Brad slipped his phone into his pocket and rubbed his hands together in anticipation. 'Right, then. What are we waiting for? We better go pay our friends a visit.'

Natalie bounced her knees and rubbed the back of her neck. Jarrod saw the fear in her eyes and guessed her university classes hadn't quite prepared her for the real world. 'You'll be fine, Natalie. Stay close to us. Okay?'

She stiffened and nodded, looking like she wanted to run and hide. Jarrod didn't blame her. He knew the feeling all too well.

Within minutes, Jarrod and Brad were driving ahead of Cassie and Natalie's departmental vehicle on their way to the Riverside Caravan Park, a cesspit on the outskirts of town. Police calls to that location were higher than the rest of the town combined. It attracted transients and with them all the shit that clung to their lives. The residents had no character references or money for a security bond and were usually flagged on rental blacklists for trashing properties or skipping on rent. The park management exploited people who had nowhere else to go. They offered no-questions-asked, bond-free rent for dilapidated caravans with an annexe or cabins, with access only to a communal shower and toilet block. They charged more for these than for a decent three-bedroom Housing Commission rental in town.

The residents were trapped in a generational cycle of

unemployment, debt, crime, substance abuse and domestic violence, but the innocent children suffered the most – like baby Zalia.

FOUR

JARROD swung the car into the main entrance of the caravan park and pulled up outside the reception office. A braless fat woman with tangled hair and dirty bare feet bent down to a little boy, no more than five years old, and whispered something in his ear. The boy, dressed only in a pair of grotty underpants, ran off. The caravan park's early alert system was already in overdrive. Residents had an innate sixth sense for identifying unmarked government vehicles from a mile away.

A shirtless man with a beard and heavily tattooed upper body sat in the annexe of a caravan, drinking a can of bourbon and cola. He gave the visitors a hard look, then shot to his feet. He puffed his chest and sucked in his gut, swinging his arms by his sides like a silverback gorilla.

Jarrod remained at the wheel while Brad got out and inspected the site plan mounted on a sign. The park manager peered out through the office curtains, his face contorting into a scowl. It was common knowledge he received kickbacks and favours from the more unsavoury residents in return for hiding them at the park. It was a waste of time asking him for information about park residents.

They ignored the unwelcoming "keep out" and "residents only" signs. Hopefully, they'd get to the site before Mundy and Hewitt were tipped off. Brad pointed to site sixteen on the map and traced his finger along a path through the maze of roads that led back to the "you are here" marker. He climbed into the car and the Children's Services vehicle pulled up alongside.

'Follow us,' Jarrod called out through his window. 'We'll find the site and contain the area first. Stick behind us and stay with your car. You ladies ready?'

Cassie and Natalie nodded and took deep breaths, their faces stricken with anxiety.

Brad yanked the radio handset from its hook and booked off at that location, just in case they needed backup. Their tyres crunched on gravel as they negotiated the tight roads winding between rows of caravans in various states of disrepair. People sitting around card tables drinking cheap wine and warm beer eyeballed them as they drove by. The park was littered with rubbish and rusted car parts. Stray cats and dogs wandered aimlessly, withered and mangy. Knee-high weeds filled the spaces between caravan sites.

Up ahead, a battered combi-van came into view at the end of a row. More residents stared, heads rotating like sideshow clowns as they drove past. Beside the van, a man and a woman sat on plastic milk crates smoking hand-rolled cigarettes. Jarrod recognised Karl Mundy and Kimberley Hewitt from their mugshots. He stopped the car, the Children's Services officers pulling up behind.

Jarrod surveyed the scene. A cast iron plate was positioned over two columns of bricks, forming a crude barbecue. A ribbon of smoke rose into the air from a recent campfire. Mundy was a tall, wiry man, his arms covered in tattoos. He wore a Jackie Howe singlet, skinny jeans and thongs. His oily hair was tied back in a ponytail, dripping between his shoulder blades.

Hewitt was a ruddy looking woman for her age, with an acne-scarred face and unkempt hair draped over her face. Her mug shot showed she had two missing front teeth, probably at the hands of Mundy or another abusive partner. She was barefoot, with baggy shorts and a tattered T-shirt. Her thin frame stooped forward on the crate, her face haggard.

The pair exchanged a guarded look and unsteadily rose to their feet. Jarrod counted at least six empty beer bottles.

'No sign of the baby,' said Brad. 'I don't like this.'

'What's there to like? Come on, let's get this over with.'

Brad sighed and they swung open their doors. They got out and ambled towards the pair, trying to appear casual and friendly while scanning for threats. The plan was to attempt a civil conversation to offer support and negotiate alternative care for the baby.

Jarrod's experience had taught him to exhaust negotiations before resorting to force. Some parents, destitute and hopeless, accepted the offer of support. A willingness to comply was often the key to a better outcome for the child. He hoped like hell they could reason with Mundy and Hewitt, but he had a bad feeling. He always had a bad feeling.

Mundy held his arms straight by his sides, hands clenched into fists. Veins in his forearms bulged. Jarrod noticed the onlookers had disappeared back under whatever rocks they had crawled out from. It was the first rule of self-preservation on the street. *'I saw no one do nothin'. I'm not getting involved.'*

'Get inside,' Mundy barked at Hewitt, who immediately complied.

She scampered into the van and slammed the sliding door. Tattered curtains and the sun's glare on the window glass obscured the view into the van.

Jarrod and Brad held up their badges. 'G'day mate. I'm Detective O'Connor and this is Detective Harding.'

Karl Mundy stood rigid as a statue, his eyes flashing a threat.

Jarrod glanced over his shoulder towards Cassie and Natalie, standing in the relative safety behind their open car doors. 'These ladies are from the Department of Children's Services. You're Karl Mundy, is that right?'

Mundy nodded, angling his body. His eyes narrowed.

'Karl, we're here to talk to you and Kimberley about how things are going with the baby. The hospital staff are concerned you guys are not coping so well, that the baby might be sick. We're here to help.' Jarrod kept the tone of his voice neutral.

'Fuck off, pigs! You're not comin' nowhere near my baby. Now piss off.' Mundy slurred his words. He made a snorting noise in his throat. His blood-shot eyes darted from side to side to keep both Jarrod and Brad in his sights. His face reddened, a sheen of sweat forming above his top lip and forehead.

Jarrod and Brad edged closer, positioning themselves on either side to form a triangle, Mundy at the apex. He sidestepped, his gaze bouncing between the two detectives.

'Karl, we don't want any trouble now.' Jarrod held his hands out in an open gesture. 'But we need to talk to you about how things are going with the baby, to make sure that little Zalia is okay.'

Mundy cocked his head and called out to Hewitt inside the van. 'Lock it up, Kimmy. Don't let these arseholes in!'

Hewitt scrabbled about inside the van, closing windows and locking doors. Jarrod heard the faint whimper of an infant. It would have been hot and stuffy inside with no ventilation.

'Now, Karl, we just need to talk. Do you mind if we…?'

Mundy sucked air past his teeth. Jarrod's shoulders tensed and his stomach twisted into a tight knot. *This is going to end badly*.

The negotiations were over. Mundy lunged at Jarrod, his fist poised to strike. He surprised Jarrod with his speed, his first punch coming without warning. Jarrod ducked to avoid the full impact of the blow which grazed the top of his head. As Mundy swung blindly, he threw himself off balance.

Brad moved behind and grabbed him by his arms, trying to restrain him in a hammer lock. Mundy twisted his body and threw Brad hard onto the dirt. Mundy, physically superior, turned back towards Jarrod. He came at Jarrod again, his fists compressed springs, ready to explode with fury. He was almost on Jarrod, rage in his eyes. Jarrod stepped to one side and turned his body, tackling Mundy around his waist. He used Mundy's own momentum against him and drove with his legs, throwing him to the ground. Jarrod crashed on top and it became a frantic brawl.

Brad had recovered and positioned himself behind Mundy. He wrapped his arm around and squeezed his forearm and bicep against the sides of Mundy's neck, using his other hand as a vice for leverage. The lateral vascular neck restraint slowed him down, but his powerful arms continued to fight on.

Jarrod slid out his handcuffs and secured a cuff onto one of Mundy's wrists. He threw his other arm about, struggling with his remaining strength. Jarrod twisted the cuffed wrist and Mundy growled, spit drooling from the corners of his mouth. The pain distracted him enough for Jarrod to grab his other wrist and snap the second cuff on. It wasn't textbook stuff, but enough to secure him, his hands awkwardly cuffed behind his back. Brad released his grip of Mundy's neck.

Kimberly Hewitt jumped out of the van, screaming like a banshee. 'Leave him alone, you bastards!'

She raised a beer bottle above her head and threw herself at Brad, who was still busy restraining Mundy. By instinct, Brad tucked his head into his shoulders for the imminent impact of glass. Jarrod scrambled to his feet and tackled Hewitt just as the bottle came down. He drove her against the side of the van and grabbed her arms, twisting the bottle from her grip. It fell to the ground.

Brad had subdued Mundy, pinning him with one knee between his shoulder blades. He slung his cuffs towards Jarrod and they clattered as they slid in the dirt. Hewitt fought hard, kicking and thrashing her body. Her fingernails scraped Jarrod's cheek, drawing blood. He forced her to the ground and struggled to secure her flailing arms, reaching for the cuffs until his fingers found them. He gripped the hinge and drove the top cuff onto one of her wrists. She cried out in pain as he twisted it and secured the second cuff on her other wrist.

Mundy spat a tirade of obscenities as Brad rolled him over and sat him upright onto his backside. Jarrod did the same with Hewitt when she eventually stopped struggling. Sweat trickled down Jarrod's face and stung the bleeding gouges in his cheek. He and Brad panted to catch their breath, dusting dirt off their elbows and knees. Brad winced his way to standing, gritting through the pain of his bad leg which had given him grief since Vincent Mile's bullet had torn a hole. He hoisted Mundy to his feet and frog-marched him to the back seat of the police car.

Cassie and Natalie had remained behind the cover of their car during the ruckus, waiting to retrieve the child when it was safe. Cassie hurried past and disappeared into the combi-van. 'Oh my God!' she cried.

A feeling of dread washed over Jarrod as he lifted Hewitt to her feet, walking her to the open van door.

'Don't take my baby,' Hewitt sobbed. 'You can't take this one off me as well.' Her knees buckled and Jarrod sat her down on the van's step.

'Don't move!' Jarrod peered inside and nearly gagged from the stench. The putrid odour of burnt cannabis, piss and vomit tickled his nose. The van was cluttered with empty beer cans and fast-food wrappers. A filthy mattress and stained blankets formed a makeshift bed. Smoke from a thousand cigarettes had stained the van's ceiling a sickly yellow.

Cassie squeezed past the clutter and knelt beside an infant. The tiny thing lay on her back on a pile of clothes, dressed only in a soiled, disposable nappy. She cried with a quiver between breaths, her legs thrashing. No sign of baby formula or bottles in the van.

Cassie slid her pinkie finger into the infant's hand and watched as the tiny fingers curled around it. She turned to Jarrod, her eyes glossy. She used the back of her hand to wipe tears away as they slid down her cheeks. She scooped the baby into her arms. Kimberley Hewitt whimpered outside.

'Hello, little girl, you're safe now,' Cassie whispered as she caressed the baby's fluffy head with her chin.

Outside, Kimberley Hewitt screamed once more. 'Get your filthy hands off my baby, you mongrels! You can't take her from me!'

She was dead wrong.

FIVE

HEADS turned when Jarrod and Brad walked into the station, their clothes dishevelled with dirt stains on the knees of their trousers. The scratches on Jarrod's face were crusted with dry blood.

One of the uniformed officers chuckled as they walked past the day room. 'Tough day in the office for the kiddie cops?'

Brad held up his middle finger without making eye contact. 'Bite me, Jones.'

They dragged themselves up the two flights of stairs to the Youth Crime Unit office and plonked in front of their desks. They fired up their computers and worked on the bench charge sheets and court brief documents. Mundy and Hewitt were cooling their heels in the cells, awaiting formal charges of assaulting police.

Later in the afternoon, Cassie called from the hospital.

'Hey, Cassie. How's the baby?'

'Hey, Jarrod. Yeah, she's doing good. The paediatrician's confident she'll be fine. We'd gotten to her just in time. She was dehydrated but they've stabilised her.'

Jarrod sensed the uncertainty in Cassie's voice. 'Are you and Natalie okay? That was a bloody rock show out at the caravan park.'

'We're fine. Natalie was a bit shaken up, but she'll bounce back. She's never been involved in anything like that before, but our manager has arranged a debriefing for us.'

'We did the right thing. You know that don't you, Cassie?'

'I know,' she sighed, unconvinced. 'It doesn't get any easier, this bloody job of ours. I'm glad we got that baby out of there. But it just makes me sad, cases like this. I've seen a lot of this over the years, maybe too much.'

'Yeah, I know what you mean. Those jobs are tough. But we just have to do the best we can, you know, making judgement calls from the information available. You made the right call on this one.'

'Yeah, I guess.' She sounded disheartened.

'So, what now? How long will the baby be in hospital?'

'The paediatrician said it depends on how long it takes for the withdrawals from her mother's prenatal drug abuse to subside. We've arranged temporary foster parents, a young couple who've just been approved as carers. We'll be applying for a temporary child protection order and placing her into their care as soon as she's released from hospital.'

'I don't expect the magistrate will have any issues granting the order, given the circumstances.'

Cassie cleared her throat to gather her composure. 'What about Mundy and Hewitt, what's happening with them?'

'They'll stay in custody tonight and we'll oppose their bail in court tomorrow, at least until their first remand date. But it depends on what arguments their Legal Aid solicitor comes up with. If they get bail, we'll need to put in proper security arrangements at the hospital. Last thing anyone needs is them turning back up at the maternity ward trying to take the baby again.'

'I need to speak with them, to serve papers. Can I do that there at the police station?'

'Sure, I'll arrange it for you when you're ready to go. There's a secure interview cell in the watchhouse.'

'Okay. Thanks, Jarrod. I don't know what we would have done without you and Brad there today. You guys okay? They bunged on a real turn.'

'We're good. And don't mention it, that's what we're here for. And Cassie?'

'Yes, Jarrod?'

'You and Natalie did good out there today. Nasty business, but it had to be done.'

After the call, Jarrod and Brad spent the next two hours finishing the documentation for court. Cassie returned to serve the paperwork on Kimberley Hewitt in the watchhouse. By then she had calmed down and listened to the conditions of the temporary child protection order, her eyes glazed and emotionless. Away from Mundy's influence, she seemed more willing to cooperate.

By seven o'clock, Jarrod and Brad were finally getting ready to leave. Their shift was supposed to finish at four. Daniel Barkley's court case that morning was a distant memory, the day just another blur in an endless run of long shifts. All for the love of the job, apparently.

Brad flicked the light switch, leaving the office in darkness behind them. 'You thirsty? I could use a cold beer.'

'Sorry, mate. I don't think I'm up for it tonight. I'll take a rain check.'

'What's the matter? Jayne and the kids are away this week, aren't they? You're a free unit. You slowing up, old fella?'

Jarrod grimaced when his knee clunked as he took the first stair. 'I guess that's what it is. I just need to go home, jump in the shower and climb into bed.'

'Yeah, righto. I'll see if any of the CIB boys are keen for a beer.'

'Take it easy. I'll see you in the morning.'

Brad disappeared down the corridor towards the CIB office and Jarrod negotiated the rest of the staircase, each step jolting his bruised rib cage. He wasn't in the mood for chitchat with the uniformed crew and slipped out the back door unnoticed. His aching body protested as he climbed up into the driver's seat of his truck.

Soon he was home. His footfalls echoed off the walls, the house silent without the usual chatter of his family. Jayne had taken the kids out of school to visit her sister in Sydney who'd just had a baby. They left that morning and would be gone for the rest of the week.

He missed them so much already. Katie was now seven-years-old and in grade three. Matty would turn four soon and was growing up so fast, his dad's little buddy.

Held to the refrigerator with magnets was a colourful masterpiece Matty had painted at kindergarten. Apparently, the picture was of a dinosaur, but Jarrod couldn't even tell if it was the right way up. Beside it, a certificate of merit was proudly displayed. "Awarded to Katie O'Connor for excellence in her spelling test."

Katie was a naturally bright little girl and already doing so well at school. She loved reading books and often did her entire week's homework in one night, preferring to do her maths quiz and spelling test than to watch TV with her little brother.

Matty was content to run around with no pants on, crashing into walls with a bucket on his head. Graced with the attention span of an avocado, he often did three things at once to amuse himself. His spontaneous bursts of energy ran out of steam around dinner time, like a burnt-out firecracker.

Jarrod threw his keys onto the kitchen bench and sunk into the couch in the lounge room. He fished his mobile phone from his trouser pocket and dialled.

'This better be a secret admirer,' said Jayne when she answered, her voice echoing down the phone line.

'Hello, sweetheart. Sorry to disappoint you, it's just the father of your children.'

'Oh, well, you'll do. How was your day? You sound tired.'

'Yeah, it's been a long day.' He didn't have the energy to elaborate, and besides, it would make Jayne worry even more. He just wanted to hear her voice. 'So, how's Carly and the baby?'

'They're great, the little bub is so beautiful. They should get out of hospital in a day or two. Katie and Matty just love him. I think they want one of their own,' Jayne teased.

Jarrod laughed but flinched under his breath when a sharp pain shot through his ribs. 'Yeah, well, don't get any ideas, lady.'

'The kids are right here. Katie wants to say hello.' Jayne passed the phone over.

'Hello, Daddy. We miss you.'

'Oh, sweetheart, I miss you guys so much. Are you having fun?'

'Yep, we catched a train into the city. The little baby is so cute. He's got fluffy black hair. I'd love a baby, Daddy.'

'Would you, sweetheart? I think our family is just the right size, don't you?'

'I guess so. Mummy took me shopping and she got me a new skirt and some pretty hair bands with flowers on them. I can't wait for you to see them.'

As Katie chatted, innocent and full of life, Jarrod's exhausted mind wandered. A flashback thrust his thoughts to another moment in time when it could have all ended. A vision, seared into his brain, re-emerged. The cemetery. The sinister squawks of a black crow. Vincent Miles staring at him with hatred in his eyes. A gun pressed to Katie's head. The gunshot and the madman's blood pooling at the base of a headstone. The angels. The rain. Jarrod closed his eyes and chased away the images. Katie had been through so much in the last year, waking most nights screaming and crying, haunted by nightmares. The worst was behind her, the nightmares less frequent. She had inherited her mother's traits – resilience and bravery. He was so proud of his little girl.

'Daddy, Matty wants to say hello, bye-bye.' His mind snapped back to the present.

Before Jarrod had a chance to say goodbye to Katie, Matty was on the other end, panting into the phone and rambling on about something to do with trains. He then kissed the handset mouthpiece and said, 'Bye, Daddy.'

Muffles and then Jayne's voice. 'Sorry about that, they're a bit hyped. You won't get much sense out of them at the moment.'

They chatted a while longer before Jayne's mobile phone beeped, an alert that the battery was going flat. They said their goodbyes and

Jarrod found himself alone once more.

He had a long shower, the hot water stinging the scratches on his face, a harsh reminder of a day he thought would never end. Afterwards, he retrieved a labelled container from the freezer and heated a meal Jayne had precooked for him. He washed it down with a cold beer and fell asleep in front of the television.

Around midnight, he dragged himself up off the couch and shuffled to the bedroom where he collapsed onto the bed. He slept soundly that night, comforted in the knowledge little baby Zalia was safe, for now at least. He'd done his job.

His nightmares stayed at bay that night.

SIX

JARROD woke re-energised. Although he missed the usual morning chaos, getting ready for work was far more efficient without the distractions of tantrums, spilt breakfast cereal and a crowded bathroom. He felt guilty admitting it but eating breakfast in peace for a change was bliss. He even had extra time to swing by a coffee shop on his way to the station to grab a decent latte. After arriving at the office bright and early, he took a moment to savour his coffee while his computer booted up. He scanned the log of occurrences from overnight for jobs that needed priority follow up. A car had been stolen and used in a ram raid at a bottle shop. CCTV footage inside the store showed grainy images of three hooded figures gaining entry after reversing the car through the glass door. Their skittish movements and slight frames pointed to juveniles. Jarrod squinted at the freeze frame images, trying to identify any of them. A few usual suspects came to mind. Attending police had marked the file for further investigation by the Youth Crime Unit.

Brad moped into the office just after 8AM, his eyes hiding behind sunglasses, face the colour of dishwater. 'Morning. Hope you feel better than I do. I'm never drinking again, ever.'

Jarrod gave him a sideways glance and returned his focus on the computer screen. 'You said that last time.'

'I mean it this time. Ugh! I think a goat snuck into my room and shit in my mouth while I slept.'

Jarrod sipped his coffee. 'It could be worse, though.'

'How's that?'

Jarrod swivelled his chair and smiled. 'It could be me who's hungover.'

'You suck, you know that?'

'What time did you get home, anyway?'

'Not sure exactly. They kicked Dawsey and me out of the pub at closing time, around midnight I suppose.'

Jarrod's desk phone rang. He answered. 'Youth Crime Unit.'

'Is that O'Connor?' a voice grumbled.

Jarrod closed his eyes and sighed when he recognised the gruff voice on the other end.

'Mr Barkley. What a pleasant surprise.' Jarrod's tone said he was lying. 'Just when I thought it was going to be a good day. You ringing to make a complaint about our little conversation in the park yesterday?'

'What? Nah, fuck that. That's the least of my worries.'

Jarrod kept his voice even. 'So, what's up?'

'You remember my daughter, Lisa?'

Jarrod thought for a moment to recollect the girl. He had cautioned her six months earlier for shoplifting, peer pressured into it from memory. Otherwise, she was a cleanskin and nothing like her arsewipe of a brother. But she was a troubled kid, aloof. From what he remembered, she was into the gothic or emo look, whatever they called it these days, dyed black hair and brooding. Her way of trying to fit in, he guessed.

'Um, yeah. I haven't seen her for a while, but I remember her. What's up?'

'She hasn't come home. It's not like her.'

Jarrod pulled out his notebook and pen. 'How old is she now? Fourteen?'

'No, she's fifteen now. Just had her birthday.'

'Man, where does the time go?'

Barkley grunted into the phone.

'So, when did you last see her?'

'Yesterday morning, at seven-thirty, before Daniel and I left to go to court. When we got home around midday, I just assumed she was at school. But she didn't come home in the afternoon. I'm telling you, it's not like her. She's a good kid.'

Jarrod had never heard such genuine concern in Barkley's voice. 'Do you think she could have stayed with some friends?'

'Maybe, dunno. The thing is, I don't really know who her friends are. She keeps to herself, spends most of her time shut away in her room.'

'Does she have her phone?'

'Yeah, it's always with her. I tried ringing it, but a message says it's turned off or out of service. She's got a prepaid, maybe she's run out of credit.'

'Hmm, strange. She should still be able to receive calls if she ran out of credit. Maybe just a flat battery. We might be able to triangulate her last known location, but generally the telcos only permit those searches in emergent situations.'

'What's it take to be classed as an emergency? Maybe when a copper's kid goes missing, or a bloody politician? But not for my family.'

Jarrod sighed. 'No, it's not like that. It depends on the circumstances. What's her phone number?'

As Barkley read out the number, Jarrod scribbled the digits in his notebook.

'What about school? Did she turn up yesterday?'

'That's the thing, I don't really know for sure. I went and celebrated yesterday after we won Daniel's court case, had a few beers with some mates. Anyway, I got home late with a skin full. You know how it is.' His voice trailed off.

Jarrod paused. 'Tell me how it is.'

Barkley cleared his throat. 'Anyway, Lisa's door was closed, so I assumed she was in bed. I checked her room this morning and she was gone. Her bed hadn't been slept in. I rang you straight away. It's too early to call the school.'

Jarrod asked all the routine questions for the missing person report and reassured Barkley that Lisa would most likely turn up soon. He told Barkley he'd ring the school himself and if she wasn't there, he'd come out to the house personally to follow up. It was more than likely Lisa was hiding out at someone's house, but it paid to cover one's arse and not make assumptions. No shortcuts. As much as he wasn't thrilled about seeing Eric and Daniel Barkley again, he had to take the report in person. The bottle shop ram-raiders would have to wait.

Jarrod waited until after 9AM to ring Lockyer High School. The number had its own speed dial button on his desk phone. The administration office transferred his call to Principal Colin Day. 'Jarrod, good morning. How can I help you, mate?'

'Morning, Col. Sorry to bother you, but Lisa Barkley's father just reported her missing. He says he hasn't seen her since yesterday morning. Can you check to see if she was at school yesterday? I also need to find out if she's turned up today.'

'Sure thing, just hold on. I'll log into the daily attendance register.'

Colin put the phone down with a clunk. After some tapping on a keyboard and muffling in the handset, he came back on. 'Sorry to hold you up, Jarrod. Computer's a bit docile this morning. Now let's see. Lisa Barkley, she's in year ten. Nope, looks like she was away yesterday, marked absent this morning as well.'

Jarrod made an entry in his notebook. 'What's her attendance like normally?'

'Lisa's a good kid, reserved, but she gives us no trouble. She has quite a poor attendance record more recently, but with her family background it comes as no surprise.'

'Yeah, poor kid. Who could blame her for doing a runner from that house?'

'Yes, but at least she's still in school. Not like her brother, Daniel.

He spent more time hanging around the school causing trouble after I expelled him than when he was enrolled as a student.'

'Yeah, I remember. So, what about Lisa's friends? Are there any kids at school she hangs around with who might know where she is?'

'There's a group of kids she's pretty tight with. They can usually be found sitting in a huddle under the same tree away from the other students; loners. The goth crew, you know the sort?'

'Yeah, I know 'em. Are they at school today?'

Colin went through the register, saying out loud the names of students until he found the ones he was looking for. 'Surprise, surprise. It seems they're all here today.'

'What about yesterday?' Jarrod expected to hear they were absent, maybe skipping school with Lisa.

Colin paused before his computer mouse clicked some more. 'Well, that's one for the books. They were all here at school yesterday as well.'

'If needed, can I come and speak with them at the school?'

'Sure, that won't be a problem. I can tee that up for you.'

After the call, Jarrod turned to Brad. 'I'm heading out to the Barkley place. You're staying put this morning, can't have you breathing on people. Not a good look.'

Brad rubbed his temples with a pained expression. 'No arguments from me.'

'Don't forget to give the prosecutor's office a call to find out if Karl Mundy and Kimberley Hewitt get bail.'

'Roger that.' Brad gave a three-fingered salute.

The phone rang again as Jarrod grabbed the car keys and headed for the door. 'Get that, will ya. If it's for me, tell 'em I'm not here.'

Brad shot Jarrod a pained look and reluctantly answered the phone.

SEVEN

IT didn't take long to drive to the Barkley home, a tired-looking worker's cottage. Remnants of flaking paint clung to the exposed weatherboard, suggesting the house used to be white. A rusting Holden Kingswood with no wheels had been jacked onto piles of bricks in the front yard. Long grass grew beneath the car's body, entangling the chassis. Discarded car parts and old tyres were strewn about the place.

Jarrod climbed the rickety wooden staircase, negotiating the rotting steps. The railing wobbled when he placed his hand on it. Up on the veranda, a weathered table held a coffee tin full of cigarette butts. A derelict chair waited, the worn seat padding moulded to the shape of Eric Barkley's arse.

Before Jarrod could announce his arrival, an unshaven Barkley appeared in the front doorway, his thinning hair squashed flat on one side of his head and sticking up in a matted mess on the other. He squinted against the sunlight. The dank aroma of oily food and body odour permeated from the gloom inside and mingled with the fresh morning air. The pungent smell snuck into Jarrod's nostrils and down his throat, leaving a sickly taste in his mouth.

With one hand Barkley rubbed his eyes with nicotine-stained fingers, with the other he scratched his balls. Wiry hairs protruded from his ears and nose. His beer belly bulged beneath a stained singlet, and he wore a pair of shorts that looked two sizes too small for him. His skinny arms were covered in homemade tattoos and a pair of rubber thongs clung to his feet, revealing gnarled toes with overgrown nails.

Jarrod spoke first. 'Mr Barkley.' He tried a half-baked smile, but Barkley did not respond in kind.

'O'Connor. Good to see you're not wasting taxpayers' money for a change. Not picking on innocent kids today?'

Jarrod folded his arms and raised one eyebrow. 'And you last paid tax when, exactly?'

Barkley scowled and they stood in awkward silence.

Jarrod let out a long sigh. 'Listen, can we just cut the bullshit today? I'm here because of Lisa. She *is* still missing, yeah?'

Barkley broke eye contact and gave a solemn nod.

Jarrod pulled out his notebook. 'So, you told me over the phone that you last saw her at seven-thirty yesterday morning.'

Barkley nodded, gazing out towards the street.

'Did she say anything?'

Barkley's eyes wandered, then came back to rest uneasily on him. 'Not really. Well, kinda. She was in one of her moods and we had an argument.'

'What about?'

'Oh, I don't bloody know. All we seem to do these days is argue. She was walking around the house in one of her snotty moods and I probably told her to pull her head in. I can't remember exactly what was said. Nothin' in particular.'

'Who left home first?'

'Daniel and I were still here when she left. It's got me stuffed why she left so early. Getting her out of bed in the morning is usually near impossible.'

'Did she say where she was going?'

'Nope. She just said, "I'm out of here," and then she walked out the front door. She never tells me where she's going, and I don't ask.'

'What did she have with her? Was she carrying any bags?'

'Yeah, she had her black canvas backpack, the one she always takes with her. I don't know what she carries in that damn thing half the time.'

Jarrod jotted down the information in his notebook. 'Was she dressed for school?'

'Well, that's hard to tell. I can never get her to wear her school uniform. Always has to be wearing her goth clothes. Black jeans and T-shirt, black boots and black overcoat. Even in this hot weather.' He thought some more and nodded decisively. 'Yeah, that's what she was wearing, the same bloody garb.'

Jarrod made more notes and looked up at Barkley, whose eyes were now locked onto his.

'I just want my girl to come home. I'm worried about her.'

Jarrod held his gaze. 'I'll do everything I can to find her. You have my word. Now, is there anything else you can remember that might be important?'

His eyes widened. He drew a U-shaped loop on his chest with a finger. 'She was wearing a silver chain around her neck with some sort of pendant on it, like a logo.' He scratched his head, trying to remember. 'I think it was a Mercedes Benz symbol, you know like the ones the kids snap off the bonnets of cars?'

'Yeah, I know the ones you mean. Those things are in high demand.' Jarrod jotted down more notes. 'I haven't seen Lisa for a while. How does she wear her hair these days?'

'Well, it's dyed jet black, shaved short at the back with this annoying long bit that dangles in her face. She's also into black eyeliner over white face makeup. She looks like bloody Morticia from the Adams Family.'

'Do you know of anyone she could be staying with?'

Barkley shook his head. 'No. No one that I know of.' He looked back inside the house and sighed. 'She never brings any friends home, probably too embarrassed of this dump. She just spends all her time in her bloody room listening to heavy metal crap hours on end. She won't even come out to eat with Daniel and me.'

Jarrod thought back to when he interviewed her about the shoplifting incident. He remembered how scrawny she was and he wondered if she had an eating disorder. Who'd really know what was going on in this lonely girl's life. Her mother had run off years ago – left alone with her deadshit brother and father without a female role model.

'Where's Daniel this morning?' said Jarrod.

'He's got his weekly appointment with his youth worker. Has to keep up his community service hours or he'll be back in court.' His nostrils flared and Jarrod sensed his growing agitation. 'You know, that burglary wrap you bricked him on. He still reckons he had nothing to do with it and I believe him. You coppers are unbelievable. You just love picking on Daniel.'

'Yeah, well Daniel reckons a lot of things that aren't true. His fingerprints on the glass and the stolen alcohol we found in his room had something to do with why I arrested him. You know, that thing called evidence?'

'Evidence my arse.'

Perhaps if you spent less time defending the little shit and more time pulling him into line... Jarrod swallowed the words down. No point trying to reason with the man. 'Getting back to Lisa, have you seen or heard anything from her at all since seven-thirty yesterday morning? Think hard, it's important.'

'No, I haven't. I wouldn't have called you if I had.'

'Has Lisa ever run away before? I didn't see any previous missing persons reports on our system.'

'No, not like this. She usually just goes and sulks in her room after we've had a blue.'

Jarrod hesitated, broaching the next question carefully. 'Can I see inside her room?'

Barkley opened his mouth, about to object.

Jarrod cut in. 'Just in case there's something that might explain why she left and where she might be.'

Barkley's eyes narrowed, a crease forming on his brow. 'Her room only. You go nowhere near mine or Daniel's rooms. They're out of bounds. You got that?'

'Understood.'

'I don't trust you blokes. Last time I got a visit from the coppers they searched my house. Pinched me for having a bit of weed. Can't a man smoke a bit of pot for medicinal reasons in his own home?'

'Not in the eyes of the law. Besides, should you be smoking weed with two teenagers in the house?'

'You kidding me? Those little shits probably smoke more than I do.' Barkley waved a hand in defeat. 'Fuck it, I don't give a shit. Come in. Do what you have to do.' He walked inside.

Jarrod followed down the hallway. A path had been flattened into the shagpile carpet.

'Don't mind the mess, I haven't tidied up yet today,' said Barkley, dismissing the years of dirt and grime as merely a bad housekeeping day. The house probably hadn't seen a vacuum cleaner since Mrs Barkley took off to find a better life.

The cluttered, three-bedroom cottage was in a constant state of chaos. In the lounge room, a sad recliner hunched in front of the television. Another ashtray brimmed with butts and ash on top of a TV dinner stand. Positioned against the far wall, a tattered couch also served as a bed, a pillow with oily hair stains at one end, an arm rest with grimy feet marks at the other. Sunlight lasered through the windows around puckered edges of orange and brown drapes. They walked past the kitchen, Jarrod glancing to notice a pile of dirt swept to one corner and dirty dishes in the sink.

Barkley led Jarrod past the first two bedrooms. He pointed to the closed doors in turn. 'Mine and Daniel's rooms. Out of bounds, remember?' He nodded at a plain white door at the end of the hallway. 'Lisa's room.'

'Do you ever go into her room?' said Jarrod.

Barkley's eyes lowered and his posture slumped. 'No way.' He seemed flustered. 'If she ever says that she's lying. I usually just bang on her door and tell her to come out. Who knows what I'd find if I went in there. I don't *want* to know. I keep out of her shit and she keeps out of mine, that's our arrangement.'

Jarrod sensed the man's unease. Something was off. He tried to breathe through his mouth to restrict the God-awful smell. 'Can I look inside?'

'If you're game.' Barkley kept his distance from the door. 'Go on then, open it.'

Jarrod reached for the knob and it creaked as he turned it. Stale air escaped from the dark room as he pushed the door open. He stepped inside and blinked to adjust his pupils to the gloom. He felt for the light switch and flicked it on. The light bulb, painted red, hung low from the ceiling and cast an eerie glow. Jarrod felt a ping of guilt for violating Lisa Barkley's private world, her sanctuary. The walls had been crudely painted purple and black curtains were draped over the window, blocking out the daylight. To Jarrod's surprise, the room was tidy in contrast to the rest of the house. She took pride in her room, her own little patch in the world. Framed prints on the walls depicted fantasy worlds, cascading waterfalls, tranquil rainforests and exotic birds. One picture stood out from the rest. A unicorn, pure white with a spiralling horn, watched over the room from above the head of Lisa's bed. Its red eyes followed him around the room, its vigilant gaze a promise of protection.

Lisa's bed had been neatly made, her trinkets laid out on a dressing table below an oval shaped mirror. Gothic jewellery, serpent rings and crucifix pendants competed for space alongside pink hairbands and glitter lip gloss she'd outgrown. There were no photographs, none of her family, nor candid shots with friends.

She had her own computer, nothing elaborate, just a basic monitor, keyboard and hard drive tower. The unit was set up on a small writing desk, the chair stowed away with care.

He pressed the power button and the monitor hummed as the

Windows chime sounded and the computer booted up. A password field appeared on screen.

Barkley poked his head inside the door. 'I bought that computer brand new for her. I'm still paying the bloody thing off. She hounded me about it, needed it for school she reckoned. She spends hours online. God knows what she's doing on it half the time, or who she's talking to.'

'Do you know the password?'

'Nope, and neither does Daniel. She didn't trust us, so she put a password lock on it. I don't know how to use the bloody thing anyway. Daniel's more interested in pulling car engines apart, he's got no interest in computers.'

Yeah, stolen cars, Jarrod thought.

He scanned the room and had a cursory look inside the drawers and cupboards. Nothing stood out, no notes or obvious clues.

Jarrod turned to Barkley. 'Can you tell if any of her belongings are gone, anything that would indicate she was planning to leave? Has she packed clothing, her toothbrush, that sort of thing?'

'All her things are still in the bathroom. I haven't noticed anything else missing from around the house.' Barkley joined Jarrod inside the room, peering inside the wardrobe and drawers. 'There's nothing missing as far as I can tell, other than the clothes she was wearing and that black bag she takes everywhere.'

Jarrod made another entry in his notebook. 'I'll go to the high school later to chat to some kids who might know where she is. I've got all the information I need to file the missing person report. Oh, one more thing, do you have a recent photo of her I can circulate and upload to our system?'

'Um, no, not really. We don't have any recent photos. She covers up her face and refuses to let anyone take pictures of her. She's self-conscious, don't know why. I'll have a look, hang on a tick.' Barkley pulled his phone from his pocket and scrolled through images in his gallery. 'There's this one. Man, she looks so young in this photo. It's the most recent one I have. She was still in primary school.'

As he passed the phone to Jarrod, their eyes met. His lips curled into a sad smile, a side of him Jarrod had never seen before, a crack in his hard man façade. A beaming little girl with freckles and brown ponytails smiled up at Jarrod. It was a warm, genuine smile, using her eyes. She wore her school uniform with so much pride. She vaguely resembled the teenager she would become, her bright blue eyes unmistakable.

'Okay, if that's all we've got to work with, it will have to do.' Jarrod passed Barkley his calling card. 'My mobile number is on the card. Can you text the photo to me?'

Barkley wiped the corner of his eyes with the back of his hand, tears welling. 'Yeah, sure.'

'Can you stay home for me? In case Lisa turns up. Ring me if you hear from her.'

Barkley nodded, staring back at the photo filling his phone screen.

Jarrod headed for the door. 'I'll make more inquiries at the school and at the local teenage haunts around town. If I hear anything, I'll let you know. You have my word.'

Barkley looked up from the phone with desperation in his eyes, his hands shaking. 'I know what you think of me, O'Connor. You look down on me. You think I'm a shit parent. Don't you?'

Jarrod held his gaze. 'I'm not here to judge. My only concern is finding your daughter. Just let me do my job.'

Barkley stared at Jarrod through glazed eyes, as though trying to read his thoughts. He finally nodded. 'She's my little girl.' He grabbed Jarrod's wrist. 'Promise me you'll bring her home to me.'

'I'll do everything in my power to find Lisa. I promise.'

Barkley released his grip. 'I'll hold you to that.'

EIGHT

JARROD drove to Lockyer High School and parked in his unofficial spot in the staff car park. He walked into the Administration office and tapped on the counter window. From behind a computer monitor, the receptionist lowered her chin and peered over bifocal glasses. Her face brightened with a look of recognition, and she motioned for him to slide the window open. 'Morning, Jarrod,' she said as he leaned in through the opening. 'You here to see Colin?'

'Morning, Judy. Yeah, he's expecting me.'

She gave a "one moment" gesture with her index finger, dialled her phone and spoke into a headset mic. 'Police are here for you.'

A few minutes later, the Staff Only door opened, and Principal Colin Day appeared. 'Sorry to keep you waiting, Jarrod. I was just making a few calls.'

They shook hands. 'Not at all, thanks for seeing me straight away.'

Colin led Jarrod into his office where they sat on comfortable chairs around a coffee table. 'Any news on Lisa Barkley?'

Jarrod shook his head. 'I went and saw the father. He couldn't offer any reason for her not coming home. There was an argument but nothing to indicate she had run away. It's odd. I'd like to speak to those friends of hers you told me about.'

'I expected you might. I just called their class teachers to send them up to the office. I called their parents to clear it with them.'

'Excellent, thanks. What are their names?'

'The first one is Tammy Heidenreich, not a bad kid but lacks motivation. She's also fifteen. Her boyfriend is Seth Francis and his mate is Jason Barlow. Both are a year older in grade eleven. The boys have never been in trouble and are both quite bright. They cop a hard time from the footy meatheads. They're a quiet little group, very much on the outer. You can imagine the sort of ribbing they get from the other kids about their hairstyles, black clothes and choice of music, but they don't seem fazed by it.'

'How long has Lisa been hanging around with these kids?' said Jarrod.

'Just a few months. She struggled to fit in and gravitated towards them. They seemed to have accepted her into their fold.'

'You said Lisa has a poor attendance record. Where would she go when she wasn't at school?'

'I sent the guidance officer around to her house a few times and I telephoned her father. Lisa would lock herself in her bedroom refusing to come to school. It's unusual for her to take off like this.'

'Has she wagged school with the other kids in this little goth gang?'

Colin raised a foot onto the other knee, clasping his fingers around his shin. 'I looked into that after I spoke to you this morning. Tammy and Seth skip school together occasionally, but their absent days don't match up with Lisa's absent days. There's no pattern of them skipping school together. I've already spoken to these kids in the grounds this morning and they say they don't know where Lisa is. Anyway, I'll see if they're outside. How do you want to play this?'

'Let's keep it informal. I'll speak to them as a group.'

'Sure.' Colin got up and opened his door. He poked his head out and spoke to someone waiting outside. 'Come on in, guys. There's someone here to talk to you.'

Colin stepped aside and pulled the door wide open, introducing each of the motley crew as they filed inside. Seth Francis led Tammy Heidenreich by the hand, followed by Jason Barlow. At first glance, Jarrod had to stifle a chuckle. The three teenagers could have just walked off the set of the Rocky Horror Picture Show. Dressed in school uniforms, white face makeup beneath black eyeliner and lipstick gave them a ghoulish appearance. Matching dyed black hair hung over their faces, each flicking fringes out of their eyes. Although a little comical at first, Jarrod's heart sank for the freakish looking kids hiding behind the sullen façade.

Colin positioned three more chairs around the coffee table and invited the kids to sit. Tammy's jaw worked feverishly on gum, making an annoying squelching sound with each chew.

'What did you want to see us for, sir?' asked Seth. His respectful manner surprised Jarrod.

'This is Detective Jarrod O'Connor. He wants to talk to you about your friend, Lisa Barkley.'

The three teenagers turned their heads and eyeballed Jarrod with suspicion. He flipped out his police badge. Tammy stopped chewing.

Seth turned to his principal. 'What's wrong with Lisa? Is she okay?'

Jarrod broke in. 'Her father has reported her missing. He hasn't seen her since yesterday morning. Look, you guys are not in trouble, we're concerned for Lisa. Her father wants to know she's safe, that's all.'

Tammy averted her eyes to her shoes and fidgeted her hands. 'Her father's worried?' she scoffed. 'That's a joke.'

Colin leaned forward. 'What do you mean by that, Tammy?'

She looked at Seth and Jason, and then back at the principal. 'Nothing, it doesn't matter.'

Jarrod pressed. 'Do any of you know where she is?'

The three teenagers shook their heads in unison. Seth spoke again. 'She hung out with us on Friday. But we haven't seen her since school finished that afternoon.'

Tammy's eyes met Jarrod's. 'We thought she was angry at us for some reason. She can be moody some days. She, like, kind of snubbed us over the weekend.'

'Why do you think she might be angry at you?'

Tammy shrugged. 'Dunno.'

'Did she say anything about skipping school yesterday?' Jarrod directed the question at all three of them.

Seth spoke up. 'No. We don't know why she wasn't at school yesterday. Sometimes she just doesn't show up.'

Tammy and Jason nodded their agreement.

'Did you hear from Lisa over the weekend? Any phone calls or messages? Has she been on social media?'

'No,' said Tammy, her eyes drifting away. 'I haven't heard from her at all. She sometimes texts or snaps me on Snapchat but I've heard nothing from her. She hasn't posted on the other socials.'

'What about you, Jason? Have you seen her around?' Jarrod singled him out because he seemed too shy to speak up for himself.

He lowered his eyes and spoke in a quiet voice. 'Um… ah… nope, sorry, sir. I haven't seen her since Friday.'

Jarrod inhaled a long breath. 'Well, the thing is, guys, Lisa left home yesterday morning at about seven-thirty and she didn't go to school and didn't come home in the afternoon. We don't know where she spent the night. Do you know where she might have gone?'

Seth responded first. 'No, we would tell you if we knew. This is freaking us out too.'

'Yeah, like, it's so whacked for Lisa to do this,' said Tammy. 'She's stayed over at my house before but as far as I know she's never stayed over at anyone else's. In case you hadn't noticed, the four of us aren't the most popular kids around here, so we stick together. If we don't know where she is, then no one else around here would.'

Jarrod looked at each of them and paused, trying to gauge if their body language would betray them. If they were hiding something they were convincing liars. 'I need you guys to level with me. If you *do* know where she is, it's important you tell me. Do you understand?' The three nodded like pre-schoolers.

'The thing is, I have been lied to before by young people who were protecting their friends, you know, kids who had run away and didn't want to be found by their parents. Sometimes friends can make promises. The problem is it causes parents a lot of unnecessary worry and it wastes valuable police resources.'

'We *are* telling you the truth, sir,' said Seth. 'We're not covering for her, hey guys?' Tammy and Jason shook their heads.

Jarrod noticed Tammy's deepening look of concern. 'Are you okay, Tammy? Is something troubling you? Is there something you should tell me?'

Tammy looked at Jarrod and held his gaze. Her eyes glazed as she fought against the forming tears. 'No, sir. I'm scared, that's all. I'm scared for Lisa.' She leaned her head on Seth's chest. He put his arm around her as she cried. Jarrod had no further questions for Lisa's friends. They seemed to be telling the truth. He thanked them for their cooperation and Colin sent them back to class.

Jarrod's concern for Lisa Barkley rose several notches. He crossed the car park, the midday sun beaming down on him, heat radiating from the bitumen. A ball of trapped hot air hit him as he opened the car door. He sat in the car and turned on the ignition, opening the window to allow the stifling air to escape while he waited for the air conditioning to kick in. He loosened his tie and undid his top button. Rolling up his shirt sleeves he used his forearms to wipe the sweat from his brow.

His mobile phone rang and he sighed when he saw the caller's name on the screen. He knew something must have been wrong for Detective Senior Sergeant Ross Benfield to be calling.

'Hey, boss. What's up?'

'O'Connor. I'm glad I reached you. Can you talk?' Jarrod knew that urgent tone all too well.

'Yeah, I'm good. Just about to leave the high school from a missing person inquiry. What is it?'

'A body's been found… you need to get out there. That's all I know. I'll meet you there.'

NINE

JARROD parked outside the abandoned house, tucked away on a quiet country road. He'd heard the rumours. Apparently, the interstate owners ran an investment scam and disappeared overseas before the Federal Police could catch up with them. Local tradesmen had downed tools when payments dried up, deserting the house before it even got to lock-up stage.

Two patrol cars were out front, one blocking the driveway and the other parked further down the road. Behind them were Ross Benfield's unmarked police vehicle and a twin-cab truck with Lockyer City Council insignias on its doors. Jarrod booked off on the radio, got out of the car and approached the house.

A junior constable met him on the footpath, writing his name on the crime scene register before waving him through. 'The boss and the other guys are around the back. They're expecting you,' said the constable. 'I was told to direct you through the house. The far side's blocked by overgrown vegetation and no one's to go down the driveway side so tyre tracks aren't disturbed.'

'You got the fun job, I see.'

The young constable's eyes dropped to the register pad in his hands and he smiled back at Jarrod. 'Yeah, I'm the designated shit-kicker on shift. Senior Sergeant Benfield threatened he'd ream me a new arsehole if I let any unauthorised people through.'

Jarrod chuckled. 'I bet he did. You'll be right mate, we're all just shit-kickers when it comes down to it. Just keep that register accurate and don't speak to the media if they show up. They'll have to stay out here on the road. If they try to get in your ear tell 'em the boss will speak to them later. He gets paid the big bucks to give the media briefings.'

'Roger that,' said the constable with an assured nod.

Jarrod ducked under the police tape strung across the front boundary of the property. A brick mailbox stood guard, a lone sentry stranded by the fence that was never built. As he approached the hollow shell of a house, the sound of his footfalls bounced off the walls inside. The property had a tranquil yet solemn quietness about it. The modern home with grand entrance pillars had shrunken from the world, as if it had chosen solitude for itself. It had the makings of a fine home but had been robbed of its potential and left to perish under the elements.

Wild clumps of vegetation encircled the house, the structure serving only as a shelter for wildlife. The rendered brickwork and tiled roofing were unfinished and windows and doors were never installed. Tall thistles sprouted from the gravel driveway and spindly weeds invaded the front yard. The house had been built close to the road for easy access to the five-acre block, swallowed within a thicket of bushland. Trees swayed, their leaves and branches whispering in the breeze. There were no other houses within sight, the neighbouring properties hidden beyond nearby hills.

Jarrod entered the house through the front doorway. The unhinged door leaned against the wall just inside. Dust filled his nostrils and clung to the back of his throat as he walked down the hallway, glancing inside empty rooms littered with offcuts and rubbish. Gyprock panel joins had been plastered over but never sanded. Exposed pipes protruded from the concrete floor where the kitchen plumbing was to be installed. A stack of floor tiles waited to be laid. Sawdust and plaster particles, disturbed by his movements, swirled in the stagnant air.

As he came to the back of the house, Jarrod welcomed the fresh air drifting in through the recess where the rear sliding door should have been. Outside, Ross Benfield and two uniformed officers talked in a tight huddle. Two other men, wearing high-vis council work shirts, stood to one side, smoking cigarettes and chatting to each other. Jarrod walked through the open space onto the bare earth outside, his shoes now covered in clay dust.

Benfield acknowledged his arrival. 'Jarrod, welcome to today's shit show.'

'Hey, boss. What have we got?'

Benfield turned and pointed towards the bushland behind the house. 'Dead girl, dumped in the dry creek bed at the back of the property.'

Jarrod felt a sudden weakness in his legs.

Benfield pointed to the council workers. 'Those blokes were inspecting the property because of complaints from neighbours about the state of this place. They saw the body and called it in straight away. I got here just before you. That's all we know so far.'

'Whose been in the crime scene?'

'The workers say they saw the body from up on the ridge but didn't go anywhere near it. Our first response crew did the right thing and secured the scene and called for the SOCO.'

Jarrod shielded his eyes from the sun with the palm of his hand. 'Any I.D. on the body?'

Benfield shook his head. 'That's why you're here. Looks like she's just a kid. We're just waiting for Larry. He shouldn't be long. I want you to be lead on this.'

Jarrod recorded versions and personal particulars in his notebook from the council workers. Soon after, the house echoed with the stomping of boots and Sergeant Larry Carson emerged, dressed in his Scenes of Crime overalls and carrying a black plastic hardcase. He set the case down and adjusted the wide brimmed police hat covering his bald head. 'Gentlemen. What have we got?'

Benfield gave Larry the same briefing and turned to Jarrod.

'O'Connor, you stay here and work the scene with Larry. I'll get the uniformed boys to remain on guard at the outer perimeter. Shit's gonna hit the fan real quick. I need to make some calls before the media get wind of this. I'll organise more manpower. The brass'll be breathin' down my neck for updates.' Dialling his phone, he stomped off and disappeared inside the house.

Larry unclipped the latches of the equipment box and produced a pair of overalls, rubber gloves and disposable booties. 'Put these on, don't want to contaminate the scene any more than it probably is.' He closed the lid and headed off towards the pocket of bush leading to the creek. 'Let's go. There's a body waiting for us.' He didn't wait for a reply.

Jarrod stepped into the overalls and slipped the covers over his shoes. As he peeled on the rubber gloves, his body temperature climbed, his skin clammy with sweat. He negotiated low-hanging branches and lantana until he caught up with Larry. Jarrod squinted against the blinding sunlight and slid on a pair of sunglasses. The air was full of grit, eager to get at his eyes. He stood alongside Larry, who surveyed the scene from the gully ridge. A steep embankment fell to the sun-baked creek bed, strewn with rocks and logs swept downstream during the last flood. It was about twenty metres across from the base of one bank to the other. Larry pointed to the lonely figure lying face down on the clay, exposed to the beating sun.

His finger drew a line in the air from the body up to indentations in the sandy bank.

'There, see that? That clearing just over on the ridge. The body was rolled from up there before coming to rest at the base. Let's take a look.'

Larry walked to the edge of the clearing and set his box down. He crouched and parted stems of grass with his pen, inspecting the dirt beneath. 'This is our secondary crime scene.' He gestured to a spot a few metres away with a raised chin. 'The offender would have been standing just over there. The vehicle came to a stop right here, parked, tossed the body and then drove back out over the same tracks.'

Jarrod bent over with his hands on his knees, beside Larry who was on his haunches sweeping his hand over the grass and prodding the ground with the pen. 'Ground's rock hard under the grass. I don't like our chances of getting any tire impressions.'

Larry stood and traced the path of the tyre tracks in the air with his pointed pen. Parallel lines compressed the knee-high grass through a gap in the bush, back out past the side of the house towards the driveway. He gave the loose end of a roll of crime scene tape to Jarrod to hold while he paced out a large grid, using trees as corner poles. He snapped a series of photographs of the compressed grass as well as high shots towards where the body lay in situ.

Larry walked along the ridge, looking for a safe point to climb down the slope. 'Right, we can approach the body from here.'

Jarrod followed him down the slope, using exposed tree roots as foot holds to avoid losing traction in the loose sand. They both made it to the bottom without slipping onto their backsides.

Larry crouched to inspect the creek bed. 'There's no other tracks or footprints. Doesn't look like anyone else has been down here.'

He looked back up the sandy slope, holding his hand in a salute above narrowed eyes. Lateral impressions had been pressed into the sand all the way down the slope where the girl's body had tumbled to her final resting spot.

Larry stood and craned his neck, scanning the scene in more detail. 'We'll need to mark out a crime scene perimeter from the body up towards the slope where she rolled. Who knows what physical evidence was lost in the sand.' His eyes met Jarrod's. 'What's up? You're very quiet.'

Jarrod's throat was dry from the sandy dust. Anxiety welled in his stomach. He hoped the dead girl wasn't Lisa Barkley, but even if it wasn't, she was someone's daughter. It would be his job to deliver the death message.

Jarrod studied the body. 'I can't quite tell from here, but I might know this girl.'

Larry gave a knowing nod and let it be.

Jarrod followed Larry, who approached the body as though traversing a mine field. He stepped in Larry's shoe impressions to avoid contaminating the scene. Larry stopped just short of the body and put his equipment box down. He opened the lid and produced his camera, taking photos of the girl's body from various angles.

She lay on her stomach, her face turned away. She was a thin girl with pale skin and dyed black hair. Her black T-shirt was pulled up, exposing a red bra strap. The skin on her back was scraped from being dragged. Her left arm extended out straight above her head, the hand resting in the sand. The other arm was awkwardly twisted under her body as though her shoulder had been dislocated.

The lower half of her body was naked, except for black Dr Martin boots on her feet, the laces still fastened. Her ankles were crossed and the feet pointed inwards, the toes of the boots dug into the sand.

Jarrod stepped around to the other side of the body. His heart sank at the sight of the girl's face. Her eyelids were open and a mass of ants clumped inside her hollow eye sockets. Blood caked around a slash to her left cheek. Despite her bloated face, he immediately recognised her. There was no doubt. It was Lisa Barkley. The lower side of her face rested in the sand, her lips were blue and purple blotches of congealed blood had formed under her skin around the ears and on the back of the neck. Dark brown bands of ligature marks criss-crossed around her neck, the skin broken with reddish abrasions.

Dry blood crusted over a small patch of ivory skull bone where a clump of hair and skin had been excised. The poor girl had suffered a brutal death, her body rolled down an embankment into a barren creek bed, discarded and left to be eaten by ants and crows. The indignity of it all was horrible.

From the corner of his eye, a metallic object glistening in the sun caught Jarrod's attention. It poked out from the sand, about halfway down the embankment. Jarrod asked Larry for a clip seal evidence bag which he dug out of his equipment box. Careful not to disturb the sand, Jarrod edged his way up the slope and leaned over for a closer look. A silver pendant and chain were half buried. He reached with a gloved hand and pinched the pendant with his thumb and forefinger, pulling it free from the sand. A Mercedes Benz symbol glinted in the sun and dangled from the broken chain. He let it fall into the evidence bag, sealed it, and held it up into the sunlight to study it closer. Auburn strands of hair were entwined within the links of the chain.

He stood, brushed the sand from his knees and took the bag over to Larry. He held it up for Larry to take a closer look. 'These hairs in the chain are still intact, complete with follicles at the base of each strand.'

'They look like head hairs to me,' said Larry. 'And different colour to the girl's. Probably got tangled with the chain in the struggle.' The corners of his mouth lifted with a hint of a smile. 'Sheath cells attached to the roots can be used for DNA profiling. Our killer might have left his calling card.'

Jarrod jumped when his phone vibrated in his pocket.

'I just heard,' came Brad's voice when he answered. 'Do you need me to come out and give you a hand?'

'Just stand by, mate. Benfield will let you know if he needs you. He's rounding up the CIB and uniforms. I'll need you to hold the fort in the office. Stay put for now.'

'Okay. What about the dead girl? Who is she?'

Jarrod hesitated. 'Lisa Barkley.'

'Ah, hell. Does the old man know yet?'

'No, not yet. I'll go and see him when I'm done here.'

'Righto, well sing out if you need me for anything.'

'Oh, there is one thing. I need you to send a request to Police Communications to run an urgent triangulation for the last known location of her mobile phone. Call me as soon as you hear back from them.'

'Roger that. Go ahead with the number.'

Jarrod read out the number from his notebook and ended the call.

He and Larry continued working the crime scene to prepare the body for removal from further exposure to the burning sun. The air shimmered above the scorched creek bed in heat hazes. Persistent flies buzzed around their eyes and mouths and crickets chirped in waves in a loud crescendo. Under Larry's direction, Jarrod rolled Lisa Barkley's body onto her side to inspect the underside of the torso. Larry bagged soil samples from underneath the body and took more photographs. He taped paper bags over the girl's hands to prevent loss of physical evidence and over the boots for potential forensic soil sampling. Nail scrapings would later be taken by the pathologist during the post mortem examination.

When they were done, the government undertakers were given clearance to remove the body. With great care, they wrapped Lisa Barkley's half naked, battered body in a plastic sheet and zipped her inside a human remains pouch. With well-rehearsed precision, they lifted the body bag onto a stretcher and carried it up the sandy slope and out of sight, followed by Larry lugging his equipment box. Beyond the ridge, a sliding van door slammed shut and gravel crunched under tyres as Lisa Barkley's body was driven away.

Jarrod scaled the worn path up the embankment and scanned the dry creek bed one last time. The sun had started its slow burning run down the sky, casting long shadows beneath a canvas smeared with red and gold. Someone approached, trampling a path through the undergrowth from the direction of the house.

Detective Sergeant Murray Long emerged into the clearing and stood alongside Jarrod, a good foot taller. He didn't bother with greetings. They stared out over the empty creek bed, lapsing into a distracted silence.

'Benfield told me you're the lead on this one,' said Long finally, his tone matter of fact. His eyes remained fixed on the grid of crime scene tape pegged around the depression in the sand from Lisa Barkley's body.

Jarrod nodded.

'You know the girl?'

'My missing kid.'

Long inhaled slowly through his nose and exhaled. 'Right then. I've got a bunch of uniforms and SES volunteers ready to go. Where do you want them?'

Jarrod pointed. 'I want line sweeps of the bushland along this ridge and the embankment, from the bend up there for a hundred metres downstream. I want another group doing hands and knees grid searches in the creek bed where the body was found.'

Long nodded. 'We'll bring in shovels and sieves for the sand.'

Jarrod then pointed to the compressed vehicle tracks in the grass. 'Larry still has to work the tyre tracks. Keep everyone away from there.'

'On it.' Long turned and looked at Jarrod, making eye contact for the first time. 'You go do what you gotta do. I'll take care of what needs to be done here.'

Jarrod held his gaze. 'Thanks Murray. I need to go and tell her father.'

'Sucks to be you.' Long smirked with a wink and disappeared back towards the house. 'Righto, you mob, listen up.' Murmuring voices quietened to a hush as Long barked instructions.

Jarrod's phone rang, insistent. He took a quick glance at the screen, shading it from the sun. 'What now?' he said under his breath. He answered. 'Yeah, boss. What's up?'

'I'm out front. Media got tipped off. They're camped on the street. We caught one journo trying to sneak around the perimeter. It's a bloody circus.'

'It was inevitable. Can you get onto the Police Media Unit to put in a request with the TV stations to keep their choppers away? Last thing we need is them blowing sand everywhere.'

'Already on it. I've briefed Police Media over the phone. They're sending a media officer out from the city. In the meantime, I'll do a brief stand up to keep the vultures at bay. Did you I.D. the girl?'

'It's Eric Barkley's daughter.'

'Your missing kid?'

'Yeah. Hey, boss, when you do your press conference, can you withhold the gender and age of the victim? At least until I've had a chance to speak with her father. Don't want him finding out from the media. I'll also need to bring him in for a formal I.D. of the body.'

'Of course, but I can get a uniformed crew to do that, Jarrod. You've got your hands full.'

'No, that's okay. I'm done here and I should be the one to deliver the news. I promised the old man I'd personally keep him informed.'

Benfield exhaled into the phone. 'Alright then, it's your call. I'll give the media the usual spin and make appeals for public assistance. We'll release more details once the family have been notified.'

'Any luck with the neighbours?'

'Not yet. We've had crews out door-knocking, but so far no reports of any suspect vehicle activity out here.'

'It's strange,' said Jarrod.

'What is?'

'Why would the killer dump the body out in the open to be found?'

'Maybe he panicked?'

'Or maybe he wanted her to be found.'

'Who knows what the twisted fuck was thinking? If we find a motive, we'll find our man.'

Jarrod thought some more. 'I spoke to some kids at the high school this morning. Lisa Barkley's friends.'

'What did they know?'

'Nothing. They seemed genuinely concerned.'

'Yeah, well don't be fooled. Keep an open mind. Chances are the victim knew her killer, or killers.'

'I won't rule anything out just yet. Anyway, first things first. I need to go pay the old man a visit.'

'Okay, good luck with that. Don't rule him out either, or his shitbag son. Both could be suspects. Anyway, I better go deal with the media pack.'

After the call, Jarrod made his way back towards the abandoned house. Murray Long and two uniformed officers met him, leading a hoard of SES volunteers clad in orange overalls. They continued past in single file, through the bush cutting towards the crime scene.

Out front of the house, a mob of cameramen and journalists assembled before Ross Benfield, his hands clinched behind his back as he spoke into prodding microphones. Jarrod slipped by unnoticed and jumped in his car. He drove off, weaving through a congestion of vehicles. He guided the car back towards town on auto pilot, eyes on the road but thoughts elsewhere. He followed the highway, long and sinuous. The road was mesmeric, unchanging. As he drew nearer to town his stomach churned.

Dread set in at the thought of what he had to do next.

TEN

JARROD pulled up outside the Barkley house and killed the ignition. He sat in the car, one hand gripping the steering wheel, keys clutched in the other. He breathed long and slow to control his heart rate. The engine ticked as it cooled. He waited in a cocoon of silence, the air inside the car growing hotter by the second. God, he hated this part of the job. He could never find the right words. There were no right words. There was no right reaction either. Some became angry or collapsed in hysterics. Others were dumb with shock, expressionless. Disbelief and denial were common.

Jarrod had no answers for Eric Barkley. He couldn't tell him why his daughter had been brutally murdered or why her body had been dumped in a creek bed. Jarrod wouldn't be able to console him or ease his pain. Nothing he could say would soften the blow.

He finally summoned the will to haul his backside out of the car. He ambled through the front gate, looking for signs of life in the house. His mind raced. Rehearsed words jumbled inside his head. As he reached the base of the staircase, he took a deep breath. He scaled the stairs, the wooden treads creaking under his weight. As he reached the veranda, Eric Barkley appeared in the doorway. He responded to Jarrod's solemn expression with a questioning stare. Jarrod opened his mouth to speak, but the words wouldn't come. An awkward silence lingered in the air between them.

Barkley wrung his hands together. 'Have you found her?'

Jarrod broke eye contact and nodded.

'Tell me then! Where's my daughter?'

'I'm so sorry, Mr Barkley. There's no easy way to say this. We found her body. We've commenced a murder investigation.'

'What? Bullshit!'

'I wish it was. Lisa's dead. I'm sorry.'

Barkley stepped forward, jabbing a finger at Jarrod, his face contorting into a scowl. 'No… no! Don't you come here telling me this, you bastard. You can't do this to me! You have no right! Do you hear me?'

'Mr Barkley, I've seen her body. I can't begin to…' His words trailed away.

Barkley dropped to his knees, gripping the veranda railing for support as he slumped to the floor. Sobs broke free with the guttural roar of a wounded animal. Jarrod knelt beside him, patting his back in a clumsy attempt to comfort him.

His shoulders heaved until his cries tapered into a whimper. He smeared tears from his eyes with the back of his hands and looked up at Jarrod with a pained expression. 'I need to see her. Where's my little girl?'

'She's…' Jarrod began, but the words caught in his throat. 'She's been taken to the hospital morgue. I can take you there if you like.'

His eyes locked onto Jarrod's with a level gaze, his eyebrows pinching together. 'What happened to her?'

'We don't know for sure. Her body was found earlier today behind an abandoned property, just outside of town.'

He shook his head in disbelief. 'What would she be doing out of town? Why was she there?'

'We think she was driven there by whoever killed her.'

Barkley's lips trembled and his face reddened, spittle building in the corners of his mouth. He breathed heavily through flared nostrils. Jarrod could see it in his eyes, despair gave way to rage. His eyelids narrowed into slits. 'How did she die?'

'It's too early to say for certain. We won't know for sure until we have the pathologist report.'

Barkley pulled his lips back, baring his teeth. 'Who did this to her? As God is my witness, I'll rip their heart out.' He pulled himself to his feet and clenched his fists into tight balls, the whites of his eyes prominent.

Jarrod took a step back, his palms raised. He spoke in a low, calm voice. 'I can only imagine how hard this is for you, but it's important you stay calm. Losing your cool won't help. Just breathe. Please, it's not worth it.'

Barkley's rigid posture loosened and his shoulders slumped. His lips pressed together, his head shaking as he searched for answers. 'Why would anyone do this to Lisa? Why would anyone want to hurt her?'

'We don't know that yet. We have a team of police working on it as we speak. We'll throw everything we have at this. I promise you. It's very early in the investigation, but we'll do everything possible to find whoever did this to your daughter.'

'And then what? Justice?' He shook his head with renewed resolve. 'No, that won't do. Catch that mongrel and hand him over to me. I'll dispense *real* justice.'

'Please, just let us do our jobs. Don't go taking matters into your own hands.'

'If you'd done your job Lisa would be home safe, instead of lying on a morgue slab.' He spoke with venom, his words barbs.

Daniel appeared on the veranda, his eyes darting between Jarrod and his father. 'What the hell's happened? Is this about Lisa? Where is she?'

Barkley turned his head towards his son. 'She's dead, son. Your sister is dead!'

ELEVEN

NO one spoke in the car. Jarrod glanced around at his passengers as he drove. Eric Barkley's emotionless eyes stared blankly towards the road ahead. He had aged a decade in the last few hours, bloodshot eyes and puffy cheeks the aftermath of a torrent of tears. Daniel sat in the back seat behind his father and gazed out the window. Tears pooled in the corners of his eyes, deep wells of rage and grief. He sniffed and wiped his nose with his shirt sleeve, smudging tears across his face.

Jarrod had just taken them to the hospital morgue to identify Lisa, where she lay on a stainless-steel examination table, a white sheet pressed against the contours of her body. Her face had been cleaned and her eyelids were closed. She looked like a store mannequin, her dyed black hair in stark contrast to her pasty, grey skin. They had seen her through the window in the viewing room, sparing them from that god awful smell beyond the glass, a blend of disinfectant, decomposition and body fluids. Jarrod knew it all too well and it still made him gag. The foul odour always lingered in his nostrils and clung to his clothes.

Daniel had stared at his murdered sister in disbelief. He'd been strong until that point but broke down at the sight of her body. He turned away and stormed out of the viewing room.

His father had pressed his palms on the glass, his bottom lip quivering. He whispered, his words jagged and coarse. 'Oh, Lisa.

What did they do to you? I'll get them, I promise. They'll pay for this.'

When they pulled up outside the house, Jarrod broke the silence. 'Do you mind if I take another look in Lisa's room? In case I missed anything.'

Barkley stared ahead in a daze and nodded. Daniel jumped out of the back seat and slammed the car door behind him. He bounded up the front stairs and disappeared into the house. Jarrod got out and went around to the front passenger door, opening it for Barkley who moved with the frailty of an old man. He lifted his legs out of the car and placed his feet onto the curb. Jarrod took him by the elbow and helped him stand.

He tugged his arm away. 'I can walk on my own.'

When they reached the base of the staircase, Barkley groaned as he sat down on the bottom step, pulling a pouch of tobacco from his shirt pocket. 'I'm gonna roll a smoke. Do what you have to do. You know where her room is.'

Jarrod left him alone to grieve and scaled the rickety staircase. When he reached the front door, he paused and took a deep breath. So much had changed since he was last here. Only hours earlier he was making routine inquiries for what he thought was just another runaway teenager. Now a murder investigation, the perspective from which he saw things had changed. He made his way through the house and passed Daniel's bedroom. Light peeked from beneath his closed door, the walls vibrating from the base of heavy metal music.

Jarrod came to Lisa's room, flicked on the light switch and stood in the doorway. The room was the same as he had left it, yet everything had changed. He now stood in the room of a murder victim. He scanned with a fresh set of eyes for anything he might have missed earlier.

He stepped inside, the red light bulb casting a scarlet glow. The air shifted as he closed the door. He caught the gaze of the unicorn on the wall. It unnerved him as it followed his movements. He wondered what secrets it had shared with Lisa, what those eyes had seen. He rotated on the spot, running his eyes over every feature of the room. He searched the drawers and cupboards. Nothing. Frustrated, he sat on Lisa's bed and scanned the room, taking in every detail of the dead girl's life. He sensed her loneliness and isolation.

His phone vibrated in his pocket. 'Hey, Brad. What's up?'

'I got the triangulation results on Lisa Barkley's phone.'

'Great. Go ahead with the details.'

'The last ping on her phone was at 9:25AM yesterday morning from a tower at the shopping centre. No more hits after that time. Looks like it was turned off or the battery died.'

'Shit. I need you to grab some guys and head out there to search that car park. We might get lucky. Get onto the shopping centre management and see if anyone found the phone and handed it in. Also check the lost property at the police station front counter.'

'Okay, on it.'

After the call, Jarrod sat alone with his thoughts in the dead girl's room. Daniel's music thumped through the walls. Something beneath the bedding prodded his backside. He stood and lifted the edge of the mattress, revealing the corner of a hard-covered writing pad. He slid the book from its hiding place. He figured Lisa had hidden it from her father and brother for a reason.

He held the book with both hands and hesitated. He felt the gaze of the unicorn. He looked up but the creature just stared back at him, its ethereal eyes the deepest shade of the richest earth. He opened the floral cover, revealing handwritten words on the first page.

My Diary – my one true friend.

Below the words, a unicorn was sketched in pencil in stunning detail, identical to the one on the wall. The artwork was so lifelike. Lisa was clearly a talented artist. Jarrod wondered if anybody knew that about her. He turned the page and found more sketches, eagles in flight, angels, flowers and in the centre, most stunning of all, another unicorn. Lisa's sketching technique had captured the same unsettling effect. The unicorn's eyes held their gaze as he tilted the notepad.

He flicked the page. Lisa's calligraphy was beautifully delicate. She had used a thin-tipped black pen to scribe her words. He skimmed through the pages and found she had recently begun using it as a diary. There was an entry each day for the last two weeks, right up to the night before she went missing. She had shared her inner thoughts, an intimate snapshot of her last fourteen days alive. He hoped it might reveal some answers. He sat back down on the bed and read.

Monday:

My life sucks, I'm so lonely. I dream of being happy, to love life. But the dream never comes true. I hate my life. Each day comes and goes but I'm still here, in this crappy house, in this crappy life, in this ugly body. I wonder what it's like to be happy, truly happy. I wonder what it's like to be in love. I wonder what it would be like to have a true friend, someone to really talk to, someone to share secrets with. All I have is this diary, my one true friend. My life isn't worth writing about, but I need to tell someone how I feel – NO ONE LISTENS!

Today was like every other. I went to school and it sucked. I'm tired. I need to sleep now. Until tomorrow, L.B.

Tuesday:

Tammy can be such a bitch! She said I was trying to steal Seth from her, she said I was trying to move in on her boyfriend. Some so called "friend"! As if…! I don't know what she sees in him. Anyway, we screamed at each other and I told her to shove it. I came home, school sucked anyway, I wasn't missing anything. I hate all those stupid subjects and the teachers are LOSERS! I spent the afternoon in my room listening to music. Daniel and I had a fight, he's such a pig! I don't think I'll go to school tomorrow, that place is a hole. I'm not in the mood tonight to write any more, I'm going to bed. L.B.

Wednesday:

I decided to go to school today, Dad started drinking early and he was being a prick. I had to get out of this shit hole. I saw Seth and Jason and they were pretty cool about things, they said not to worry about Tammy, she was just being weird.

Tammy and I talked, we worked things out. Things are pretty well back to normal, school still sucked. We were given a history assignment today about the American Civil War, who cares about that? I sure as hell don't.

We went over to Jason's house this afternoon, the boys smoked a bit of pot. Tammy and I just listened to music, it was soooooo boring. On the way home we saw a freaky looking guy in the street. Gave me the creeps. Never seen him before. He just stared at us.

I couldn't be bothered starting this assignment, it's crap anyway. School is crap. What's the point of it all? I'm tired, L.B.

Thursday:

Dad did it again, he touched me AGAIN! I feel so dirty. The drunken bastard came into my room tonight, he stunk of bourbon. I just wish he was dead. I hate him! I didn't know what to do, I was so scared. I just froze. I just lay there while he groped me with his grubby fingers. I don't want to talk about it. L.B.

Jarrod found himself holding his breath. Lisa had been enduring her own personal nightmare. She had no one to talk to, no one to turn to for help. He felt so sad for her, and angry. He continued reading.

Friday:

Today sucked. I felt like shit after what happened last night. I didn't want to talk to anyone at school. I hate my father, the dirty paedophile. That's what he is! I wish I could talk to someone about it, but what's the use? No one would believe me. He makes me feel so dirty, he says I am special, but only when he wants to feel me up. I couldn't face him today, or anyone else. But I met someone today. He sounded nice. I hope I get to talk to him tomorrow. I can't wait. At least I've got one thing to look forward to. I hope I dream about him. L.B.

Saturday:

What a head spin, I'm freaking out. He contacted me again! We talked all day. I wonder what he looks like, I hope he's cute. It's so good to have someone to talk to… at last! We have so much in common, it's almost too good to be true. I can't sleep, I don't know what I'm feeling right now. He makes me feel so special, like I'm the most important person in the world. I'm so excited, I just want to meet him. Until tomorrow. L.B.

Sunday:

Dad was drinking all day again, he tried to come into my room tonight but I yelled at him to get out. I hate him! The cops were around here again today looking for Daniel, who knows what he did this time. I hope they lock him up forever!!! I hate my brother.

I keep thinking of HIM. He didn't contact me today, I miss him already. I hardly know him but God I miss him, could I be in love? I wonder what his real name is. He sounds so sweet, he listens to me. He said he would do anything for me, I need him right now, I wonder where he is!

I'll try again tomorrow. I don't know if I'll go to school tomorrow, see how I feel in the morning. L.B.

Monday:

Today was ok, school didn't suck as much as usual. I topped the class in my art assignment, it's the only thing I'm good at. It was a good feeling, I felt special; for a little while at least. All the other kids still think I'm weird, they make fun of me. I don't care anymore. I think I've met my soul mate!

We chatted again tonight, for hours! He really cares for me and he knows what I'm going through. He said he loves me, I think I love him back, it's so romantic. We've talked about things, secret things that I won't even share with my diary. I dream about what he might look like, I dream of kissing him. I hope he feels the same. Goodnight, my sweet diary. L.B.

Tuesday:

Boring day today, not much to tell. School ok. I spent all day with Jason. Tammy and Seth did their own thing. Jason is pretty cool, he's a better person when Seth isn't around, he can just be himself. We talked today. He's nice. I'd never thought I'd say that about Jason.

I'm home by myself tonight. Dad's at the pub pissing it up and Daniel is probably out stealing cars or some shit. How did I become part of this family? I don't believe I'm related to them. No wonder my mother left us.

I'm about to see if my soulmate is online (that's what I like to call him) I can't wait to talk to him again. Good night. L.B.

Wednesday:

I can't believe it! He wants to meet me. We haven't decided when, but he said it will be soon. He said he loves me, he wants to make love to me. I wonder what that is like, I don't know if I am ready for that. I still feel dirty because of what Dad did.

I'll wait and see. I just want to meet him!

We talked for hours again tonight. I didn't get my history assignment done tonight but who cares, I'm gonna fail history anyway. School sucks, everyone sucks! L.B.

Thursday:

I got detention today because I didn't hand in my assignment. The teacher gave me an extension to get it done by Monday, I don't know if I will bother. I don't know if I will even go back to school, the whole thing is such a waste of time. I'm never gonna get a job anyway so what's the point? Who would ever want to give a weirdo like me a job? Sometimes I just hate myself, I see myself in the mirror and what I see makes me sick. I'm ugly, so ugly!

I hope my soulmate doesn't think so. He said he doesn't care what I look like, he said he will love me no matter what. I so hope he means that. L.B.

Friday:

He tried to do it again, the creep. I just want him to stop. He touches me, he kisses me. I'm not his girlfriend, I'm his daughter! I hate him. I just want to get away from here, my soulmate will take me away, one day. He promised! L.B.

Saturday:

I spent the day in my room. We chatted again for hours. We are going to finally meet, in the next few days. I don't know if I can go through with it, what if he hates me?

I'm excited and scared at the same time.

I'm going to meet him, in person.

I can't wait. Sweet dreams. L.B.

Sunday:

We've finally decided, we are going to meet tomorrow. I don't think I will be able to sleep. I'm not going to school, Dad won't even notice. He's so caught up in Daniel's court case, I hope they find him guilty and send him away to juvenile detention.

I can't believe we are going to meet face to face.

Good night, Diary. I'll tell you all about it tomorrow night. L.B.

The night before Lisa went missing was her last entry in the diary. Each of the remaining blank pages represented a day she would never get to write about. A life cut short. She had entrusted her life to a stranger she'd met online. This person had to be the killer.

Jarrod needed to access Lisa's computer. He sat at her desk and clicked the mouse. The monitor woke from its sleep mode, crackling with static electricity. The brightness assaulted his eyes until his pupils adjusted. The cursor blinked inside a password text box in the centre of a blue screen. He sighed and folded his arms, willing a solution to present itself.

It would be a basic security function the Forensic I.T. guys could easily bypass, but the waiting time for computer examination was months. There were even delays analysing computers for priority murder investigations. He needed access now. He looked around the room hoping for some inspiration, maybe a clue what her password might be. He stared at the unicorn. He slid out the keyboard and took a punt. He typed U-N-I-C-O-R-N. The "Incorrect password" message box flashed on screen. That would have been too easy.

He returned his attention to the diary again and flicked through the pages from cover to cover. As he was about to close it, he noticed tiny letters in the bottom right corner of the back cover, written in Lisa's distinctive handwriting. He held it up to the light and squinted. The letters read *#Mona-Lisa01.* It looked like a password.

Worth a shot. He typed in the characters and paused, mentally crossing his fingers before pressing the ENTER key. The hard drive whirred and came to life as desktop icons appeared on screen. When the system had booted, a small message occupied the screen. *Welcome back Lisa.* Jarrod stared at the screen, stunned by his dumb luck.

The desktop background image was a face he recognised instantly, but the woman held a strange expression. An image of the Mona Lisa occupied the entire screen, but the portrait had been digitally modified. Her all too familiar expression had changed to a stark look of despair. Her mysterious smirk was gone, the eyes no longer staring out from the canvas. They looked down to her left, tears welling. Jarrod was taken by how dramatically her expression had been changed by the slight modifications to her eyes and mouth.

Maybe that was how Lisa Barkley had seen the world.

TWELVE

JARROD opened the mail server on Lisa's computer and found her inbox cluttered with messages from the email address kotj_L@hotmail.com. He opened the most recent email.

My sweet 'Goth-Girl', I miss you so much. I dream of making love to you. I fantasise about touching you and wish you were here to touch me. I get so hard thinking about you. Make sure you are online at 10PM tonight so we can plan where we will meet in person. Remember, I'll bring money if you need it. Attached are pictures of the things I would love to do with you,

Your soulmate.

Kotj_L

He opened the attached files. Pornographic images appeared on screen. He closed the images and clicked on other emails from the same sender. More pornographic images were attached. The person using the tag *kotj_L* vowed his commitment and love for Lisa. He said he cared for her, that he understood her problems. The emails usually led to sexual connotations.

The first emails contained innocent content, just two friends chatting about favourite movies and music artists. Lisa was vulnerable and desperate to find anyone to talk to. He preyed on that vulnerability. He soon progressed to discussing whether Lisa had tried sex and whether she was curious about it. In her initial replies, she was reluctant but later succumbed to his advances. He'd gained her trust.

Jarrod recognised the tell-tale grooming techniques.

Her low self-esteem made her welcome any special attention, sexual or otherwise. She believed this person had fallen for her, loved her unconditionally. He, on the other hand, was playing her, creeping into her life through cyberspace. He had only one thing in mind for Lisa. Evil bastards like that made Jarrod sick, preying on the innocence and vulnerability of kids.

He then remembered what Lisa had written in her diary about her father touching her and his stomach churned. The poor girl was being preyed on in her own bedroom by two monsters, both exploiting her trust. Lisa's father was no different to the creep stalking her online.

He read every email, the depravity of them making him physically ill. He then accessed her web history. Lisa had been active on a chat website. Her account was still logged in. She'd gone into a chat room called *Coolzone*. It looked innocent enough from the outside, but Jarrod knew paedophiles lurked inside those chat rooms. The sites were their hunting grounds, where they posed as kids to lure their next victim.

Jarrod discovered a vast number of chat conversations between Lisa, using *Goth-Girl* as her tag, and *kotj_L*. They moved their conversations from the common chat room and communicated privately using messaging software. The initial chats were brief but grew into more intense exchanges with each day.

kotj_L showered Lisa with compliments, subtly extracting personal information from her. At first, she was guarded about what information she gave about herself but as her inhibitions evaporated so did her suspicions of him.

Soon she engaged in sexual roleplaying games, describing how they were touching themselves and fantasising about having sex with each other. It was alarming how quickly it descended into such sexually explicit dialogue. Lisa's mislaid trust in the stranger had allowed him to infiltrate her life.

In a matter of days, he knew her first name, where she went to school, where she lived and how old she was. He told her he was a bit older and that he would be able to teach her things that boys her own age wouldn't know. He told her that he would be gentle with her so that everything he did to her would feel nice. She believed him and soon agreed to give herself to him, to finally meet him in person.

After wading through the many chat logs, Jarrod came across the most crucial of all. Their last conversation, the night before Lisa went missing.

THIRTEEN

kotj_L: hello, my sweet girl
Goth-Girl: hey
kotj_L: I'm just sittin here thinkin of u
Goth-Girl: I'm thinkin of u 2
kotj_L: U miss me?
Goth-Girl: maybe LOL
kotj_L: I need to be with you. U know I luv u?
Goth-Girl: yep
kotj_L: R u ready to finally meet me, in person?
Goth-Girl: I can't wait
kotj_L: we need to meet somewhere secret, somewhere private
Goth-Girl: where? when?
kotj_L: do u know the little park behind the shopping centre?
Goth-Girl: yep
kotj_L: I can meet u there tomorrow at 9.30AM.
Goth-Girl: I'm not going to school anyway. How will I know u?
kotj_L: I will be wearing a red cap. What will u be wearing?
Goth-Girl: black overcoat
kotj_L: I hope u have no underwear on tomorrow LOL
Goth-Girl: maybe, if u r nice
kotj_L: I will always be nice to you
Goth-Girl: I hope so
kotj_L: u can trust me
Goth-Girl: what will we do then, after we meet in the park?

kotj_L: we can go to a motel. I know a place. I have money.

Goth-Girl: ok

kotj_L: Cool. We'll meet in the park behind the shopping centre at 9.30AM. I'll be near the rotunda. Do you know where that is?

Goth-Girl: Yeah I know it

kotj_L: Don't tell anyone ok

Goth-Girl: ok

kotj_L: u promise?

Goth-Girl: I promise. So excited. C U then. Good night.

kotj_L: Good night my Goth Girl

Jarrod's gut tightened as he finished reading. He swallowed against a wave of nauseousness, his tongue like sandpaper against the roof of his mouth. That piece of shit had set his trap and Lisa Barkley walked right into it, his willing prey. Jarrod needed to get the computer analysed right away. The chat and email directories might reveal an IP address.

He left the room and found Eric Barkley sitting on the couch in the lounge room, mesmerised by the blank television screen. He seemed oblivious to the ash falling from his hand-rolled cigarette, the embers creeping closer to his nicotine-stained fingers.

'Mr Barkley, I need to take Lisa's computer.'

He stared at the television, his eyes indifferent. 'Take the damn thing. Lisa doesn't need it anymore.'

Jarrod hesitated. 'Did you know Lisa kept a diary?'

Barkley prised his eyes away from his own reflection and looked vacantly at Jarrod. 'A diary?'

Jarrod nodded and stared into the man's glassy eyes, searching his face for answers.

He took a drag of his cigarette and blew smoke out the corner of his mouth. 'I don't know about no diary.'

Jarrod moved closer. He wanted Barkley to squirm. 'She wrote about things that made her afraid. She wrote about you.'

The blood drained from Barkley's face and his sagging eyes lowered to the floor.

Jarrod leaned in and whispered, 'I know what you did to her.'

Barkley's eyes darted up and fixed onto Jarrod's. He opened his mouth to speak but hesitated. Jarrod's gaze bore down on him.

'I… I never meant to…' Barkley dipped his chin to his chest and his posture slumped. His shoulders heaved as he sobbed, his face burying into his hands.

'You'll have to live with it. You can't run from yourself.'

Jarrod stepped away, disgust gnawing away at his insides. He went back into Lisa's room and unplugged the hard drive tower. He grabbed the diary and walked out with the computer under his arm. He had to get out, the walls were closing in on him.

He stepped out onto the veranda and breathed in, grateful for the fresh night air filling his lungs. He hoped like hell he would never have to return to that house.

FOURTEEN

JUST after 8.30PM, a man wearing a navy suit and matching tie appeared in the open doorway to Jarrod's office and rapped his knuckles on the door. He looked impressive, tall and athletic, with college boy good looks. His sculptured hair was spiked with gel. 'Excuse me, mate. Are you Jarrod O'Connor?' He held up a police badge.

Jarrod got up from his desk where he'd been studying Lisa Barkley's diary. He held out his hand. 'Yeah, come in. Joe Marshall, right?'

The city detective accepted his handshake with a hearty, almost painful, grip. 'That's right. The guys downstairs sent me up. Am I interrupting?'

'No, no. Not at all. I've been expecting you. Thanks for travelling out here so soon. I could use your help.'

'No problems. I'm happy to get out of the city any chance I get. Makes me claustrophobic. I needed some country air.'

'Ah, don't be fooled. Lockyer looks like a quiet country town from the outside, but I reckon there's something in the local water, makes people go loopy. Cases like this one, hysteria can spread fast.'

'Sounds like you've got your hands full.'

'To be honest, our arses are hanging out of our pants. Any help we can get is much appreciated. When can you start?'

'Do you have the hard drive here?'

'Yep, right here.' Jarrod gestured to the computer tower on the floor beside his desk.

'I'll get my gear from the car and we can start straight away.' Joe took off his jacket and hung it over the back of a chair.

'Sounds great,' said Jarrod. 'I was just about to make a coffee. You up for a brew before we get started?' He held up the plain labelled tin of instant coffee. 'It's not the hipster latte you're probably used to.'

'Caterer's Blend? My favourite. That stuff has gotten me through many an all-nighter. Chuck in plenty of sugar though, will ya?' He winked and the corners of his mouth stretched to form a subtle smile.

'I'll shout you a proper coffee in the morning. The café up the street does the best coffees in town.'

'You're on. I'll just go grab my gear from the car.'

'Need a hand?'

'Nah, mate. All good.' Joe disappeared out of the office, his footfalls echoing down the stairwell.

Jarrod had a good feeling about this bloke. He had phoned the Child Exploitation Taskforce's forensic computer unit earlier in the evening and Joe agreed to drop everything and travel up from Sydney. He had the software and expertise to extract the data needed from Lisa Barkley's computer.

Brad wandered into the office, yawning. 'Hey, mate. Sorry, no luck on the phone. We searched every inch of that car park, and it hasn't been handed in.'

'Shit. Let's hope it turns up.'

'Who's the suit I passed on the stairs?'

'Kiddie porn computer tech. Up from the city to scan Lisa Barkley's computer.'

Brad tilted his head with a raised eyebrow. 'What do you hope to find?'

'Lisa was being groomed online. She was due to meet someone at nine-thirty yesterday morning at the park behind the shopping centre.'

'Has to be him, right?'

'I'd bet my left nut on it. Oh, that reminds me. I need you to ring the afterhours security office and get hold of surveillance footage in and around the centre around that time. We might get lucky with some vision.'

Brad slid his hands into his pockets and sighed. 'So, we won't be going home anytime soon?'

'Nope. It's gonna be a long night.'

'Righto. On it.' Brad sat at his desk and made the call.

Joe returned, breathing heavily after lugging up an equipment box and laptop computer bag slung over his shoulder.

Jarrod took him down the hall to the tearoom where they made coffees. When they returned to the office Brad was heading out the door, car keys jingling in his hand.

'Security is downloading the surveillance footage as we speak. I'm heading down to their office now.'

Jarrod introduced Brad to Joe, and he set off down the stairs.

They returned to the office and Joe unpacked his gear. After connecting a power source and cables to Lisa Barkley's computer he ran a diagnostic on his laptop. He was soon accessing email directories and chat caches on the hard drive.

'Bloody hell, this bloke really brainwashed the poor kid,' said Joe as he read through the chat conversations.

'Yeah, the sick bastard groomed her from day one.'

'He must have thought he'd struck the jackpot when he stumbled across a local girl.' Joe spoke as he typed madly on his keyboard. 'I assume he *is* local, based on his knowledge of the meeting point, I mean?'

'Yeah, we've made that assumption. He's either local or he's someone who visits here enough to know the layout of the town. They planned to meet only the night before, so he must have been within driving distance.'

Joe ran anti masking software to track the source of the emails and the identity of the user Internet Protocol where the chat directories originated from. Working the mouse, he scrolled through directories for about twenty minutes. He then leaned back in the chair, shaking his head in frustration. 'Cunning bastard.'

'What is it?' said Jarrod.

Joe bit his bottom lip and took a deep breath. 'The system this guy is using has some pretty impressive firewalls. He's set up a complex system of anonymous proxy servers. I decoded the first set of directories, but it then bounced all over the place. He's using encryption software which rebounds his IP number all over the network. It's impossible to track the original source.'

'Are you telling me we can't trace him?'

'Here, I'll show you.' Joe ran another application. 'My software has the latest IP tracing tool using mapping technology to pinpoint longitude and latitude co-ordinates. Each IP address is unique, and every computer connected to the web is assigned an IP address.'

'Yeah, so what's your point?'

Joe rolled his chair over to Jarrod's computer and logged onto the internet. He entered a URL address and a website opened. 'Here, look at this.'

Jarrod read the on-screen message over Joe's shoulder. *Your IP address is 154.113.238.12. You are located in Lockyer, New South Wales, Australia – latitude 27.6 longitude 154.018. You are connected to the Internet through: NSW Gov.*

'What you're looking at here is your IP address. This website traces your location via your internet connection. It's that simple. Look at this.'

Joe scrolled down the webpage and clicked a map icon. A world map filled the screen. Two crosshair lines intersected at the exact location on the map where the town of Lockyer was positioned. Jarrod was stunned how quickly his geographic location could be identified.

'Now compare that to what this guy is using.' Joe rolled his chair back across to Lisa Barkley's computer. 'See this IP address your suspect is using? It's an anonymous proxy server, a phantom. It was easy enough to extract the number from his emails but look what happens when I key in his number.'

Joe typed the number into web tracker software on his laptop. The text read *IP location is UNKNOWN*.

He scrolled down to the world map and the crosshair lines bounced all over the screen. First, they settled on a remote Indonesian island before jumping across to the East coast of the USA. The crosshairs fixed on a position for a second and bounced across the screen again.

'I'm sorry, mate. I can't trace him.' Joe pushed with his legs and rolled the chair out from the desk.

'What about the Hotmail email address? Can't we trace that?'

'Nope, the same software applies to the Hotmail address. My software can analyse an e-mail and its headers, even Hotmail, but not this guy. He's covered his arse far too well. I'll give him credit for that; impressive.'

'We have to nail this prick. Is there anything else we can do?'

'This firewall lets him roam the network without leaving a digital footprint. I've seen this kind of software before. There're a few different varieties on the market, but nothing I have can decode this one. He must have paid top dollar for it. He's got programs running simultaneously which scramble the network, making it impossible to decode.'

'Shit! What now?'

'There is one thing we can do,' said Joe, with a glimmer of hope in his eyes.

'What is it?'

'I hope you had no plans tonight. We're going fishing.' Joe's lips parted with a wry smile. 'Let's play this guy at his own game.'

Jarrod nodded. He liked the sound of that.

FIFTEEN

TWENTY minutes later, Joe had created a covert IP address for his laptop using his own masking software. He went into the *Coolzone* chat room, posing as a fourteen-year-old girl. A long shot, but there was a chance the suspect might return to his old hunting grounds.

'You do realise this is a million to one shot?' said Joe, not lifting his eyes from the screen.

'Yeah, I know the odds. Do we have any other choice?'

'Not really. The odds aren't that bad when you think about it. These idiots often prowl several chat rooms at once until they hook up with some unsuspecting kid. They often use the same usernames or a similar derivative. This bloke might rear his head again, you never know.'

'Would he be that stupid? I mean, while the heat is on straight after the girl's body was found? You'd think he'd lie low.'

'Remember, these blokes don't think like you and me. He's got the taste for it, and he knows just how easy it is to handpick victims online. He might be active again sooner than you think.'

'What have we got to lose?' Jarrod rolled a chair over beside Joe, who was registering a username.

'What name do you want to use? If you were a fourteen-year-old girl, what would you like to be called?'

'I've not really given that much thought. How about we call ourselves Christine?'

'Christine it is. She'll like horse riding, Lady Gaga and boys with blonde hair.' Joe entered the username fields and interests. 'We'll say she comes from Sydney. We don't want to make ourselves too obvious.'

Soon, Joe was engaging in live chats with people from all over the world. Every time someone responded to his username a chime sounded. The chime ding-donged every twenty seconds or so.

"Hey sweet thing, have you sucked cock before?" came the first response. The message had an attachment. Joe clicked on the icon and a close-up dick pic appeared on screen.

'These bastards are incredible,' said Joe, shaking his head. 'We could have been a real fourteen-year-old kid just trying to chat with other kids. These chat lines are full of scum like this.'

He ignored the response, which had been sent from bigcock69. There were several responses like this, no grooming at all, just perverts sending explicit propositions. Others were more subtle, but their intentions were quite clear. A response from studguy02 said, *"Hi Christine, are you lonely? I'd love to be your friend. Whatchya up ta?"*

"Not much. Just cruizin. Wat u doin?" Joe typed.

studguy02: *"I bet ur so pretty, what r u wearing right now?"*

"Just baggy shorts and a t-shirt."

studguy02: *"Do you have underwear on? Do you have big boobs?"*

"LOL. That's embarrassing, why do you want to know?"

studguy02: *"I just want to imagine what you look like. I'm getting horny already."*

"Horny! LOL. Why?"

studguy02: *"Why? U sound so pretty. I'd love to meet you. Have you had sex with boys?"*

"Maybe. LOL. What if I have?"

studguy02: *"I can show u stuff those boys don't know. We could do things that would feel sooooo nice."*

Joe leaned in and yelled at the screen. 'Sicko!' He turned to Jarrod. 'I'd love to reach in and grab this guy by the throat. Can you believe how brazen these guys are? This could be someone's daughter sitting in her bedroom while her parents are watching TV in the next room. This is how easy it is. Kids on the net are so vulnerable.'

All the while, the chime sounded as more responses came in. It was overwhelming. Joe played around for a while with these people, not going too far with any of them. He kept a close eye on the usernames, but nothing resembled the suspect.

He stayed in the chat room using the fake profile of fourteen-year-old Christine for about an hour. The sheer number of perverted responses was sickening. He and Jarrod took turns at chatting with the sickos online, but they were just wasting time. Jarrod had given hornyguyxxx the brush off when he noticed Joe deep in thought.

Joe rubbed his chin. 'k-o-t-j underscore L. Any ideas what that might mean?'

'No idea. It could mean something, or it could be nothing. Maybe an acronym? Who knows?'

Jarrod and Joe just sat there, staring at the screen.

Brad walked in and gave them a strange look. 'What are you blokes so mesmerised about?' He blew the steam rising from a mug of coffee. 'Find anything?'

Jarrod's eyes remained fixed on the screen. 'Nope, we can't trace him. We're combing chat lines to see if he reappears, but it's a needle in a haystack. How about you? How did you get on with the CCTV footage from the plaza?'

Brad held up a disc. 'The security boys outdid themselves. They had it ready for me. It's all on this.'

Brad stood behind Jarrod and Joe, and they all stared at the computer screen. The hypnotic hum of the monitor broke the silence.

'King of the Jungle,' said Brad.

Jarrod looked up at him. 'Huh?'

'King of the Jungle. That tag name you're staring at. Kotj,' said Brad, as if it was obvious.

Joe looked at Brad and then back at the screen. 'You've *got* to be shitting me. King of the Jungle, it's so bloody simple. But, what's with the underscore L?' Joe leaned closer to the screen as if that would help him find the answer.

'Dunno.' Brad lost interest. 'I'm off to stare at security videos. I'll use the monitor in the scenes of crime office.' He strolled out and disappeared down the hallway.

'What does King of the Jungle L mean?' Joe said, thinking out loud.

Jarrod doodled the letters on a pad. 'What's the King of the Jungle?'

Joe raised his eyebrows. 'The lion.'

Jarrod nodded. 'Lion.'

'What's with the L then?'

Their eyes met and they both exclaimed in unison, 'Lion-ell'

His name was Lionel.

SIXTEEN

ROSS Benfield had scrambled a task force of local and city detectives. At 10.30PM the station conference room filled with long-faced detectives for the first briefing. A Mexican wave of yawns circled the room. Everyone had that pink-eyed look, shoulders slouched. Benfield went around the room as each team leader gave their update.

Murray Long and his team had returned from the crime scene after hours of searching the creek bed and surrounding bushland. His shoes were caked in dry mud, his trouser knees ruined by grass stains. So far, they'd come up with nothing, but would resume searches at first light. The scene remained under police guard. Lisa Barkley's missing clothing and belongings hadn't been located.

The Police Media Unit had issued a media release naming Lisa Barkley as the murder victim and included the most recent photo of her. The public were being urged to come forward with information of sightings of Lisa on the morning of her disappearance. Intelligence officers were manning the phones to triage information from callers.

There was no information at hand relating to the killer's vehicle and door knocks at the neighbouring properties were fruitless. No one had seen or heard anything. The killer had driven a vehicle into an abandoned property, dumped a dead girl's body in a dry creek bed and driven out again, all unnoticed by anyone. He was a ghost.

Jarrod introduced Joe Marshall to the group who explained, in simple terms, why the suspect's email address and IP number couldn't be traced. He explained how he and Jarrod had been using themselves as bait to hook the predator who'd been prowling teen chat rooms. He revealed their breakthrough of a possible first name, which would be the priority line of inquiry. Brad had begun the mind-numbing process of scouring security videos, which so far had yielded nothing. There were still hours of vision from multiple camera angles to be viewed. Lisa Barkley's last known movements were still being pieced together. Jarrod planned to interview her friends again the next day in case he'd missed anything. They might remember something.

The post mortem examination order had just been issued by the Coroner and the autopsy would be performed by the forensic pathologist the next morning. The sense of frustration in the room was palpable. The spotlight was on them. The media circus had kicked into top gear and they were under immense public pressure to hunt down Lisa Barkley's killer.

Ross Benfield had been leaning against the lectern at the front of the room during the briefings. His face sagged with exhaustion. 'Righto people, good work. I appreciate it's been a long day. Go home and get a few hours' sleep. That's an order. I'll see you all bright and early tomorrow.'

The room emptied amid tired murmurs and sighs. As Jarrod stood, his knees clunked. Everything in his body felt heavy from his arms to his feet. He lolled his head from side to side, his stiff neck protesting.

'Have you got somewhere to stay?' he asked Joe.

Joe frowned, dark shadows under his eyes now prominent. 'Um, no. Not yet. I didn't have time to book a motel room.'

'I can offer you a bunk at my joint. The wife and kids are away visiting my sister-in-law. There's a spare room. You're more than welcome to crash there.'

'Sounds good,' Joe said. 'Best offer I've had all day. I've got an overnight bag in the car.'

They gathered their things from the Youth Crime Unit office and switched off the computers. They'd chatted online with deviants enough for one night. Jarrod's skin was still crawling. He had an urge to scrub his hands with bleach and disinfect the computer mouse and keyboard after the filth he'd seen online.

'I couldn't do your job dealing with those twisted fucks every day.'

'I guess you become hardened to it,' said Joe as they reached the top of the stairs. He stopped and faced Jarrod. 'But the kiddie porn is the worst. Man, we've uncovered some sick shit on the dark web. It's a commodity. They trade it like shares on the stock market. We've dismantled some major child exploitation rackets, but for each one we shut down, more rear their heads. We're throwing resources at it but it's a losing battle. These guys are smart, always one step ahead.'

'I've heard it said that trading in kiddie porn is a victimless crime. That's such bullshit,' said Jarrod. 'There are real kids out there getting abused and those fuckers are creating the demand for more images.'

'Exactly. And that's our focus, finding the victims. We've managed to identify some kids and get them out of abusive situations. You've got the offenders who get their kicks trading kiddie porn, and then you've got the ones who start acting out, like our guy Lionel. Whether or not they act out, in my book they're all paedophiles.'

'I'm with you on that,' said Jarrod. 'Come on, let's get the hell out of here.'

Soon they were rumbling home in Jarrod's Forerunner. When they arrived, Jarrod showed Joe the spare room and gave him a fresh towel.

He called Jayne, her familiar voice reassuring, but her words edged with concern.

'Please be careful, Jarrod.'

'I will. You know me.'

'I know you better than anyone. That's what worries me. Promise me you won't get in too deep this time. Not like last time.'

'I promise. But I have to do my job.'

'I know, but just don't let it consume you. We can't go through all that again. It's not all on you. The responsibility isn't yours alone.'

A silence hung on the line between them. 'But she's just a kid. I owe it to her to find her killer.'

Jayne sighed. 'I know. That's why I love you. Do what you have to, but please, just be careful. Nothing reckless, you promise?'

'Scouts honour.'

'You were never in the scouts,' said Jayne lightly. He could tell she was smiling. 'Just get some sleep and make sure you eat properly. There's plenty of food in the freezer.'

'I will. Give the kids a kiss on the head for me, will you?' he said.

'I will. They miss you. So do I. We'll be home in a few days.'

'Goodnight, sweetheart,' Jarrod whispered into the phone.

After the call he grabbed a quick shower and fell into his bed. He reached over and stroked the void usually filled by Jayne. He hugged her pillow, her fragrance soothing. As each limb became heavy and the beat of his heart slowed, the comfort of his bed lured him into a deep sleep.

SEVENTEEN

AFTER grabbing coffees and rolls on the run from the bakery, Jarrod and Joe arrived at the office by 7.30AM the next morning. They logged back into the chat rooms under the assumed covert identity. For hours they roleplayed in more sordid chat conversations with online deviants. Yet, their suspect Lionel failed to rear his head. The situation looked hopeless. They still had very little to go by.

The intelligence officers ran profile checks on state and federal police databases for registered sex offenders with Lionel featuring in the name or aliases. There were hundreds of hits from across the country. Each needed checking. They needed to narrow down the search parameters. So far, they were acting on just a hunch. The name Lionel could be a red herring.

At 10.30AM, Jarrod's desk phone rang. He swivelled his chair and answered.

'Good morning, Jarrod,' came a man's sing-song Indian accent. Jarrod recognised Dr Kaushal's cheery voice. The Government Medical Officer also doubled as the town's forensic pathologist.

'Good morning, doctor. Thanks for calling. Do you have any news?'

'Oh, yes. I've finished the Barkley girl's autopsy.'

'Cause of death?'

'Ligature strangulation. She also suffered blows to the head and upper body. From their severity, I believe your killer was in a rage state. But the poor girl fought for her life.'

'How can you tell?'

'Defensive bruising on her forearms and abrasions on her back are all indicative of a struggle. I took scrapings from under her nails and looked under the microscope. Definitely skin.'

'So, she scratched him?'

'Most likely. However, there are scratches around the ligature marks. Best not to draw conclusions yet. These may have been self-inflicted as she clawed to extricate herself during strangulation.'

'Enough for DNA testing?'

'Absolutely. We'll soon know if it's the victim's or the killer's DNA.'

'Any indication of what was used to strangle her?'

'Hard to say for certain. Possibly a cord or cable, or something similar. No blistering consistent with rope burns.'

'Was she…' Jarrod hesitated.

'Sexually assaulted?'

Jarrod paused. 'Yes.'

'I'm afraid so. Trauma was consistent with rape. I've taken swabs and pubic hair combings for DNA analysis.'

Jarrod sighed. 'Okay, thanks, doctor. I'll come over soon to collect the samples myself.'

Jarrod welcomed the distraction and the chance to stretch his legs. Joe still worked the chat rooms and Brad was busy viewing the shopping centre security footage. Jarrod swung by the major incident room that had been stood up in the station conference room. He briefed Ross Benfield who co-ordinated the allocation of investigations logs. Teams of local CIB detectives and investigators on loan from the Homicide Squad were chasing down every lead. The station hummed. Uniformed logistics officers triaged the influx of job logs coming in.

There were calls from people who had bad feelings about their neighbours. Other callers provided information about suspect vehicles or theories about the murder. Calls even came in from self-declared psychics claiming to have had visions of the murder scene and dead girl. Everyone had an opinion. Social media speculation ran rampant. Media had whipped themselves into a frenzy. Every shred of information had to be followed up.

Jarrod never cared much for visiting the morgue and today was no exception. It was a detached facility at the back of the base hospital, unseen from the car park. No more elaborate than a large outhouse, the drab brickwork had recently been given a facelift with a varnish-like coating. The terracotta roof tiles were repainted in a ghastly mustard colour. The morgue sat alongside an imposing, factory-like structure with incinerator chimneys towering forty metres high, spewing white steam. This part of the hospital was hidden from public view, concealed within a cluster of industrial buildings.

Jarrod parked outside the mortuary building and took a deep breath, anxiety growing. He crossed the car park on foot towards the front entrance. A flyscreen door swung ajar, its hinges creaking. He pushed it open and rapped his knuckles on the heavy front door. A sign on the door shouted, "RESTRICTED ACCESS". He looked up at the security camera. A buzzer sounded, followed by the click of a locking mechanism. He pushed the door open, the stark odour of hospital grade disinfectant and death swirling around him as it escaped into the outside air.

A first-year constable gave him a wave from behind the reception desk. The poor lad had drawn the short straw, taking one for the team as the rostered morgue officer.

'Hey sarg. You here for the murdered girl?'

Jarrod nodded. 'Yeah, mate. Is the doc about?'

'He's out back.'

Jarrod walked by the glassed-in viewing room, where Daniel and Eric Barkley had formally identified Lisa's body. Dr Kaushal emerged through a set of opaque flap doors, suited up in surgical scrubs, disposable cap and white rubber boots. He wiped his bloodied gloves on an apron which reminded Jarrod of the ones worn by butchers.

'Ah, Jarrod. I didn't expect to see you so soon.' His jovial voice was muffled behind a facemask and splash shield. He held his hands up, fingers pointed to the ceiling. 'You'll have to excuse me. I've just opened up my next client.' Jarrod could see from the man's squinting eyes that he was smiling.

'Come with me. The samples are ready.' The doctor backed up and parted the flap doors with his backside, holding them open as Jarrod gingerly stepped through.

The naked corpse of an elderly man lay on a stainless-steel examination table, rib cage splayed open and organs exposed. The dead man's head rested in a U-shaped cradle, his arms straight by his sides. His mouth gaped open, exposing toothless gums and swollen tongue. Lifeless grey eyes peeked out through half-closed eyelids. Surgical cutters and scalpels were laid out on a metal tray. A coiled hose with spray nozzle hung on a bracket on the lime green tiled wall. Identical floor tiles were contoured towards drainage covers below the cutting table. Jarrod wondered where Garth was – the lanky morgue attendant.

'Garth is off collecting another body from ICU,' said the doctor, as if reading Jarrod's mind. 'Heart attack victim, I believe.' He wobbled his head and chuckled. 'With the rate of coronary disease, we're never short of customers.'

Dr Kaushal removed his gloves and splash shield and patted the dead man's shoulder. 'I'll be right with you, Mr Simmons,' he said with a sincere smile. 'Just entertain yourself for a moment.' He walked along the rows of refrigerators, counting out the hatch door numbers as he went.

He stopped at hatch number six. 'The young girl is in this one.' He grabbed the handle and tugged it open, the seal suction releasing its grip. 'Could you please give me a hand? The bloody rollers have seized up, like everything else around here.'

Dr Kaushal gripped the railing on one side and gestured for Jarrod to grab the other. Together, they heaved the body tray out along the clunky rollers. A white sheet was draped over the contours of a female body. Kaushal folded back the sheet exposing Lisa Barkley's battered face, her hollow eye sockets and pale face haunting under the glow of fluorescent bulbs. Her black hair shone, wet and slicked over a bloodied patch of bare skin.

'What do you make of the missing scalp?' said Jarrod.

'The scalp was sliced off post mortem. Superficial. Very crude, but enough to remove a patch of skin and hair the size of a fifty-cent piece. Not the handiwork of someone who knew what they were doing.'

'A souvenir?'

'You're the detective. But, yes, that would be my guess.'

Kaushal tilted his head to the side to study the girl's face. 'Although your victim died from strangulation…' he lifted her chin with a pistol grip and rolled her head to one side to expose the ligature marks, '…she was unconscious at the time, judging from the skull fracture.'

Jarrod frowned. 'Skull fracture?'

'Yes, at the back of the head. It may have been to subdue her when she was struggling. The blow wasn't enough to kill her. I've documented it all in the photos which I'll send to you.'

'Any idea of the implement used?'

'Blunt object. That's the best I can give you. Anything else would be speculation on my part.'

Jarrod breathed through his mouth in a futile attempt to mask the foul smell of that horrid place. 'You said on the phone she was raped.'

'Correct. I believe she was assaulted, dragged, raped and strangled. Probably in that order.' Dr Kaushal then pulled back the white sheet, further exposing Lisa Barkley's bruised body. He lifted her shoulders and rolled her onto her side, exposing the abrasions on her back. Jarrod's mind flashed to the grim sight of her battered body lying face down in that sun-baked creek bed.

The doctor looked up at Jarrod. 'Seen enough?'

Jarrod nodded.

'The samples are over on the bench.' The doctor covered up Lisa's body and Jarrod helped him slide the tray back into the refrigerator. The thud of the closing hatch echoed off the wall and floor tiles. Jarrod followed Kaushal to a steel bench at the end of the room.

'I've laid them out in order. The samples are all labelled. There are organ tissues and blood samples for toxicology screening.' He pointed to the row of samples, stored in screw-top specimen cannisters and swab tubes. 'The swabs and fingernail scrapings are all there.'

'And the T-shirt, bra and boots the girl was brought in with? Where are they?'

'Oh, of course. They are packaged up in this.' The doctor bent down and handed him a large brown paper evidence bag. The weight of the boots was heavy in Jarrod's arms. He looked inside to verify the items.

Jarrod called for the constable to come in and sign the samples over to him. The constable placed the samples into a polystyrene cooler box and taped down the lid, signing across the seals.

With the specimens and exhibits in hand, Jarrod was relieved to be leaving the air-conditioned chill of the morgue. He walked out into the warm sunlight, back into the world of the living.

When he arrived back at the station, he lodged the evidence with the station exhibit officer who placed the perishable specimens into a padlocked fridge. They were booked in to be delivered to the scientific section in the city on the next police transport vehicle. The strands of hair, pendant and soil samples found at the crime scene were also being sent for analysis.

He headed back upstairs and nearly collided into Brad as he ran out of the scenes of crime office, his face bright with excitement.

'Jarrod, you're back. Good. You gotta come look at this. I've found something on one of the security videos. I found Lisa Barkley!'

EIGHTEEN

JARROD stared at the zoomed-in image of Lisa Barkley filling a computer screen. She had been captured on security footage standing in line at an automatic bank teller machine in the shopping centre plaza. Brad had freeze-framed the colour image and zoomed in so that Lisa's face was visible. Her fringe dangled over her eyes. She was draped in a black overcoat and a backpack hung from one shoulder.

The time on the screen said 9.15AM, just 15 minutes before she was due to meet her online predator. Seeing her like this, so alive, was unsettling.

Jarrod then noticed the man. From the end of the line, the man watched Lisa. Every other person in the plaza went about their business, caught up in their own lives or gazing at phone screens. But not this man.

Jarrod stabbed a finger at the screen, touching the man's face. 'Him! That guy there. Zoom in on him.'

Brad clicked the mouse and zoomed in on the man's face. As the image expanded, the picture quality deteriorated. The man's face become a blur of colour pixels. Brad zoomed the image back out to give the clearest picture. The dark recesses of his eyes contrasted with his distorted, pale face.

It was difficult to tell if the poor picture quality had created this effect, but to Jarrod the man's face appeared disfigured. The man was Caucasian, quite tall and had an athletic build. He wore jeans and a dark grey hoodie. Scraggy auburn hair jutted out at the sides from beneath the hood. Lisa stood two people ahead of him in the queue, oblivious to the fact she was being watched.

'Now that we know where she was at nine-fifteen, can you isolate the various camera angles around that time?' said Jarrod.

'Already done.' Brad produced the map and unfolded it out over the desk. 'Here, check this out. The security manager gave me this overlay map showing the positions and angles of each camera. Lisa's last phone ping was at nine twenty-five at the shopping centre, yeah?'

Jarrod nodded.

'So, I used that as a reference point and searched all the cameras thirty minutes either side. It was a needle in a haystack and much of the footage was grainy, so I had to go back over it in slow-mo in case I missed anything. That's why it's taken so long. But once I found her at the ATM I pieced together the video clips to retrace her steps in chronological order. I've edited the clips into one video sequence.'

'How did you know how to do that?'

'The editing software is intuitive. A bit of trial and error, but I worked it out.'

'You *are* full of surprises. What other hidden talents have you not told me about?'

'None that I know of. Anyway, watch this.'

Jarrod dragged a chair over and spun it around so that his elbows leaned on its back, straddling it like he was riding a horse.

Brad double-clicked on a video file. Lisa Barkley was first captured as she walked in through the northern entrance of the shopping centre. The vision jumped to more camera angles showing her ambling through the shopping centre. She walked into a bakery and came out holding a drink and taking a bite from something in a paper bag.

'Pause it,' snapped Jarrod. 'Get the name of that bakery and make a note to get their in-store security footage.'

Brad made notes and clicked play again. The video showed Lisa making her way along the main plaza, stopping to look at clothing on display on racks outside a discount store. She then peered through the window of a video game store. She was in no rush, killing time. Jarrod then spotted the hooded man from the ATM queue.

'Stop. Go back.' Jarrod pointed to the man on screen.

Brad played the footage back to where Lisa had gone to the bakery and clothing store. In the distance, just in camera shot, the man appeared. He was following Lisa through the plaza.

They studied the footage as Lisa crossed the plaza towards the ATM. The man emerged on screen, following Lisa at a distance. He joined the queue behind her at the ATM and his stare never deviated from the back of her head. Lisa withdrew cash and walked away towards the Southern exit. The man left the queue and followed Lisa.

The last vision showed Lisa walking out towards the car park which backed onto the park, the proposed meeting place. The man stopped at the exit and did a strange thing. He looked up at the camera. A horrid smile appeared on his disfigured face, seemingly just for the camera.

He turned and disappeared out of camera view towards the car park, behind Lisa Barkley.

NINETEEN

DETECTIVES were dispatched to the shopping centre to distribute still image printouts from the security footage and to review in-store security vision at the stores Lisa Barkley had visited. Images of the suspect were shown to shop owners and shopping centre staff, but no one recognised him. A media release was issued with appeals for public information, the image of the man's face saturating social media. Television stations, both local and national, delivered the breaking news of the "police manhunt" for Lisa Barkley's killer. Online news bulletins shouted, "Breaking news: Murder suspect revealed by police."

Jarrod didn't mind all the hype. At least the suspect's photo was getting the exposure he wanted. They now had a suspect profile to work on and it was only a matter of time before someone recognised him. It was the first real break in the case. The investigation had momentum and the dedicated Crime Stoppers hotline went into meltdown. Half leads came in, but nothing concrete. They still didn't have a name, and the image didn't match any of the registered sex-offenders on the state database. Interstate checks were still underway.

Jarrod checked in on Joe Marshall, who had spent most of the day covertly chatting in teen chat rooms. Joe was like a sniffer dog chasing a scent, fixated on finding Lionel. He slumped in a reclined office chair, his shoes discarded and his socked feet up on the desk. His fingers worked the laptop nursed in his lap.

Jarrod took a seat beside Joe. 'Any luck?'

Joe replied without looking up. 'This guy I'm chatting with right now. He's offered to fly up from Melbourne with a spare return ticket and two grand to have sex with him in a motel. He thinks I'm a fifteen-year-old girl named Karly.'

Jarrod shook his head. 'Sick bastards. Acting out their sordid little fantasies behind a keyboard.'

Joe gave Jarrod a sideways glance as he typed. 'So, I hear you guys had a breakthrough. Do you have a name yet?'

'Not yet. No one has come forward with anything concrete. I've got a strange feeling about this guy.'

'How do you mean?'

'Dunno, I can't explain it. The way he smiled at the camera, I sensed something. Maybe we're underestimating him.'

'Come on, mate, how smart can this guy be? He's probably left his DNA all over the girl's body and we know what he looks like. It's only a matter of time before we track him down, you'll see.'

'I guess so. I hope you're right. Even so, something about him just doesn't sit right with me.'

Joe twisted in his chair and raised an eyebrow. 'The guy's a predator and a rapist.'

'I mean, he's been so careless. This makes him more dangerous, more desperate. She was beaten, raped, strangled and her body dumped in a creek bed, out in the open to be found. He controlled his rage, followed her, waited for the right opportunity, and then struck. All the planning, the encrypted online profile, the patient grooming. Doesn't fit with a man in a rage state. Something's off.'

Joe slid his feet off the desk and squirmed upright in his chair. 'Take Ivan Milat. Australia's worst serial killer, that we know of at least. His MO was to hand-select victims who wouldn't be noticed missing straight away, backpackers, hitchhikers, drifters. He was opportunistic but calculating. Accounts from his victims who escaped described him as friendly at first, but just out of the blue a switch would flick in his head, like Jekyll and Hyde. He killed his victims with brutality, in a rage. He was methodical and impulsive, all at once.'

'You think our guy can turn the rage on and off as well?' said Jarrod.

'It's possible. Maybe he doesn't fit any particular profile.'

'Yeah, I suppose. But the guy on the security footage doesn't match my mental picture of an online child groomer.'

'So, what *was* your mental image?' said Joe. 'A nerdy accountant type or bank manager? Guy in a suit? Or an old perv?'

'I dunno.'

'Just don't make assumptions, that's all I'm saying.'

Jarrod glanced at the laptop screen. 'Has our mate, Lionel, surfaced yet?'

Joe pursed his lips and shook his head. 'Nope. You'll be the first one to know if he does. I'll keep at it. He might rear his head again.'

Jarrod stood. 'I need to get out of here for a while… to clear my head. Ring me on my mobile if you come up with anything, will ya?'

'Sure thing.'

'Do you need anything? Coffee?'

'Nah, I'm good. I've had my caffeine fix for the day. But, if you've got a spare body, I wouldn't mind someone giving me a hand to collate all the intel I'm collecting on these online paedophiles. Even if they're not linked to your killer, my unit will run an operation on them when I finish working on your case.'

'Yeah, sure. I'll see if Brad is free to give you a hand.'

Jarrod needed to get out of the station. The place caved in around him, suffocating him. He drove out, going nowhere in particular. He cruised the streets and stared at people in cars, pedestrians, joggers and bicycle riders. They stared back at him, mirroring the same wary expression. In every face he searched for that disfigured man, that smirk etched into his memory, a vivid snapshot he couldn't erase.

Jarrod watched a group of high schoolers strolling along the footpath, skylarking and whistling at friends across the street. They weren't carrying the weight of the world on their shoulders, not yet anyway. They were still carefree, not giving a shit. Lisa Barkley should have been with them.

Jarrod drove into the car park of the shopping centre and parked. He just sat and watched people. No information had come in about the killer's vehicle. He must have parked nearby. He had enticed Lisa Barkley into a vehicle in broad daylight without being detected. Jarrod then remembered the online conversations between Lisa and the killer.

Had she gone with him willingly? That was the only explanation. But that guy? The creep in the security video footage? Surely not. As much as Jarrod cringed at the thought, he had to accept it was the most likely scenario. Lisa wanted to be loved for who she was. The guy she had fallen for online had said the same thing. Maybe she accepted him, turning a blind eye to his appearance. The killer must have been convincing enough to persuade her to get into his car. He was roleplaying right until the end. Right until he turned on her, when he strangled and raped her.

The afternoon sun beat down on the windshield and the car became a sweatbox. Jarrod got out and headed over to the Northern entrance of the shopping centre. His reflection met him in the automatic glass doors before they swooshed open. A wall of cool air hit him as he walked inside. He noted the position of the security cameras as he strolled down the main plaza, following the last known path of Lisa Barkley.

He didn't know what he expected to find. The CIB detectives and uniformed police had already canvassed the plaza. He needed a greater sense of Lisa Barkley's last movements, and to get inside the killer's head.

He wandered past the ATM but there was no line up today. Before exiting the Southern entrance, he looked up at the camera, just as the killer had done. He walked out into the car park, squinting to adjust to the brightness. Heat rose from the bitumen, the late afternoon sun retaining its fierce bite.

He crossed the sprawling car park until he came to an oasis of grass and shady trees. An earlier search of this area had yielded nothing. He headed for a nearby Jacaranda tree and sat on the grass in the shade, imagining Lisa waiting there for the stranger.

Jarrod wondered where he had taken her. Did he plan on killing her or did something just go horribly wrong? He thought about what Joe had said about Ivan Milat. Lisa had been groomed and lured, the rendezvous patiently planned, only to be attacked in a fit of rage. The profiles were at opposite ends of the spectrum. Could one person possess both characteristics? There was no other explanation.

The cool breeze was comforting. He closed his eyes. For a moment he allowed himself to relax, to rest his exhausted mind and body. He jumped with a start when his mobile phone rang. It was Joe Marshall.

'Jarrod, you need to get back here right away. I have him online. Lionel's back!'

TWENTY

WHEN Jarrod arrived back at the office, he found Joe and Brad seated in front of the laptop. Murray Long and Ross Benfield watched over their shoulders. Joe leaned forward, on edge. His keystrokes were sharp and purposeful. The others nodded at Jarrod then turned their attention back to Joe who stopped typing. Jarrod stood beside Murray, his eyes drawn to the screen. Joe called himself Caitlin. From somewhere in cyberspace letters appeared on screen forming words and sentences.

'*So baby, I know we could be friends, and soooo much more. I can make you feel sooooo good*,' the next sentence read.

Joe diverted his gaze. The whites of his eyes were glazed, the pupils tiny black dots. 'It's the same guy, Jarrod. It *has* to be. And get this, he's changed his username to leo/L.'

'Leo. Lion. Lionel,' said Jarrod.

'He's already given up that he lives in the city,' continued Joe. 'I told him I was from Lockyer. I've been chatting with him for about forty minutes, running my tracing software but can't get an IP number. It's the same encryption firewall.'

Jarrod was speechless. Joe's focus returned to the screen, and he typed a response. The others watched on in stunned silence.

'I need to be careful,' said Joe. 'I don't want to scare him off.'

'*That sounds nice. I don't have many friends*,' he typed.

'*Either do I. U sound so special. I know I could luv you. I can picture your naked body. I'd love to touch you*,' came the reply.

'Holy shit. This prick doesn't muck around,' muttered Brad.

'*I've never done that with a boy before*,' typed Joe.

'*Don't u worry about anything, my sweet. It will be so nice. Do u think we could meet?*'

'*Meet? I dunno. What do you look like?*' Joe typed.

'*Oh, that's a surprise. I have to go. Can you meet me here in this chat room at 7.30pm tonight?*'

'*Ok. See you then. Bye. Luv Caitlin.*'

'*Bye for now, my princess.*'

A chime sounded and the username disappeared. The cursor flashed, and just like that, he was gone. He had been right there, within reach, but still so far away.

'Do you think we spooked him?' said Benfield.

'I don't know, boss.'

'What now?' said Murray.

'All we can do is wait.' Joe leaned back in his chair and clasped his hands behind his head. 'Let's see if he comes back at seven-thirty.'

A collective sense of unease clung to the walls in the office.

Benfield broke the silence. 'Well, there's plenty of work to be done while we wait. Get back to the MIR you lot. There's a pile of investigation logs waiting for you. Nothing gets missed. We're gonna tighten the noose around this guy's balls.'

TWENTY-ONE

DETECTIVES crowded around Joe and his laptop, the tension palpable. He rubbed his hands together and steepled his fingers. He cracked his knuckles, limbering up for round two.

At 7.30PM he logged on, again role-playing as Caitlin.

CAITLIN/ has now entered the room, appeared a generic prompt as Joe entered his fake username.

'*Hello Caitlin, R U up for some sex*?'came the immediate reply from some arsehole. Joe ignored the comment and waited, his fingers poised on the keyboard.

Minutes crept by. Joe was soon ignored by the other chatters, who continued with their meaningless dribble.

'This isn't looking good,' said Murray.

'Give it more time, Joe,' said Jarrod.

The cursor blinked against Joe's username. He turned to Jarrod and let out a defeated sigh. Twenty minutes slid by and still no sign of Lionel.

'I think we've lost him,' said Joe.

Detectives in the room murmured their frustration.

'Wait! Look. That's gotta be him,' said Brad.

leo/L has now entered the room.

Jarrod held his breath so that even the person on the other end wouldn't hear him breathing.

Joe waited.

'*Are u there Caitlin?*' typed 'leo/L'.

Joe clapped his hands together and they all jumped. 'We're in boys. It's time to rock and roll!' he shouted. 'If only this prick knew he was talking to a room full of coppers. I'm coming for you now!'

Joe was on a roll, exchanging sexual inferences until the role playing intensified. Their guy wanted "Caitlin" so badly and declared his love for her. He promised her the world. He would give her anything she wanted in return for sex. "Caitlin" reluctantly agreed. The guy wanted to meet tomorrow.

They were so close to taking him down, but one false move and he'd slip through their grasp. Any hint of a ruse and he would be gone. For the next thirty minutes, no one uttered a sound as Joe considered every reply before typing it in, knowing one mistake could scare the guy off. He had to remain in character. Any deviation or over persistence would be a fatal mistake. So far, leo/L had shown no signs of hesitance, becoming cockier the longer the conversation progressed. He let his guard down as Joe reeled him in.

'*So I'll meet you at St. Charles park at 10AM tomorrow?*'

'*OK. I know where that is.*'

'*U know you can trust me,*' the text read.

'*I know. I'm excited about meeting u. U promise u will bring the money?*' typed Joe.

'*$300, that's what I promised. Think of all the things you could buy with that. Do u promise to get naked with me?*'

'*Yep, I will, I promise.*'

'*I will meet you at the picnic shelter near the duck pond. I'll be wearing a red cap. How will I know you?*' the text read.

'I'll be the one shoving a Glock up your arse, you sick bastard,' said Joe.

Nervous laughter broke the tension in the room.

'*I'll wave when I see you,*' Joe typed.

'*10AM it is then. See you in the morning my sweet.*' Lionel logged off.

'Right, we've got a lot of planning to do between now and then,' said Benfield. 'We're going to surround this guy with a net so tight a fart won't escape his butt cheeks. Tomorrow morning, we take this guy down!' Benfield turned and headed for the door. He paused in the doorway without turning around. 'Good job, men.' He strode out into the hallway.

'What now then?' said Brad to no one in particular.

'Well, for starters,' said Joe, 'we're gonna need a girl to be our bait.'

TWENTY-TWO

JOE'S face bore the toll of sitting in front of a computer screen for hours on end. Jarrod tossed him the keys to his house and sent him home. Jarrod's mind was too active to sleep, and he needed to write up case notes to organise his thoughts.

By 10PM he yawned uncontrollably. He'd given Jayne a call, her voice comforting but making his heart ache all the more. Loneliness pressed heavy on his shoulders. His head was foggy, as though sent to oblivion from alcohol, but he hadn't touched a drop. His body cried out for sleep, and he yielded to exhaustion. He closed his official diary and pushed his chair in, switching off the lights as he left the office.

Downstairs, he checked in with the uniformed officers who were sipping instant coffees to get them through the rest of their night shift. He headed out the back door and as he walked through the police station car park, he drew in the balmy night air. He absent-mindedly looked up. A full moon's glow brought a comforting beauty to the graphite night sky.

His thoughts swirled as he ambled down the station driveway towards his truck parked out front. When he reached the footpath, a darting movement in the laneway between the police station and the neighbouring office building caught his eye. Stopping under a streetlight, he squinted towards the laneway to adjust his vision to the gloom. He sensed he was being watched.

He moved into the laneway. 'Who's there?' he called.

He spotted another movement, a subtle shift in the shadows.

Footfalls grew louder. A figure sprinted towards him with a weapon raised to strike.

Jarrod spun and tucked his head behind his forearms. A blow struck his right wrist. Bone cracked. Crippling pain shot up his arm. Too stunned to even blink, he stumbled into the laneway and fell to one knee, leaning his good hand on the ground for support. He cradled the other against his chest.

A boot thrust into his stomach, forcing the air from his lungs. Winded, Jarrod wheezed. The man came at him again. This time the laces of his boot struck the side of Jarrod's head. His knees buckled and he slumped to the concrete, rolling to evade the barrage of kicks that followed. Sound rushed in his ears and pain flooded his nerves. His vision swam, his mouth filling with blood. He coughed, blood speckling the ground. His head pounded in time with his heartbeat.

Survival instincts took hold. Fight or flight. He would fight. His legs wobbled as he rose to one knee. His senses toggled back one by one. His attacker stepped closer, the weapon poised to strike again. The moonlight glinted off the galvanised steel of a wheel brace hellbent on caving in his skull.

With his good hand, Jarrod gathered up his trouser leg, clambering for his ankle holster. As his fingers curled around the grip of his gun, his thumb searched for the holster clip. The man bounded in again, striking the wheel brace against Jarrod's ribcage. He went down a second time, his Glock still secured in the holster. As Jarrod lay prone, the man stomped on his shattered wrist, the searing pain nearly sending him into unconsciousness. Pinning Jarrod's arm under his boot, the man bent down and yanked at his gun, fumbling with the holster clip until the Glock slid free. The man examined the gun with curiosity. He bounced it from hand to hand, testing the gun's weight. He gripped it awkwardly with one hand, finger on the trigger, the muzzle pointed at Jarrod. A set of crooked teeth emerged in the moonlight behind lips contorting into a smile.

The man cocked his head and spat at Jarrod's feet, wiping his mouth on his sleeve. 'Not such a big man now,' he sneered.

Jarrod blinked, his vision strobing, head throbbing. The world spun. The man leaned down, his face a distorted blur haloed by the streetlight. Jarrod had heard that voice before but couldn't place it.

'How long did you think it would take before I hunted you down? Copper bastard!'

Jarrod grimaced and tried to speak. A single word escaped his lips. 'Wha… what?'

'I've been waiting for you, pig,' the man spat. 'I've got nothing to lose, nothing to live for because of you.'

Jarrod's brain misfired with confusion.

'Did you think you could just come and take my baby with no payback?' The man aimed the gun at Jarrod's face.

The voice registered as the features of the man's face came into focus. In a heartbeat, Jarrod understood.

'You're the first one on my hitlist,' said Karl Mundy, scowling. 'Once I've killed you, I'm coming after your partner. Then those two sluts from welfare, they'll be next. I'm gonna enjoy making them squeal like stuck pigs.'

Mundy discarded the wheel brace, clattering and clanking as it bounced on the concrete path.

Jarrod gasped, his eyes fighting to regain focus.

Mundy stepped over Jarrod, one foot on either side of his feet, and aimed the gun at his forehead. Jarrod held his hand up and squeezed his eyes closed, waiting to enter a world of nothingness. He couldn't believe his life would end like this. In a single moment it would all end. The faces of Jayne, Katie and Matty flashed in the back of his eyelids. A single thought entered his mind. *Not now! I'm not ready to go.*

Click. But the boom of a gunshot never came.

'What the fuck?' said Mundy, his words high-pitched.

Jarrod peeked through one eye. Mundy snatched the trigger again, a look of bewilderment plastered across his face. He shook the gun as though it were a broken toy. Jarrod's senses tingled with electricity, super charged from escaping certain death. Hesitation would be his end, action his only salvation. His body responded to the lifeline the universe had thrown him. He kicked his leg upwards, the toe of his shoe connecting with Mundy's balls. It was unorthodox but an effective distraction.

'Arrghh!' Mundy reeled over, clutching his gonads with his free hand.

Jarrod rolled and sat upright, reaching for the gun with his good hand. Grabbing the barrel, he twisted it upwards to weaken Mundy's grip. He thrust the Glock downwards and prised it free from Mundy's grasp. He scrambled to his feet and pointed the gun at Mundy who took a step towards him, rage and hate in his eyes. Mundy panted through the pain in his testicles and hesitated, his eyes darting between the gun and Jarrod's eyes.

Mundy chuckled like a madman, his face twisted and deranged. 'That gun don't even work. You're so fucked now.'

Jarrod needed to clear the misfired round, but his broken wrist was useless. He tapped the butt of the magazine against his hip, rotated the gun and slid it down the side of his body until the rear sight blade snagged onto his belt. He pushed downwards and used his belt to rack the slide and release its springs with a snap, seating a fresh round in the chamber. The dud bullet ejected and clinked on the concrete at Jarrod's feet.

He gripped the Glock and raised it towards Mundy's chest, his arm shaking. 'It might work now,' he said, his ribs screaming with every intake of air. 'Take one more step and let's see what happens next.'

The smile dissolved from Mundy's face.

Jarrod crept backwards until his heels found the laneway fence. Mundy blocked the path to the street. Jarrod had nowhere to go, his jelly legs unable to carry him any further. They faced off, stalemate. Mundy took a sideways step and glanced down at the wheel brace. He bent down and picked it up, gripping it with both hands as though he had stepped onto a baseball plate. He lined up for one last strike, calling Jarrod's bluff.

'Don't do it!' yelled Jarrod, his voice raspy. 'Drop it or I'll shoot!'

Mundy shrieked and rushed at Jarrod, the iron bar fixed to strike. Jarrod squeezed the trigger and the crack of the gunshot echoed in the laneway like a stockman's whip. The wheel brace fell to the ground as Mundy clutched his chest, blood spurting between his fingers. Stopping in his tracks, he gazed at Jarrod with a questioning stare. Blood gurgled from his mouth. He dropped to his knees, his upper body rolling forward until he slumped to the concrete, writhing as life drained from his body in a pool of crimson. A guttural groan escaped his lips, his final breath a slow hiss. He went still.

Jarrod's knees buckled, and he sank to the ground beside Karl Mundy's lifeless body.

TWENTY-THREE

THE paramedic's voice was muffled in Jarrod's ears, like she was talking under water. She handed Jarrod a Penthrox inhaler. 'Suck on the green whistle, mate. It's an analgesic. It'll take the pain away. Soon you'll be in La-La-Land. It's good shit.' She placed the green cylinder in Jarrod's hand and raised it up to his mouth. 'Just breathe in and out.'

He followed her instructions until a wave of blissful dizziness clouded his vision. His arms and legs felt like they belonged to someone else. Drowsy thoughts staggered in his head like a drunkard's and then faded as euphoria set in. He was high as a kite, but at least the pain in his wrist, ribcage and head eased.

Blue and red lights strobed, catching paramedic and police uniforms as people fussed about and talked on radios. The paramedic's face lowered closer to Jarrod's, her mouth moving, but her muffled words not registering in Jarrod's brain. He smiled like a village idiot and gave a dopey thumbs up.

'Won't get any sense out of him, he's tripping out on the whistle,' said the paramedic. 'Let's load him up.'

Jarrod blinked, and he was in the back of an ambulance. He blinked again and was lying on a bed, bathed in hard fluorescent light and surrounded by a blue curtain. It was like he had teleported to the hospital emergency ward. One arm was splinted and bandaged, the other down by his side. He strained to lift his head, heavy as lead. 'Oh shit,' he slurred when he saw his blood-drenched shirt.

'Don't worry, it's not your blood,' said a doctor without raising his eyes from a chart.

Images flickered in Jarrod's head like a faulty light bulb. Awareness seeped back in. The muzzle flash of a gunshot, Karl Mundy's motionless body and lifeless eyes, blood the texture of golden syrup pooling around Jarrod's knees and seeping into his clothing as he applied pressure on Mundy's wound. His fingers were still sticky with blood. The coppery smell filled his nostrils and nearly made him gag.

'The green whistle is wearing off, so we'll get you connected to a morphine drip once you've had your X-ray.' The doctor looked up and gave a half smile. 'But you'll live.' He pulled the curtain aside and disappeared into the ward.

The X-ray revealed an impact fracture of the radius, but to Jarrod's relief, surgery was unlikely. His right arm was set in a cast from below the elbow, encasing his wrist and hand so that only the fingers and thumb could wiggle. He'd be in the bloody thing for eight weeks. Luckily, he was left-handed. Small mercies. His cracked ribs would give him grief for several weeks, but he'd just have to suck it up and let them heal in their own time, so the doctor had told him. He touched the swelling around his right eye and winced. He'd have an impressive shiner by morning.

He was cleaned up, changed out of his bloody clothes into a hospital gown, and moved to a private room. Snug under a heated blanket, semi upright in a tilted bed, he dozed. Wooziness took hold with the sensation of falling from a great height. He slipped into a dreamscape, a place in the gaps of consciousness. A presence woke him with a start. He looked around the room, disoriented. He could have been asleep for one minute or eight hours. There was no way of telling. Blinking, he cast his eyes around the room until awareness returned. Someone knocked on the door. Ross Benfield's tall form filled the open doorway. He looked more exhausted than usual. Over recent months there was a weariness that followed him, a noticeable weight that seldom lifted.

'The shit you'll do, O'Connor, to get out of a bit of work.' Sarcasm laced his words.

'Hey, boss. Come in,' croaked Jarrod. 'What time is it?'

Benfield pulled up his shirt sleeve and squinted at his watch. 'Nearly 2AM. Did I wake you?'

'That's okay, just dozing.'

'How you holding up, lad?'

'I'm alright. Ribs hurt like a bitch, but the painkillers are taking the edge off.'

Benfield dragged a chair across the room and sat alongside the bed, looking around to satisfy himself they were alone. He leaned in and spoke, cigarette breath clinging to each raspy word. 'I need to know what happened, Jarrod. Are you up to it?'

Jarrod nodded.

'Okay, run me through it so I'm ahead of the game before Internal Investigations arrive from the city. They'll be here soon.'

Jarrod's eyes searched the ceiling, retrieving memory fragments from a distant corner of his brain. 'It was Karl Mundy,' he said after some thought. 'A few days ago, we went out with Children's Services and removed his baby under a child protection order.'

Benfield listened intently, nodding to urge Jarrod to continue.

'So, tonight I was leaving work and he jumped me in the laneway with a wheel brace. He was waiting for me.'

Out of the fog, Jarrod remembered, blurry images came into focus with more clarity. 'He got my gun and tried to shoot me, but it didn't go off. It was racked and loaded. I don't understand.'

Benfield produced a clip seal plastic bag from his shirt pocket and held it up to the light. 'You might want to keep this as a lucky charm once Ballistics are finished with it. Found it at the scene.' Inside the bag, a bullet dangled innocuously, its brass casing corroded with a tinge of green. 'My guess is the firing pin struck the primer, but it didn't fire. Judging by the colour I'd say it's been a while since you changed your ammo.'

'Yeah, I've been meaning to do that. Been a bit busy.'

Benfield leaned back in the chair. 'Bloody hopeless. You know the policy on changing old ammo.'

Jarrod nodded.

'Your complacency saved your life. You're one lucky bastard, you know that?'

Jarrod shrugged.

'How did you get the gun off him?'

'Kicked him in the nuts and snatched it from him. Had to reload one-handed. I warned him, but he came at me again with the wheel brace. He was going to kill me, boss. I had no choice, I had to take the shot.'

'I know, mate. Nothing else you could have done, under the circumstances.'

'So, he *is* dead then? They couldn't revive him?'

Benfield nodded. 'Dead at the scene. The boys in the station heard the gunshot and raced out. They called the ambos, but Mundy was already gone.'

Jarrod's heart sank. 'Stupid bastard. I didn't want to pull the trigger.'

'He forced your hand. It's not your fault. He chose his own path.'

'What now? How screwed *am* I? Tell me straight.'

'We've got your back, son. You'll be fine, don't stress. When Internal Investigations get here, just tell them what you told me and don't leave out any detail. A police union bloke is on his way to represent you, so don't agree to an interview until he gets here. Is that clear?'

Jarrod nodded. His gut wrenched with dread.

'Media have already got wind of it,' said Benfield. 'I'll brief the Chief Superintendent. He'll hold a press conference in the morning. I've been in touch with our media unit to put out some holding lines.'

Benfield rose to his feet and patted Jarrod on the shoulder. It was an awkward but well-intentioned gesture. 'Rest up.'

He hesitated. 'I'm sorry, but I've been instructed to stand you down from operational duties until cleared by Internals.'

'Instructed by who?'

'The Chief Superintendent. He wants a transparent investigation. He's just following procedure.'

Benfield turned to leave the room.

'Wait!' called Jarrod. 'The Barkley murder is my case. You can't take me off it now. Not when we're so close.'

'Jarrod, we're taking that guy down in the morning. You're not up to it. Period.' He shook his head and frowned as though he'd made his mind up. 'No, Jarrod. You've been through a lot tonight.'

'Please! I need to follow it through. I need to be there. I'm doped up on painkillers. A few hours' sleep and I'll be right as rain. I *have* to be there. At least let me be there as an observer. I won't interfere.'

'Why, Jarrod? We've got plenty of good people.'

'I made a promise to Lisa Barkley's father. I need to see it through.'

Benfield stared at Jarrod and sighed.

'Come on, Boss,' Jarrod urged. 'We're so close to getting this guy. I need to be there when we make the arrest.' He grimaced as a sharp pain bit his ribs.

'Look at you, Jarrod. You're all banged up.'

Jarrod stared at him. 'You won't even know I'm there.'

Benfield sighed again, deeper and more exasperated this time. 'Fine! Don't make me regret it. I'll take the heat from the Chief Super. You'll be an observer only. You won't be making any tactical decisions. Got that?'

'Understood.'

'As far as anyone else is concerned, you'll be at home convalescing. Murray Long will take the lead in tomorrow's operation. Try to get some rest. I'll send Harding by in the morning to pick you up. Have you spoken to your wife?'

'Not yet. I'll call her soon.'

'Do it now, before she gets wind of it through the media and panics.'

'She'll lose her shit.'

'I expect nothing less. I'll see you in the morning.' Benfield turned and walked out before Jarrod could thank him.

Jarrod reached for his mobile phone and dialled Jayne's number. As it rang, he took a deep breath to quell the dread. The call scared him more than having to stare down the barrel of his own loaded gun.

'Jarrod, what's wrong?' she snapped when she answered.

'Can't a man call his wife?'

'Not at two o'clock in the morning. What is it?'

'I'm fine. How are the kids?'

'They're asleep. They're fine. Now stop stalling. What is it?'

Jarrod hesitated 'I'm in hospital, but…'

'What! Are you alright?'

'I'm alright,' he cut in. 'Just a broken arm, cracked ribs and a shiner.'

'*Just* a broken—' She clipped her words to stop herself going totally nuclear. 'How did that happen? Were you in an accident?'

'No, nothing like that.'

How to explain it?

'I got jumped as I left the station. A guy who didn't like me. Tried to cave my head in with a wheel brace.'

Jayne's voice went up another octave. 'What? You could have been killed!'

Jarrod paused. A clumsy silence clung to the phone line.

She spoke again, this time with more control. He pictured her gritting her teeth to mask her rising anxiety, like she did when the kids were testing her patience. 'What aren't you telling me? What happened?'

'He tried to kill me,' said Jarrod, his voice low. 'I had to shoot him.'

Jayne gasped into the phone. He pictured her placing her hand over her mouth.

'He's dead.' Jarrod's voice wavered. 'I killed him.'

'Oh, sweetheart. I'm so sorry. That must have been terrible. You must feel awful.'

'I had no choice.'

'I know. Of course you didn't.'

They talked it through. Eventually, she calmed down and promised to call again in the morning.

After the call, he sunk his head into the pillow and let the morphine drip do its job. The throbbing in his arm subsided, the fractured bone secured within the cast. A mild-mannered man in jeans and crinkled polo shirt knocked on the door. He looked dishevelled and apologetic. The regional union rep had clearly been dragged out of bed. Jarrod waved him in, and they ran through the usual preamble, going through his rights and support services available.

Soon after, two men in suits with poker faces appeared in the doorway. Neutral and business like, they introduced themselves as detective inspectors from Internal Investigations. They reminded him of his requirement to answer all questions truthfully, as refusal would be considered misconduct. The bedside interview followed formal protocols, and he answered their questions in as much detail as he could. The investigators were by the book and meticulous, pressing for details as Jarrod told his story.

When the lead investigator turned off his recording device, the hint of a smile broke his stony façade. 'You're all good, mate,' he said. 'We've reviewed the station CCTV footage. We just needed your version of events to corroborate what we already knew. Seems clear this was a justified use of force.'

He turned to his colleague, who nodded in agreement, the man's face wearing a frown as if it had been cast that way.

The lead investigator spread his hands in a conciliatory gesture. 'We'll have to jump through all the usual hoops, forensic analysis of the scene, witnesses, you know the drill,' he said. 'We may need a further interview with you to clarify anything new that comes up. The final investigation report will take a few months and it'll get dragged out in a coronial inquest. It's important you don't talk to media or make any public comment. We'll stay in touch. Any questions?'

Jarrod shook his head.

'Oh, one more thing,' said the detective inspector. 'You *will* get your wrist slapped for not following policy to keep your ammunition in a serviceable condition. A breach of discipline report will go on your service record.'

'Understood,' said Jarrod.

The investigators and union official left him in peace, and he closed his eyes, desperate to calm his mind. He rubbed his temples to ward off a headache.

Sleep soon found him.

TWENTY-FOUR

AFTER a few hours of drug induced sleep, Jarrod woke to a delivery of scrambled eggs, cereal, coffee and orange juice. As he ate, the ward outside his room buzzed with activity. Trolleys clanked, telephones rang and bed curtain runners clattered. Hearty cackling of nurses filled the corridors over the relentless ding-donging of patient call buzzers. A nurse removed the drip and helped him shower without getting the cast wet. A doctor on the morning rounds popped in and gave him the all-clear to be discharged.

'You probably still have a concussion, and you need to rest those ribs. Go home and take it easy,' the doctor had ordered.

'Shall do,' Jarrod lied.

His phone vibrated. Jayne was calling.

'Did you get any sleep?' she asked.

'A few hours. I'm feeling a lot better.'

'Liar. Don't be a hero. Go home and get some rest.'

'Uh huh.'

'Jarrod! You're going into the station, aren't you?'

'I have to, love. The Barkley case. We're getting close.' He thought about the operation planned for the morning. *Better not tell her about that, not yet anyway.*

'Can't the other guys do it? It's not all your responsibility.'

'But it is! It *is* my responsibility. I promised the girl's father.'

Jayne sighed. Her voice softened. 'I know. Do what you have to do, just don't run yourself into the ground.'

'I won't. I'm fine, really.'

'I'm getting the kids packed up and we'll head home later today. I promised I'd take them up to the hospital this morning to nurse the baby. I'll drive back after that.'

'Spend time with your sister. Don't rush home on my account. Give everyone a kiss for me.'

After the call, Jarrod got out of the bed and sat in a visitor's chair. He was checking emails on his phone when Brad poked his head in the room. 'The things you'll do to get out of work.'

Jarrod looked up. 'It wasn't even funny when Benfield said that last night.'

'It could be worse,' smiled Brad, stepping into the room carrying a sports bag.

'Don't even say it.'

Brad burst into laughter. 'It could be me.' His expression faded into a look of genuine concern when he noticed Jarrod's black eye and cast. 'Jesus. You okay, mate? I heard what happened.'

'Yeah, I'll live. Not really sure how I'm supposed to feel after killing a man, though.'

'Don't be hard on yourself, mate. It was Karl Mundy. He was a shit stain on society. You did the world a favour. I might start calling you Dexter.'

'Not funny. I keep second guessing myself, questioning if I could have done things differently. Killing another man is a hell of a thing.'

'You did what you needed to do to stay alive. Just like when you shot Vincent Miles. It was you or them. You made the right call both times.'

'Yeah, well, it still feels like shit.'

'I know, mate. You need to talk to someone, get professional advice. Shit like this could really mess with you. Maybe talk with a human services officer?'

'No thanks. Those bleeding hearts have never seen an angry man in their lives. How can they help me? By talking about how I feel?

Bloody waste of time.'

'Maybe, but you should keep it in mind. All I know is they helped me after I got shot.'

'Righto, I'll think about it,' Jarrod lied again, hoping that would end it.

'Have you spoken to Jayne?' said Brad.

'Yep. She had a cow.'

Brad chuckled. 'Oh, man. I bet. And how did your interview with the toe cutters go?'

'All good, I think. The investigation will take months to wrap up. You know how drawn out these things can be.'

'You'll be cleared, I'm sure of it.'

'I wish I had your confidence. It's not over, not by a long shot. Coronial inquest, media scrutiny. They'll be looking for someone to blame. They'll exploit the whole "victim of the child protection system" bullshit. Did you see today's headlines?'

'Uh, huh. "*Young father slain by police*" is a bit rich,' said Brad.

'God damn sensationalism. Bloody vultures.'

Brad placed the overnight bag on the bed. 'Best you don't read any more of that shit. It'll do your head in.'

Jarrod gestured at the sports bag with his chin. 'You bring some clothes in for me? Internals seized my clothes for gunpowder residue testing. They even took my shoes.'

'Oh, yeah,' said Brad, unzipping the bag. 'I swung by your house and Joe let me in. I grabbed what I thought you'd need.'

Jarrod got up and inspected the contents. 'Not bad. Shoes, clean jocks, socks, trousers and shirt. You iron them?'

'I'm not your girlfriend. Although I did pack a toothbrush and deodorant. Thought you'd need those.'

'Good man. Thanks mate.'

Jarrod dressed into his clean clothes. Brad watched, bouncing on the balls of his feet with a questioning look.

'What?' said Jarrod.

'You *do* know you should be going home to rest? What are you trying to prove, going to work today?'

'Don't you start on me. I already had this conversation with Benfield last night. He gave me clearance to come on the operation this morning, as an observer.'

'As an observer? Yeah right. Shit, Jarrod. You sure you're up to it?'

'I'm fine. Nothing will stop me from seeing this bastard go down. I just need to make it through today. When we nail this guy, it'll be over. I'll worry about resting then.'

They left the hospital and were soon pulling into the police station driveway. A gaggle of cameramen and reporters loitered under the gigantic Moreton Bay fig at the front of the station, casually chatting and nursing takeaway coffee cups.

'Shit. Circus is in town,' said Brad. 'Chief Super's due to give a press conference.'

Jarrod recognised a few faces from the local rag and radio stations, as well as A-list city reporters from the major networks. A small marquee had been set up in the laneway and cordoned off with police tape. Two forensics officers were still working the scene of the shooting. A uniformed constable on guard duty gave Jarrod and Brad a nod as they drove in the driveway. The media paid no attention to them. It occurred to Jarrod they probably hadn't learnt the identity of the police officer involved in the shooting. It was only a matter of time before his face and name were plastered all over the news. Jarrod glanced at the crime scene through the car window and prised his eyes away. He looked out the opposite window, trying to compose himself.

Brad parked in their usual bay and killed the ignition. He turned to face Jarrod. 'You gonna be okay?'

Jarrod took in a deep breath. 'Yeah, come on. Let's get this done.'

TWENTY-FIVE

BY 9:45AM, they were all in position at St. Charles Park. An octagonal shaped gazebo with a slate roof overlooked a natural basin of brownish water surrounded by undulating slopes and shady Golden Wattle trees. Waist height railings with latticed panels enclosed a picnic table and bench stools. Wild ducks and water birds usually emerged from the lily pads whenever bread was on offer, now they stayed hidden, roosting in trees on a small island at the centre of the pond. Maybe they sensed something was amiss.

Jarrod sat alongside Ross Benfield in the back of a white transit van parked at the far end of the car park, peering out through tinted windows. He was already going stir crazy cooped up in the tight space, the stale air laced with Benfield's Old Spice aftershave. With his arm in plaster and body aching, Jarrod resigned himself to his role as observer. His hands trembled from lack of sleep and being jacked up on painkillers. Benfield co-ordinated the communications side of the operation. Jarrod wished he could be outside with the other officers.

Constable Kirsty Loudin had volunteered to be the bait. Posing as Caitlin, she was dressed in tight-fitting black jeans, a black T-shirt and sneakers, her hair loose and wild. She checked her concealed radio and made her way down the slope towards the picnic shelter. When she reached the picnic shelter, she sat up on the table where there was a better view of anyone approaching. She chewed gum and bopped her head as she played with her phone, pretending to be listening to music. From a distance, she could be taken for a teenager. With good approach visibility and concealment options in the surrounding trees, the location of the shelter gave them a tactical advantage for the operation. Their officers in the field could close in on the suspect, cutting off all escape routes. Diving into the pond would be his only escape option but he wouldn't get far. They'd be on him by the time he got to the other side.

'Can you guys hear me?' Kirsty spoke into her concealed microphone.

'Kirsty, we're right here,' responded Benfield. 'We can all see you. We'll be there in a flash if you need us. Are you okay?'

'I'm out here alone, live bait for a killer. Of course I'm okay, Boss.' The crackling radio didn't mask the nervous sarcasm in her voice.

The voice of Murray Long cut in. 'We're all in position, Kirsty. This bloke won't get near you, we'll be onto him before he knows what's going on. Just hang tight.'

All they could do now was wait. Every now and then a jogger or dog walker went by and then disappeared out of sight. Minutes ticked by. It was now 10AM. Kirsty slid off the table and leaned out over the gazebo railing, fidgeting with her radio earpiece.

'Take it easy, Kirsty,' Murray spoke into his radio, his voice light. 'We're watching. Relax.'

'I'm alright. You guys just keep an eye out.'

Ross Benfield spoke into his radio. 'Listen up, all units. Radio silence from this point on. If the suspect is spotted, call it in. Otherwise, quit the chit-chat. Forward Command out.'

An eerie silence filled the airways. Kirsty paced around the table. The park seemed deserted. Anxiety churned in the pit of Jarrod's gut, his palms sweaty. Jarrod checked the time on his phone. 10:10AM.

'Come on, where is this guy?' Jarrod said under his breath.

The radio crackled to life. Murray Long whispered into his handset. 'Oscar Bravo Two. Male Caucasian approaching from southern end of the park, heading towards the target point.'

'Oscar Bravo One, suspect now in sight,' came Brad's voice.

'Steady now all units, wait for my command,' directed Benfield.

Jarrod then saw him. A man in a red cap emerged from the trees into a clearing, walking down the grassed slope towards the picnic shelter. Sunglasses concealed his eyes. Jarrod couldn't make out his face from that distance.

'I can see him now,' whispered Kirsty into her microphone. 'You guys better be on your toes.'

The man scanned his surroundings as he drew closer. He stopped about twenty metres from the gazebo and stared at Kirsty, a long unsettling gaze. He then swivelled his head, spooked. Kirsty waved at him, flashing a forced smile. He looked over his shoulder and backed away.

'Move in now, all units, move in!' ordered Benfield over the radio.

Kirsty reached into her pocket and flipped open her badge. 'Police!' she yelled.

The man turned on his heels and ran. Murray Long and Brad Harding emerged from their position behind a line of shrubs and ran towards the man, cutting him off.

'Police! Don't move!' commanded Murray.

The man's shoes slid on the grass as he tried to change direction. He stumbled, clambering to escape. Joe Marshall and Liam Dawes emerged from behind the toilet block and ran at him from the other direction. He veered up the hill towards the car park. Benfield slid open the van door and he and Jarrod bundled out.

'Police, don't move,' yelled Benfield.

The man halted and looked around, panic-stricken. He panted, sucking in gulps of air. Officers closed in all around him. He relented, dropping to his knees on the grass with his hands in the air. Murray and Brad tackled him and within seconds he was lying on his stomach, hands cuffed behind his back. They stood over him in a circle.

Murray and Brad gave him a pat-down search.

'He's clear,' said Brad.

'Sit him up,' said Jarrod.

Murray and Brad rolled him over and pushed his upper body forward to a sitting position, his knees bent.

Jarrod pulled the red cap off the man's head and removed his sunglasses. The man looked up at him, fear in his eyes.

They had the bastard.

TWENTY-SIX

LIONEL Collins slumped on a chair in the interview room, a defeated man. From the other side of the two-way mirror, Jarrod watched him chewing his fingernails and bouncing one knee, his gaze ping-ponging around the room. The diminutive fifty-four-year-old stroked his mutton chop sideburns out of nervous habit, then ran a hand through his oily fringe, smearing it across the top of his scalp. He repeated the ritual over and over, hands shaking like an alcoholic suffering withdrawals. He licked his lips past nicotine-stained teeth, his tongue darting out like a lizard's. His business shirt was dishevelled, his tie loosened and askew.

A life insurance broker from the city, he drove to Lockyer twice a week as a consultant for a local financial advisor. He lived alone, ex-wife, no kids. Loner.

Jarrod had pestered Benfield until he agreed to allow him to be present in the interview, with the condition that Joe Marshall be the lead interviewer. Jarrod and Joe entered the interview room, startling Collins as the door swung open. Joe dropped a thick manilla folder on the table with Collins' name written in bold on the front. That had been Jarrod's idea. Jarrod sat opposite Collins, watching him squirm as Joe loaded the digital recording device with blank CDs. Joe sat beside Jarrod, eyeballing Collins from across the interview table.

Collins broke eye contact and bit deeper into his fingernails, shifting in his chair as though sitting over a blowtorch.

Joe reached over and pressed the record button, followed by three long, high-pitched beeps. He introduced everyone in the room before running through the pre-formatted preamble questions. Collins was read his rights and he declined a lawyer.

'Mr Collins,' Joe began. 'Can I call you Lionel?'

Collins nodded.

Joe steepled his hands on the table and looked Collins in the eye. 'Right now, a team of detectives with a search warrant is searching your home. Your computer has been seized for forensic examination. What can we expect to find?'

Jarrod sat in silence, his stare bearing down on Collins who refused to make eye contact. He studied Collins' body language. Shoulders slouched, staring at the floor in silence like a scared little boy caught in a lie. A minute passed before Joe spoke again. 'Tell me about the girls you've been chatting with online.'

Collins didn't answer straight away. His eyes lifted and darted between Jarrod and Joe, calculating his options. With a look that said he'd settled on a decision, he started to ramble. 'Is there anything so wrong with wanting female company? I haven't hurt anybody. I just wanted female company. You can understand that, can't you? These girls on the internet, they're such teases, so willing.'

Jarrod stared all his disgust at him without paying attention to a word the man said.

'Tell me about Goth Girl?' said Joe, deadpan.

The blood drained from Collins' face and he slumped back into his seat. 'What do you want to know?'

'Just the truth,' said Joe. 'Start from the beginning. Tell us about her.'

Collins looked up at the ceiling, considering his answer. 'We started chatting online. She agreed to meet me at the park behind the shopping centre, but the little bitch didn't even turn up. Bloody tease.'

Jarrod's hackles raised. He wanted to pummel the weasel into a pulp. He opened his mouth, about to speak, but Joe cast him a look of admonishment which said he needed to shut his trap.

Jarrod felt his ears grow hot and suppressed the angered response against the back of his clenched teeth. He held his shit together, crossing his arms in silence.

Joe's face changed, a hardness joined by an intensity, a concentration. 'That girl was murdered, Mr Collins,' he said, letting his words hang in the air while studying Collins' reaction.

'What?' Collins blinked, wrong-footed. The skin around his cheeks rippled in a wince, confusion in his eyes. 'Murdered?' He let out an audible gasp.

'Three days ago.' Joe kept his voice measured, cautious. 'Her body was found dumped in a dry creek bed out of town.'

Collins shifted in his chair again, running his fingers through his greasy hair. 'Wait, I heard about a murder here in town. A young girl.' His eyes widened with a sudden realisation and he jolted upright. 'Is that what this is about? Oh, Jesus, no. You can't pin that on me, no way. I'm telling you she didn't turn up. I never laid eyes on her.'

'You said she didn't turn up. What happened when you got to the park?' said Joe, still eyeing Collins.

'Nothing. I waited in the park for about thirty minutes, but she never arrived.'

'What time did you get there?'

'Nine-thirty, like we'd planned.'

'What did you do then?'

'I went back to the local office here in town. I worked there for the rest of the day and then drove back to the city that afternoon. You can check.'

'Can you verify that?'

'Um, yeah, I can. I stopped for petrol on the city outskirts on my way home. The receipt is still in my wallet. You guys have my wallet, check it.'

Joe and Jarrod exchanged glances. 'We will,' said Joe.

'Did you see her at all? The girl who called herself Goth Girl?'

'No.' He was adamant. 'I didn't know what she looked like. Still don't. She was going to wear a black overcoat. I was wearing a red cap. That's how we would know each other. But she didn't come.' Collins looked down at his shoes, dejected. 'I should have known she was leading me on.'

'She was a fifteen-year-old girl,' said Joe, his voice low and calm. 'I put it to you, Lionel, that you planned on meeting her for sexual purposes. We have the online chat records.'

'It wasn't just me, she was up for it. She led me on, said she wanted to meet, so I went along with it. But I had nothing to do with her murder. You have to believe me!'

Jarrod leaned forward on his elbows as Joe continued to press hard with several lines of questioning. Collins never budged, denying any involvement in the murder. He gave consistent answers about his movements, rock solid to every detail. If he was lying, he was a master of deception. He admitted to everything they needed to charge him with two counts of procuring a minor. He looked gutted when Joe told him that Caitlin was a covert police officer.

After the interview, they left Collins to marinate alone in the interview room and studied him through the two-way mirror.

Jarrod leaned against the glass, hands in his pockets. 'What do you think? Is he our killer?'

'Has to be. He's just admitting to what he knows we can prove. He's full of shit, a con artist.'

'Something feels off.'

'He's a sicko, of course it feels off. Everything about him is off.'

'Look at him. You believe he's a killer?'

'Hell yes. Maybe she turned him down? Threatened to report him? She tried to leave, and he flew into a rage and killed her.'

'Forensics are searching his car as we speak. We'll have to wait to see what they find.'

Jarrod looked at Joe. 'The guy in the shopping centre security footage. That's really bugging me.'

'What about him?'

'He's the one I expected to turn up at the park today, not Collins.'

'Probably just a random weirdo in the shopping centre, staring at a pretty girl,' said Joe.

'That's not what my gut tells me. Think about it. Her last sighting was at nine-fifteen. She was meant to meet Collins in the park at nine-thirty. The last phone ping was at nine-twenty-five. She could have been grabbed in the car park.'

'It's one hell of a coincidence she gets grabbed on her way to meeting Collins,' said Joe.

'Yeah, I know. But possible.'

'It's a stretch, but it's your investigation. I'll take the pinch for the child grooming charges. I'll oppose his bail. He'll stay in the bin at least until his court appearance tomorrow. That should buy you some time to keep working the Barkley case.'

'Righto, good plan. Without any more evidence, we won't be able to hold him on murder charges. When you take his DNA sample, can you dispatch it to the lab for priority processing?'

'Yeah, sure thing. I'll organise an urgent transport to the city. The lab's staffed twenty-four-seven these days. They can generate profiles in a few hours, for urgent requests. They've got this new rapid testing software developed by the FBI in the States.'

'Really? Sounds promising. Appreciate it, thanks mate.'

Brad returned to the office and offered to walk Joe through the local charging procedures and paperwork. They led Collins away to the watchhouse in handcuffs.

Jarrod sat alone in the office, his head and ribs throbbing. The restrictive cast was uncomfortable and his fingers tingled. He swallowed more painkillers with a swig of cold coffee, hoping they would kick in. His phone vibrated in his pocket. It was Jayne.

'Oh, shit,' he sighed. He'd forgotten to call. He braced himself for the fallout.

'Please don't tell me you're still at the office?' she said when he answered.

He could hear the rumble of car tyres on bitumen and the drone of a car. She was calling on hands free as she drove.

'Okay, I won't tell you I'm at the office.'

'Jarrod!'

'I'm coming home soon.'

'You better be. How *are* you? I mean, really. After what happened last night?'

'It hasn't sunk in yet. Had a big job on today, been distracted.'

'What's so important that the other guys couldn't have taken over?'

'The murder. We had a suspect.'

'Oh.'

He told her about Lionel Collins.

When Jayne sighed into the phone, Jarrod knew what she was thinking. Another unsolved case meant he'd hardly be home until they had an arrest.

'We'll be home soon. The kids miss you. So do I,' she said.

'I've missed you, too. I'll be home soon. I'll get a lift. Doctor said I can't drive for twenty-four hours because of the drugs.' He looked at the cast on his arm. A*nd good luck driving a manual*, he thought.

'Where's your truck?' she read his mind.

'Still parked here at the station.'

'Okay. Well, see you at home. Wait, hold on. Say hello to Daddy.'

'Hey Daddy,' Katie and Matty's muffled voices chorused in the background.

Jarrod smiled. 'Hey monsters. I'll see you at home soon.'

After the call, Jarrod leaned back in his chair with his feet propped on the desk. He closed his eyes and massaged his temples. The nagging headache behind his eyes was the kind that stopped all traffic to the brain. He pushed through the discomfort and made a few phone calls.

Joe and Brad were chatting when they returned from the watchhouse.

'You look like shit, mate,' said Brad. 'You need to go home.'

'Don't *you* start,' said Jarrod. 'How's our friend?'

Brad smirked. 'Cooling his heels in a cell.'

'And, good news,' said Joe. 'I just got off the phone from one of our computer techs who raided Collins' townhouse. They broke through his computer firewall. Penetrated his encryption software and found all the incriminating evidence we need. He's also been networking with some real sick bastards, trading kiddy porn. This job's gonna snowball. We've uncovered an entire paedophile ring, heaps of names. Plenty of sphincters will be puckering when we start kicking in doors. My boss has spoken to your boss. I'm to take the lead on the child exploitation side of the investigation.'

'Makes sense. You guys are the experts. That's good news, I guess,' said Jarrod.

Joe studied Jarrod's expression and frowned. 'What's up?'

'I just got off the phone with the office lady at the local finance office Collins works out of. His story checks out. On the day he was meant to meet Lisa Barkley he was back at the office just after 10AM. She remembers it clearly. Says she wasn't expecting to see him back so early. That morning, he told her he had a meeting with a client and would be out all day. That's why she was surprised when he came back. He was only gone for about an hour, tops. He then spent the rest of the day in the office and left to drive back to the city at five o'clock.'

'Maybe he hid the body in his car?' said Brad.

'He drives a two-door Suzuki Swift,' said Jarrod. 'Boot is tiny. No way, not possible.'

Brad's eyes lit up with an idea. 'Maybe she went with him to a motel room where he killed her. He could have come back later to dump the body in the creek bed.'

'Maybe. We can't rule anything out. We need to check with local motels and pubs, tie down his movements. He has an alibi for most of that day. Can you follow up on that, mate?'

Brad nodded. 'Yeah sure.'

'But that's not all,' said Jarrod.

'What is it?' said Brad.

'I also spoke to Larry Carson. After a first sweep, Collins' car looks clean, but he'll need to strip it right down to do full forensics on it. Could take a week.'

Jarrod turned to Joe. 'I need to talk to your man in charge of the search of Collins' place, to talk him through items missing from the Barkley homicide crime scene. They need to know what to look for.'

'No problems,' said Joe. 'I've got his number.'

Jarrod stared at a spot on the wall, lost in his own thoughts. Dread weighed heavy in the pit of his stomach.

'What are you thinking?' said Brad.

'We have to keep an open mind, not get too tunnel-visioned on Collins, not ignore other possibilities. I want to I.D. that bloke from the shopping centre security footage. Have we had any response from the media release?'

'We've had a few leads to follow up, but nothing concrete,' said Brad. 'We still don't know who he is. How can someone with such a distinctive face not be known by anyone? It's like he's a ghost.'

'Well, we keep looking for him. Follow up every lead.'

'You won't be doing that today,' said Brad. 'You're going home, Benfield's orders.'

Joe Marshall shook their hands. 'It's been a pleasure working with you guys. My boss wants me back in the city. There's not much more I can do here. I'll tidy up the brief for Collins' first court appearance and then I'll head back to the city. I can show myself out.'

'Thanks, Joe,' said Jarrod. 'I'll keep you updated if anything else comes in that implicates Collins with the Barkley murder. Thanks again for everything.'

'No worries. We'll wait to see if he gets bail in the morning. You look after yourself now, and that family of yours. Oh, speaking of which, I cleaned up after myself.' Joe handed Jarrod his house keys. 'Thanks for putting me up at your place. It sure beat sleeping in a room above the pub.'

It was now 4PM. Jarrod called the detectives who were still searching Collins' townhouse in the city. It was clean. No sign of Lisa Barkley's missing clothing or phone, nothing to implicate him with her murder. He had the growing sense of unease they were headed for a dead end.

After the call, Jarrod and Brad dropped into Benfield's office for a debrief.

'Righto, O'Connor, you go home and get some rest. We've got teams working around the clock. I'll let you know if anything comes up.'

Brad held up a set of car keys. 'Already on it, boss. I'm driving him home now.'

***

As they slowed towards the house, Jarrod spotted Jayne's Mazda 3 parked in the driveway. She lugged a suitcase across the yard towards the base of the staircase, followed by Katie and Matty, their arms hugging pillows and little backpacks on their backs like turtle shells.

Brad pulled into the driveway. 'Spend some time with your kids. I'll swing by in the morning to pick you up.'

'Thanks mate, see you tomorrow.'

As Jarrod got out of the car, Katie and Matty squeal in unison, 'Daddy!' They dropped what they were carrying and ran over. Jarrod knelt and caught them as they fell into his arms, squeezing and exchanging kisses.

Katie placed her palm on his cheek, her little hand tender and warm. A furrow of concern bisected her forehead. 'Your eye, it's all purple and black.'

A reflex response popped into Jarrod's head. *You should see the other guy.* Karl Mundy's lifeless and bloodied figure flashed before his eyes, and he caught the words before they escaped his lips. 'I'm okay. It's just a bruise.'

'What happened?' she said, her eyes searching his.

He looked over at Jayne who had put the suitcase down. She shook her head, her eyes saying, "No, don't you dare tell her."

'I fell over.'

Katie cocked one eyebrow and pulled a face. She wasn't that easily fooled. 'You fell over?' she said, her words soaked in scepticism.

Jarrod opened his mouth to speak, not knowing what to say next.

'What's that?' said Matty, his eyebrows tilting to a frown. He prodded the cast with a finger.

'Daddy hurt his arm,' said Jarrod. 'This will help it heal.'

'Oh', he said, deep in thought. His face lit up as a new idea came into his head. 'We went in a train, Daddy. It was scary and fun,' he said with sudden excitement.

'I'm glad you guys had fun, but I am really glad you're home.' He made eye contact with Jayne. 'I missed you all so much.'

Her stern expression softened and a smile flickered, her stiff posture relaxing. She came over, bending down to kiss him softly on the lips. Her familiar fragrance gave him goosebumps. She sent the kids upstairs, carrying their things into the house.

She grabbed his hand and tugged, helping him to his feet. She stroked his face with the backs of her fingers, her eyes shining. 'You look like a wreck. Are you okay?'

'Just trying to hold it together, to be honest.'

She hugged him tight. Overcome by a wave of emotion, he melted into her arms. She rocked him like he was a small child. His rock.

A lump formed in his throat and his nostrils tingled. Vulnerability burst through the cracks in his outer façade, a torrent of tears burning his eyes. He didn't know what he felt, or how to control it. He felt giddy, light-headed.

'Just breathe,' Jayne whispered into his ear.

The weight of fatigue was too great. If she were to let go, he'd topple over like a string puppet.

She kissed his bruised eye. 'You don't have to do this alone. I'm home now.'

TWENTY-SEVEN

TAMMY Heidenreich walked home alone that afternoon after wasting an hour at the library. She had stared at the pages of her homework, but her thoughts swirled, a fog rolling across her mind. She got nothing done. Her mind was numb since receiving the news of Lisa's murder. Her best friend was dead. It didn't seem real. Her mind wandered back to her last days with Lisa and her heart ached. Seth and Jason had tried to console her, but they couldn't mend the gaping hole in her heart.

Jason said little. He could never find the right words. Seth just kept telling her it would be okay, but she knew it wouldn't be. He was just a boy trying to be all grown up and mature. What did he know? She needed to be alone. Being with the boys was just a constant reminder that Lisa wasn't coming back, ever.

The treads of her boots scuffed the loose gravel as she trudged along the shoulder of the back road. As she did each day, she came upon the pine forest lining the roadway. Generations ago, thousands of towering trees had been planted in rows, forming a dense forest swallowed in shadow. Her thoughts a thousand miles away, her feet steered her down the shortcut carving its way through the forest. The fifty-acre property where she lived with her parents backed onto the far side of the forest.

As she disappeared into the gloom, the air became cool and still. High above, the treetops reminded her of stoned hippies swaying with their arms in the air. On ground level, there wasn't so much as a breath of breeze. The dense forest canopy formed a dome of silence from the outside world. She felt more at ease. It was a place where life's worries dissolved away. She meandered along the track snaking its way through thick undergrowth towards her home. Ever since she was little, she never ventured from the safety of the walking track, scared she would lose her way and become lost forever.

She sensed a shift in the air behind her, and the unsettling feeling she was being watched. An eerie presence had entered her haven from the outside world. Uninvited. Unwelcome.

A dry twig snapped under the weight of a stomping foot, the cracking sound echoing so she couldn't pinpoint its location. Startled, birds fluttered from their treetop perches. She stopped and scanned, squinting to make out any shapes in the dying light. Her shallow breathing and pounding heart were the only sounds. A crunching of dry leaves broke the silence from the shadows to the left of the walking track. She kept walking, quickening her pace. The clearing at the edge of the forest that led to her farmhouse was still several hundred metres ahead. Another noise, but this time much closer. She froze with fear. She watched and waited. Nothing but silence.

Someone or something was out there, watching from the cover of trees. Her eyes darted from side to side, but in the fading afternoon light, the gloom thickened. She was about to set off again when something darted from behind a tree, circled ahead of her and disappeared. She willed her legs to move and started running along the track towards her home, towards safety.

She then saw him for the first time. A man, or something resembling a man, weaving through the trees a stone's throw off the track. She gasped to control her breathing, and her chest tightened. Her senses heightened. Every sound and movement amplified. She dropped her school bag and ran for her life. Her breathing laboured and her abdomen cramped until her chest ached. Lightheaded, a sense of vertigo sent her off balance as she looked back over her shoulder. She stumbled, furious at herself for tripping over the tree root she had stepped over a thousand times before. Regaining her balance, she ran, fighting to control the panic that had taken hold.

She was close to home now and up ahead could see the clearing at the end of the track. She ran, unsure if the man was still following her. The clearing drew nearer, towards home. To safety.

Her legs jerked to a halt and her shoes skidded in the dirt. A sudden coldness bit at her core and her body froze. A figure had stepped out onto the track, blocking her path to safety. She could only make out the man's silhouette, a sky of fire melting the horizon behind him. Golden shards of sunlight pierced the trees, creating a blinding glow around his form.

'What do you want? Leave me alone!' The forest absorbed her raspy cries.

The man let out a chilling laugh.

Tammy opened her mouth to scream, but her lungs contracted inside her ribcage like a fist, her breath jagging in her throat, unable to escape. Agonisingly close to home, she turned and ran back along the track from where she had just come. She had no choice but to try to outrun him. He ran after her and closed in. She ran for her life now, ignoring the searing pain in her chest. She could hardly breathe, but sheer terror drove her forward, willing her legs to move. She glanced over her shoulder. The man mowed her down, almost on top of her. He laughed again, humourless and taunting.

Her legs buckled and she stumbled to her hands and knees. Survival instincts pumped adrenaline through her veins. She crawled along the ground, her fingers clawing the damp earth. But her body gave in to exhaustion, her arms and legs no longer functioning. She lay helpless, her knees tucked up to her chest. She sucked in short, gasping breaths like a fish out of water, trying to quell the rising sense of panic. His footfalls slowed to a walk. He had her now. She had nowhere to go.

He stood over her and for the first time she saw his grotesque face, a face she recognised. Twisted with hatred, it now filled her with terror. Hollow eyes bore into hers, merciless, compassionless.

She swallowed against her fear. 'Leave me alone,' she repeated, without taking her eyes off him.

He brought a single finger to his lips, signalling for her to be silent. He tilted his head, as if in sympathy, and offered an approximation of a smile. 'Ssshhh. It's over now. It's time to pay,' he whispered across the gap between them, his tone malicious in its neutrality.

He edged forward and leaned over her until she could feel the warmth of his breath against her face.

She cowered but couldn't tear her eyes away. In the depths of his black, soulless eyes, she caught her own reflection.

He studied her face but said nothing, not for a very long time.

Finally, he spoke. 'It's time to die.'

TWENTY-EIGHT

TOM and Marcia Heidenreich sat on padded cane chairs on their back porch, facing the setting sun. The sky had a brilliant red haze as the day's last sunlight filtered through a smearing of clouds. It would be dark soon and their only child hadn't arrived home yet. As the daylight dwindled, the tension in the sky matched Tom's growing sense of unease. He looked at his wristwatch again.

He turned his head and considered his wife for a moment. Marcia had grown frail in the last few months, her zest for life fading with each day. Skin sagged from her bones, her eyes sunken. The cancer had spread and there was nothing the doctors could do. He spent his days trying to make her comfortable. Some days were worse than others. Today had been one of the better ones. She was in less pain and seemed content as she looked out over their precious farm.

The property had been in Tom's family for generations, handed down to him by his parents. A memory came to him, clear and well defined, as if illuminated by stage lights. Twenty-five years ago, Tom and Marcia had exchanged wedding vows beneath the farm's big old jacaranda tree. Standing under a purple canopy, he had kissed his bride in the light of a setting sun, like the one now dipping below the horizon. They vowed to spend the rest of their lives together on the farm. That thought trapped him. He couldn't move on, couldn't escape it. His happy life with Marcia would soon end. She had bravely accepted her fate and chose to spend her last days in the one place she loved most. She gave instructions for her ashes to be sprinkled under the jacaranda tree so its roots could absorb her life force.

Tom's thoughts returned to Tammy, their miracle child, who the doctors said would never be conceived. She had been their shining light. Another memory came to him, so vivid he could smell it. He remembered how, as a little girl, she would hold his hand as they walked down to the chook pen each morning to collect the eggs, plodding through the mud in her gumboots and pyjamas. She had been such a sweet child, but those days were long gone. The cheeky smile had vanished, replaced with the brooding scowl of a teenager. She rarely spoke to them, instead locking herself in her bedroom listening to punk music.

She had lost interest in tending to the horses she once adored. Tom feared he was losing her. Everything had changed since Marcia became ill. Tammy had taken the news hard and withdrew even more. Maybe it was just the initial shock, her own coping mechanism. He couldn't remember the last time he'd seen that smile of hers.

'Did Tammy say anything about coming home late this afternoon, love?' said Tom. 'I know she hasn't been overly reliable lately, but she should be home by now, shouldn't she?'

Marcia gazed out over the farm. 'She hardly spoke to me this morning.' She paused, straining to fill her lungs with air. 'You know she's been cutting school. I worry about those weird kids she's been hanging around. And that terrible business with Lisa Barkley. Tammy won't speak to me about it. She's bottling it all up inside.' Her head lolled to one side, her dull eyes meeting his. 'She's been avoiding me. It breaks my heart.'

'I don't think she's avoiding you, sweetheart. I think she just doesn't know how to cope with you being sick, and her friend Lisa…' Tom struggled to find the right words.

'She should be home soon. Give her a few minutes,' said Marcia, her eyelids heavy. She dozed off again, drowsy from the morphine.

A movement at the edge of the pine forest, down near the bottom paddock fence, caught Tom's eye. Sam, their golden retriever, emerged from the walking track and through the open gate. He carried something in his mouth. The old dog laboured up the hill towards the house as far as he could before needing a rest, then plonked his barrel frame onto the grass. The object fell out of his mouth as he panted, his drooling tongue hanging out the side of his mouth.

Each afternoon, Sam would venture into the forest, meeting Tammy on the walking track as she walked home. Tom rose from his chair and whistled for Sam to come, but he could only manage an excited wag of the tail.

Tom made his way down the stairs and across the lawn. When he reached Sam, he made out the shape of the object. He knelt on one knee and picked up the black boot. He recognised it: one of Tammy's chunky lace-ups, the ones she wore every day with her black clothes. His fingers slid in something greasy on the toe of the boot.

Maybe Sam's drool?

He rubbed his thumb and forefinger together, now coated in dark red. *Wet paint? No, blood!*

He dropped the boot and shot a look over at the gate leading into the forest, wiping his bloodied fingers on his trouser leg.

'Tammy!' he yelled. He got up with a groan and hurried into the forest. Beyond the fence it was so much darker, and he blinked to adjust his eyes. He followed the track into the forest, screaming out his daughter's name. He then came across Tammy's school bag, its contents scattered all over the walking track.

'Where are you?' he whispered to himself. He looked around, his eyes searching. 'Tammy!' he called. The trees swallowed his voice without echo, and then silence.

He went deeper into the forest, his legs heavy with fear. He stopped when he saw a figure up ahead, just off the track. At first, he couldn't make it out, but as he walked closer the cold reality hit him. He could never have been prepared for what he saw.

Bound to the base of a pine tree, his daughter dangled like a rag doll, her naked body pale and still. Her dyed black hair was matted with blood and draped over her face, her head slumped forward. A rope supported her body weight under her armpits and spiralled around her waist and thighs. Her arms dangled by her sides and her bare feet rested in a clump of dry leaves, her knees bent. She was on display, a hunter's prize kill. Her clothes were nowhere to be seen. Her other boot, scuffed and muddied, lay out on its own in the middle of the track.

Tom's arms and legs went to jelly. He reached out a hand towards his daughter as he moved closer, his heart wrenching. *Who could have done this to her? Why? She didn't deserve this.* He swept the hair off her face, her skin cold to the touch. Blood seeped from a deep gash to her left cheek, her pretty face disfigured. Tears of smudged mascara had fallen from her lifeless eyes, black streaks staining her face.

He needed to hold her, to comfort her, to free her of the indignity. He felt around until he found the knot and untied it. As the rope unravelled, he caught the weight of Tammy's body and lowered her to the ground. He fell to his knees, rocking her back and forth in his arms.

'It's okay, baby. I've got you now,' he sobbed. 'Daddy's here.'

He stroked her face with the back of his hand and looked up to the darkening sky, the first stars blinking through the treetop canopy. His groans were that of a wild beast, guttural. Primal. 'No! My God, no!'

His hand formed a fist and he punched the ground. He had never felt so powerless, utterly useless. He'd failed as a father, failed to protect his precious child. He gently lay Tammy on her side, just like he did when she had fallen asleep in his arms as a little girl. He stood and looked around. Whoever did this might still be close, watching.

He listened. Everything was strangely peaceful. He didn't know which way to turn or what to do. He turned on the spot, gazing into the gloomy forest closing in all around him. Nothing, not a sound.

'Come out, you coward. Gutless mongrel,' he yelled, the rage in his voice rising. 'Come and face me! You took my little girl. Come out now so I can rip your heart out!'

Tom coughed, gagging on the bitterness in his throat. His legs buckled and he collapsed to his knees, staring at his daughter's lifeless form. He couldn't bare the pain. He unbuttoned his flannelette shirt and used it to cover her nakedness.

He then thought of Marcia. How could he tell her? She was too frail to cope with this news. It would surely kill her. The final blow to end her suffering. His world crumbled, stripping away his own will to live. He would gladly take Tammy's place, but it was too late for that.

He felt so alone, filled with hatred and rage at the maniac who had done this to his daughter, to his family. He clutched his chest, a pain ripping through his heart as if pierced with a dagger. Red mist clouded his vision as the desire for revenge consumed every fibre of his being.

Whoever did this would pay – whatever it took.

TWENTY-NINE

JARROD nodded off on the couch as Jayne busied herself making dinner. The kids had propped themselves on the carpet in front of the TV, giggling at old Looney Tunes. Jarrod's phone vibrating on the coffee table roused him.

Jayne poked her head out of the kitchen doorway. 'Don't answer that. You need to rest. They can handle it without you, whatever it is.'

Jarrod blinked at the phone, still rattling across the glass like a windup toy. He groaned and reached over with his good hand to check the caller I.D. It was Ross Benfield.

He sighed. 'It's the boss. He wouldn't be calling unless it was urgent. I have to take it.'

Jayne gave him a disappointed look. 'Of course you do.' She shook her head and retreated into the kitchen.

He swung his feet onto the carpet and sat up, flinching as a sharp pain shot through his ribs. He gave himself a few seconds to shake off the grogginess before he answered. 'Hey boss, what's up?'

'O'Connor. Sorry to call you. Can you talk?'

'Yeah, I guess. What is it?'

'There's been another murder.'

Jarrod's mind bubbled. 'Where?'

'The pine forest out on Dawson's Road.'

'Who's the victim?'

Benfield cleared his throat. 'A teenage girl, surname Heidenreich.'

Jarrod's stomach plummeted. He leaned forward and pressed the phone against his ear. Bugs Bunny nibbled a carrot on the TV. 'What's up, Doc?' Elmer Fudd pulled a face and Matty burst into raucous laughter.

Jarrod put a finger in his other ear. 'Tammy Heidenreich?'

'Yeah, that's her. She's Lisa Barkley's friend, isn't she?'

Jarrod felt woozy. Maybe it was the painkillers, or just the shock. He couldn't tell. 'Yes. I only spoke to her a few days ago. My God. What else do we know?'

'Not a lot. That's why I'm calling you. Given your knowledge of the Barkley case, we could use your eyes at the scene. You should be the one to speak to her parents. I hate to ask, after all you've been through in the last twenty-four hours, but are you up to it? Can you come in?'

Jarrod looked at Matty and Katie, their backs to him as they watched TV. The clanking of dinner plates in the kitchen had fallen silent. Jayne was listening. He looked at the cast on his arm and wiggled his fingers. He stroked the puffy skin around his eyes. The headache had subsided. He swivelled his head towards the kitchen and then clinched his eyes closed. 'Yeah boss, I can come in.'

He waited for Jayne's reaction. Her silence said it all.

***

Brad collected Jarrod from home and drove straight to the Heidenreich property. They parked in the driveway behind a patrol car, unmarked CIB vehicle and forensics van. As they got out, a woman's howling cries emanated from inside the farmhouse. Moths, attracted to the artificial glow of the kitchen light, fluttered against the windowpane in erratic flight paths. As Jarrod and Brad walked down the side of the house, a motion sensor spotlight threw light into the yard. A uniformed senior constable standing out on the back porch directed them to the gate leading into the forest. As they approached, a junior constable on guard duty, a little on edge, shone a torch in their faces and nodded in recognition. He lifted the police tape strewn across the gate opening. The young officer shifted his weight from leg to leg, as if he didn't want to be there.

Jarrod placed a reassuring hand on his shoulder. 'You right, mate?'

'Yeah, I'm good, sarge,' he said, his expression non-committal. 'My first murder, that's all. That poor girl.' He shook his head and stared off into the middle distance. 'Seeing her like that, got to me a bit, ya know?'

'Yeah. I know, mate. It gets no easier, trust me.'

The constable pointed his torch into the treeline. 'Just follow the walking track. You won't miss it.'

As Jarrod and Brad entered the blackness of the forest, they navigated the track behind their own torchlight. They followed the path as it snaked its way through the criss-crossing rows of trees – tall, vertical and endless. The sounds of a plethora of nocturnal critters, hooting, chirping and scampering filled the grey shadows.

Up ahead, portable spotlights penetrated the darkness, positioned in a ring around a single tree. Through the haze of frenzied insects, the lights looked like flickering campfires. As Jarrod and Brad approached the outer cordon, the hum of generators grew louder. Liam Dawes and Murray Long emerged and met them on the path.

Long aimed his torch beam at their chests. 'We've been waiting for you guys.'

Jarrod squinted away from the offensive light.

Dawes lowered his torch to Jarrod's cast arm. 'You holding up alright, mate? After what happened last night?'

'Yeah, mate. I'm alright.' He flicked his chin towards the crime scene. 'So, what've we got?'

Long directed his torchlight towards a lit marquee where Larry Carson pottered around dressed in disposable booties and forensics jumpsuit.

'Girl's body is under that tarp. Larry's still working the scene.'

'Who found her?' asked Jarrod.

Long frowned, as if considering the gravity of the situation. 'Her old man.'

'Shit, poor bastard,' said Brad.

Long pointed to the tree at the centre of the spotlights. 'He found her strung to that tree, naked and already dead. He then untied her and covered her up with his shirt. Contaminated the scene, but who can blame the poor bloke.'

'Cause of death?' said Jarrod.

Long stroked the bristles on his chin. 'Looks like strangulation.'

'When was she last seen alive?'

Dawes flicked open his notebook and tilted his head, securing his pen light in the skin fold between his second chin and shoulder. 'Last seen leaving the school library around four-thirty this afternoon. Old man says she takes a shortcut home from school through this forest track.'

Long cut in. 'The killer might have known her routine and was waiting for her.'

'Any sign of her clothes?' said Jarrod.

'Nope,' said Long. 'Clothes are missing. Only her boots were left behind. Family dog brought one home. The other one was near the body.'

Dawes pointed his torch back along the track. 'We found her school bag just off the track, back towards the house. Contents had fallen out like she'd dropped it. School books and a laptop computer. We've bagged it all for prints and DNA.'

Brad gave a questioning look. 'Wait. Her bag was back towards the house?'

Dawes squinted, as if trying to improve his mental focus. 'Yeah, strange right?'

'What do you guys make of that?' said Brad.

Murray shrugged. 'Don't know for sure.'

'Anything missing from the bag?' said Jarrod.

'As far as the mother can tell, just her mobile phone,' said Long.

'We've already run a triangulation. It last pinged from the tower on the other side of the pine forest. It's a network black spot in here. No pings since. Probably been turned off.'

'Just like Lisa Barkley's phone,' said Jarrod.

'Our boy's not a total idiot,' said Long. 'Keeping 'em as souvenirs but turning them off so he can't be tracked.'

'We'll need to send the laptop for analysis,' said Jarrod. 'It might tell us something.'

Dawes sighed. 'Don't get your hopes up. The mother says it's a laptop they lease from the school, has built-in firewalls or somethin' or other. For schoolwork only, so she says.'

Long gave a humourless chuckle. 'Yeah right, and teenagers don't know how to get past firewalls?' He looked at Jarrod. 'Your mate Marshall should be able to help, yeah?'

Jarrod nodded, deep in thought. The four detectives stood in a wordless huddle, their collective gazes drawn towards the spotlights illuminating the blue tarp covering the dead girl. Jarrod spoke next. 'Who's spoken to the parents?'

Dawes looked up from his notebook. 'First responders I.D'ed the body with the father and took basic details while they waited for us to arrive.'

Long's voice broke the silence, a sharp edge to his tone. 'Benfield gave us explicit orders to secure the crime scene and wait for you to arrive to interview the parents. Seems you're still the golden-haired boy.'

Jarrod said nothing and averted his eyes towards the patch of bushland lit up like a circus ring. He took a deep breath to re-centre himself. His eyes met Long's, matching the intensity of gaze. 'Can I see the body?'

Long raised his eyebrows and pursed his lips, as if he couldn't care less. 'Sure, your crime scene, mate. Benfield's orders.' He made no attempt to hide his annoyance.

Jarrod didn't give him the satisfaction of a reply.

'Hey, Larry,' Long called out. 'You got some spare booties and scrubs for O'Connor?'

'In the hard box,' Larry called back as his camera flash illuminated the crime scene in a burst of white light.

Long turned to Jarrod. 'This shit-show is all yours. Come on, Dawsey. Let's go.' He turned and sauntered away, his gait confident.

Dawes shrugged apologetically, his smile generous and unflappable. He fell in behind Long, their torch lights fading until swallowed by the darkness.

'I should go in alone,' Jarrod said to Brad. 'Fewer people entering the scene, the better.'

'Sure, mate. Go do what you gotta do. I'll go back and check on the young connie. He could do with some company.' Brad set off behind Dawes and Long.

Jarrod kitted up and followed the evidence flags stabbed into the ground to mark the crime scene entry path. He ducked under a ring of police tape and stood alongside Larry, who gave him a sideways glance. 'You ready?'

Jarrod took a breath and nodded.

Larry crouched and pulled back the tarp. Jarrod's stomach churned at the grim sight. Tammy Heidenreich's pale, naked body lay face up in a bed of dead leaves and rotting bark, her mouth frozen in a silent scream.

'It's the same guy. Same MO.' With a gloved finger, Larry flicked away a cockroach as it crawled out her gaping mouth. Her lifeless eyes looked up at the stars through half open eyelids.

Jarrod tilted his head and followed the dead girl's gaze towards the night sky, tinted with a starry blue haze beyond the tree canopy above. A flimsy spark of hope constructed itself in his mind that her soul was at peace, smiling down from the stars. He remembered speaking with her and the two boys at the school just a few days earlier. She hadn't fooled him. Beneath her solemn emo appearance, the dyed black hair, Cleopatra eyeliner and blood red eyeshadow, she was just a shy and confused kid trying to express herself. He remembered the sincerity in her eyes, her face stricken with worry, her shoulders hunched under the weight of troubles too great for such tender years.

Larry interrupted Jarrod's thoughts. 'See here,' he said, pointing. 'Ligature marks around the throat and a small piece of scalp sliced from the top of the head. It's deep, exposing the skull. Just like the Barkley girl.' He pointed to a deep cut splicing the petal skin of her cheek. 'He slashed this girl up as well.'

'To disfigure her,' Jarrod supposed.

A frown came over Larry's face. More silence followed before he spoke again, his voice thoughtful. 'He's sending a message.'

'What message?'

'Dunno. You're the detective.'

Jarrod stared at the girl's body, words failing him. For a while, his mind reeled. 'Any luck with shoe prints?'

'Nah. The forest floor is inches thick with foliage. Though we might have more luck in daylight.'

'Any other evidence?'

'Nothing yet. We'll do a zone search in the morning once the body's been removed. Benfield's organising more personnel.'

Larry looked up at Jarrod, making full eye contact for the first time. 'You seen enough?'

Jarrod took one last look, taking mental pictures of Tammy Heidenreich's corpse, now void of the soul-spark that had made her a living person. He scanned the surrounding trees, taking in the eeriness of the moving shadows playing tricks on his eyes. Such a lonely place to die.

'Yeah, I'm done here. I need to speak with the parents.'

***

Jarrod knocked on the screen door of the back porch, noticing muddy work boots kicked off to one side. A man dressed in a flannelette shirt and work trousers came to the door, the distress on his weathered face plain to see. He looked bewildered, uncomprehending.

Jarrod held up his badge. 'Mr Heidenreich? I'm Jarrod O'Connor, a local detective. I'm so sorry to disturb you right now. May I come in?'

The man barely acknowledged him as he pushed the door open, brass hinges creaking in protest. 'Mr Heidenreich was my father. You can call me Tom. Come in.'

Tom held the door for Jarrod and turned back inside, his socked feet gliding over the polished timber floorboards without making a sound. A hint of tobacco trailed behind in his wake. He seemed to float through the house like a ghost. Jarrod followed him down the hallway into a quaint sitting room. The aromas of scented candles and pine needles mingled in the air, reminding him of a log cabin in the woods. An antique looking grandfather clock tick-tocked in the corner. A frail woman with thinning, wispy hair the colour of ash sat on a recliner chair with a crocheted blanket over her legs. She sat still, face gaunt, puffy eyes locked onto Jarrod's. They were eyes that had no more tears left to cry.

Tom sat on the armrest and held her hand. 'This is my wife, Marcia.'

The woman remained silent, her stare unwavering.

'We've already told the other police everything,' began Tom, wiping his nose on his sleeve. 'What else do you want with us? Why aren't you out looking for whoever…' His voice tapered off. He brought a fist to his mouth and his body trembled with an outpouring of despair. 'Oh, God… our little girl... who would do such a thing? She's still out there… lying in the dirt.' Equal doses of grief and rage filled his eyes. A stunned look crossed his face, as if his words were not his own.

Jarrod lingered in the doorway, considering what to say. 'I'm so sorry for your loss. I can assure you we will do everything in our power to find the person who did this to Tammy, whatever it takes.'

Tom sprung to his feet, jabbing his finger at Jarrod. 'You *will* find the animal who did that to our little girl and you'll bring them to me. Do you understand?' he insisted. 'No courts, you just bring them to me. I'll tear their heart out with my bare hands. I'll dispense my own justice!'

His wife reached for his hand and looked up at him, her eyes glistening. 'No, Tom. Don't. This man is trying to help. Please, sweetheart,' she urged.

Tom looked down at her. 'I'm sorry, love,' he said, aggression leaving his voice. He lowered himself back onto the armrest. 'I just need to know who did this and why. You can understand that, can't you?'

'Of course. I can't imagine how you must be feeling.'

Mrs Heidenreich spoke, her eyes sad. 'Please, detective. Sit.' Despite her fragility, the woman projected her voice with dignity. 'Thank you.' Jarrod sat at the end of a couch, closest to the couple. He leaned forward, elbows on his knees, hands clasped.

The woman considered Jarrod for a moment, studying his face. 'We know you have a job to do, detective. What do you need to know?'

Jarrod ran through a list of routine questions, Tammy's movements, anything she might have said, suspicious cars, signs of trespassers, strange phone calls, the usual. The distraught couple shook their heads after each question. The only information they could offer was that since Lisa Barkley's death, Tammy had been more reclusive than usual, but there were no red flags to forewarn them of the impending nightmare.

'Was it the same person who killed that other poor girl?' Tom asked, a note of desperation in his voice. 'We need to know.'

Jarrod exhaled, hesitating. 'We think so. There are many similarities.'

'Like what?'

'It's best that I don't go into those details right now, but we are working on the assumption that the same person or persons are responsible.'

'You need to speak with those boys she's been hanging around.' The way he said the word *boys* had an accusatory tone.

'Jason and Seth, you mean?'

'Yes. There's something…' he paused to find the right word, 'off.'

'Do you have any reason to think they could be involved somehow?'

Tom glanced down at his wife who remained stoic, her jaw clenched. 'Just a feeling,' he said. 'They could be bloody devil worshippers for all we know. All dressed in black and listening to music, if you can even call it music, about death and doom. Tammy has changed, ever since she's been hanging around them. It wouldn't surprise me if they were into sacrifices and satanic rituals.'

'We don't know any of that for sure, love,' said Marcia. 'They seem harmless enough.'

'Harmless? Just as harmless as those two boys who shot up that school in America and killed countless kids? I heard they were into the same sort of thing, trench coats and satanic music.'

'We'll consider all possibilities, but for now we can't jump to conclusions,' said Jarrod. 'We'll follow every possible lead.'

'Do you *have* any leads?' Tom spat with rising anger in his voice. 'Why are you wasting time here? My little girl is lying out *there*!' He stood, pointing his finger towards the window. His bottom lip quivered. 'She should be home, safe in her room, not in the forest being probed and prodded like a piece of meat. She's just evidence to you, not a person! Not someone's daughter. You police should have stopped this from happening. If you'd been doing your jobs, you would have caught the mongrel who killed Lisa Barkley and our little girl would still be alive. How many other innocent kids have to die while your incompetent mob sits on its hands?'

Jarrod listened without interruption, waiting for him to finish. His face and neck grew hot, his hands clammy. The back of his shirt soaked up a trickle of sweat running down the small of his spine. Tom's eyes burned into his like a branding iron, his gaze probing for answers. Try as he might, Jarrod couldn't dismiss the accusations as just the erratic ramblings of a grief-stricken man. He felt a tug of guilt. Maybe Tom was right.

Jarrod could only stare, his mind blank, deer in the headlights. Tom's outburst drained the momentum from him.

'Well? Do you have any leads?' he repeated, examining Jarrod's face for a reaction.

Jarrod cleared his throat. He could no longer meet Tom's gaze. 'Well, we have forensic evidence.' The words caught in his throat, jagged as a rusted fishing hook. 'There is a person of interest.'

'Person of interest! What the hell does that mean?' Tom shouted, his face a scowl.

'There was a man captured on security footage, at the shopping centre where Lisa Barkley was last seen.'

'Have you found him?'

'Not yet. We're still trying to identify him. We've put out public appeals.'

'Public appeals?' Tom scoffed. 'You should be out looking for him!'

Jarrod opened his mouth about to speak, but was cut off by Marcia who spoke unprompted, her voice even. 'Tom, please. Getting yourself wound up won't help.' She lifted a shaky hand, beckoning him to come sit by her side. The exertion of it seemed to drain her strength. Tom blinked at her frankness and went to her, taking a knee beside her chair. She stroked his cheek and his anger evaporated. No more words were spoken as they drew solace from each other, becoming one in their grief. Jarrod admired their solidarity. Marcia struck him as a remarkably strong woman despite her deteriorating health, cool-headed and considered. Tom wore his heart on his sleeve, loyal to a fault, a simple man of the land who took pride in providing for his family.

Jarrod saw the opening to probe a little more. 'Tammy's school bag.' Tom and Marcia gave him the same confused look. 'The only thing missing was her mobile phone?'

'Yes,' said Marcia, uncertain. 'Well, we think so. Those other detectives showed her bag to us. But to be honest, we wouldn't know for sure what she had in that bag when she left for school this morning.'

'Her school laptop. Did she use it much at home?' said Jarrod.

'It was supposed to be for schoolwork. That's why we got it for her. We had strict rules about it being for school email and homework research only.'

'Did she use it for social media, or chat rooms?'

Marcia gave Tom a questioning look. He replied with a shrug. She looked back at Jarrod. 'Apparently the school I.T. people put blocks on it to prevent inappropriate use. But what parent really knows what their kids are doing online these days?'

'Do you mind if we examine it?' Jarrod didn't need their permission. The laptop was evidence in a homicide case, but he wanted their buy-in, to empower them with a sense they still had some control.

'Of course,' said Tom.

'Does she lock the laptop with a password?'

'Oh, yes,' said Marcia. 'Do you need the password?'

'You know the password?'

'It was one of our rules,' she nodded, resolute. 'If she wanted a laptop, she had to tell us the password. Tom will write it down for you. Won't you, love.'

'Yes, anything to help.' Tom's tone had softened. He looked around the room, thinking on it some more. 'What do you expect to find on her laptop?'

'I don't know, but it might tell us if Tammy was communicating with anyone.'

'She uses her phone for all that sort of thing,' said Marcia. 'She's always on it. Damn thing is in her hand constantly. Snapchat and that other thingy, Instagram. I don't understand the appeal of all that social media. Kids these days don't know how to communicate face to face, eyes glued to their screens. They never look up, oblivious to the world around them.'

Jarrod nodded his agreement.

'Have your people found the phone?' said Tom.

'No, it's been turned off. Impossible to track. But we'll keep searching for it.'

'Do you need anything else from us?' asked Marcia.

'You've been a big help. Thank you. May I see Tammy's room?'

'Yes, it's the next room down the hallway.'

Jarrod rose to his feet.

'Detective, how much longer will Tammy be out there?' said Marcia. Her eyes were steady, grief replaced by determination. 'I need to see my daughter.'

'I know how hard this must be for you. She'll be taken to the hospital mortuary as soon as our forensic people are finished at the scene. Our people will take good care of Tammy, I promise. We'll make arrangements for a viewing as soon as possible.'

Jarrod moved to the doorway. 'Thank you for your time. We'll get this monster, I promise.'

Tom looked up at him, his eyes narrowing. He flexed his fingers, his knuckles white as he drew them into fists. 'Remember what I said. As God is my witness, I meant every word. You bring them to me. No courts. Promise me.'

'I can't make that promise. I'm sorry.' Jarrod turned away and left the couple alone with their sorrow.

***

He followed the hallway until he came to Tammy's room, the door ajar. As he nudged it open with his knuckle, he caught the tinge of a smoky incense fragrance. He flicked on the light and stepped inside the tidy room. A red bulb created a dark ambience, just like Lisa Barkley's room. The bed was neatly made with a teddy nestled on a stack of pillows. Posters clung to a purple feature wall, projecting moody imagery with dark colours and bursts of neon. Thorny roses, broken hearts and skulls added to the sense of melancholy. The room had a minimalist look, a sign of her lack of attachment to material things, furnished with a simple writing desk painted black, a chest of drawers and a bean bag. Dark clothing and studded belts hung in a built-in closet. Fairy lights weaved around the curtain rod above the window, black curtains pulled closed.

In the corner, a dollhouse spray-painted black imprisoned a collection of troll figurines, their wild hair ablaze with neon flames. Strange little faces with lifelike eyes peered out the windows, making Jarrod uneasy. Their knowing stares followed him as he moved about the room.

He searched the drawers and closet but found nothing sinister, no obvious links between Lisa and Tammy's murders or a possible motive. He wasn't sure what he was even looking for. He checked under the bed mattress. No hidden diary. He turned his attention to a polaroid thumb-tacked to the bedhead, four smiling faces beaming from the photo. Tammy, Lisa, Jason and Seth sat together in front of a graffitied wall, dressed in their usual goth attire, arms around each other's shoulders and pulling faces at the camera. They all seemed happy in that snapshot in time.

The room revealed nothing of note. Jarrod's mind raced, searching for answers. He leaned in and focused on the polaroid.

Seth and Jason, maybe they held the key.

THIRTY

AFTER leaving the Heidenreich property, Jarrod and Brad drove back into town and made two late-night house calls, pounding the front doors of Seth Francis and Jason Barlow. The boys and their parents all seemed rattled by the news of Tammy's murder. Both sets of parents consented to a search of their son's rooms. The boys had nothing to hide, so they said. Despite the mess and boy stink, a blend of body odour, damp shoes and sweaty socks, they found nothing in either of the boys' bedrooms to implicate them.

Given the urgency of the investigation, the parents agreed to bring their sons in for immediate interviews. For now, both boys would be treated as potential witnesses. Although wary, Jarrod had no reason to consider them as suspects, not yet anyway. He reminded himself it wouldn't be the first-time homicidal teenagers had conspired to kill their friends. He remembered an awful case in the USA a few years back where two teenage girls had planned and executed the brutal murder of their unsuspecting friend. Their only motive? They didn't want to be her friend anymore. So fickle, so callous. Jarrod knew all too well the cruelty and irrationality of teenage psychopaths. For now, all bets were off.

Jarrod and Brad were waiting for them upon their arrival, and they were escorted into separate interview rooms. As sixteen-year-olds, they were afforded juvenile safeguards. Anything they said would be inadmissible unless a parent or support person was present.

Seth took the news of Tammy's death particularly hard. She was his girlfriend, and it was clear he had real feelings for her. He buried his face in his hands, inconsolable. His mother tried to comfort him, rubbing his back and stroking his inky hair. The boy swiped at her hand, squirming away from her touch. His father sat with his arms folded, an uncomfortable rift wedged between him and his son. The Francis family ran the local post office. They were decent, well-respected people in town. Mr Francis had made no secret that Seth's lifestyle choices were an embarrassment to the family name, causing angst in the household.

Jarrod left Brad to interview Seth, closing the interview room door behind him as he headed down the hall to the next room where Jason and his parents waited. Their faces were stricken with anxiety, all on edge. Mr and Mrs Barlow were battlers, simple folk. His mother was a tiny woman, softly spoken. His father, a truck driver, had a bloated belly with tattooed tree trunks for arms. Despite his gruff appearance, he was subdued and cooperative. Jason was a blank canvas, difficult to read. He seemed numb, expressionless.

'When did you last see Tammy?' said Jarrod.

'This afternoon at school, at the front gate. She was going to the library. Said she wanted to be alone.'

'Was anyone with her?'

'No.'

'Where was Seth?'

'With me.'

'What did you boys do after school?'

'We went back to my place. Just listened to music in my room.'

'Until what time?'

Jason shrugged, staring at the carpet. 'Don't know, maybe 'til around six o'clock. Mum was putting tea on the table and Dad had just come home from work, so Seth went home.'

Jarrod made eye contact with his mother.

She responded to his questioning expression, nodding. 'He's

telling the truth. The boys were at home. I had to chip them about the loud music.'

Jarrod turned his attention back to Jason. 'How did Tammy seem when you last saw her?'

'Sad. She's been sad ever since Lisa…' He hesitated. 'Ever since what happened to Lisa.'

'Did the girls ever say anything about meeting someone?'

Jason looked up for the first time. He flicked a fringe of dyed black hair out of his eyes. 'What do you mean?'

'Well, was anything said about them chatting online, planning to meet someone?'

Jason shook his head. 'No. Not in front of me.'

Jarrod pressed with more questions. Jason answered without hesitation, no contradictions, no shifty bodily language, no red flags. Jarrod was satisfied the boy was telling the truth. He was just a scared kid, a little awkward, grieving the loss of his friends. He had nothing to hide.

Jarrod opened a folder and slid it across the table in front of Jason. The boy leaned in and squinted, studying the still image taken from the shopping centre security footage the day Lisa went missing.

His eyes widened.

Jarrod shimmied forward in his chair. 'What is it, Jason? Do you know this person?'

Jason stared at the man with the distorted face.

'Jason? What is it?'

'This man, I've seen him before.'

'Where? When?'

'Last week, when we were walking home from school. He was sitting in a park at the end of Lisa's street, the one opposite the service station. It's got a kid's play area, swings and stuff. He was just sitting on a seat, staring across the road.'

'Go on.'

'We walked past him. The girls laughed, like, making fun of him.'

'Why?'

Jason stroked his own face. 'His face. They said he was a freak, called him pizza face.'

'Do you know this man? Have you seen him before?'

'No, never. I have no idea who he is.'

'Have you seen him since?'

'No, thank God.'

Jason's father spoke. 'What? Do you think this man killed the girls? Is Jason in danger?'

'I don't know. I wish I knew more,' said Jarrod. 'We don't know who this guy is or whether he has anything to do with the murders.'

Mrs Barlow looked up at her husband, her face ashen. They exchanged a concerned look. She turned to Jarrod, a tremor in her voice. 'Should we be worried?'

Jason spoke up before Jarrod could answer, his hands jammed under his armpits. 'Is he coming after me?' His eyes bounced from his parents and back to Jarrod, his lips trembling. 'Oh, shit, shit. He's coming for us, isn't he?'

Mr Barlow's mild demeanour instantly shifted. He slammed his meaty fist on the desk, his nostrils flaring. 'Mongrel will have to get past me first. Let him try. It'll be the last thing he ever does. If you coppers won't protect my boy, then I will.'

'Now, let's not jump to conclusions,' said Jarrod, his voice low. 'I can understand why you might be concerned, but please, stay calm.'

'That's easy for you to say,' said Mr Barlow. 'It's not your family under threat. How would you feel?'

Images flashed in Jarrod's mind, a living nightmare he had tried to suppress. His wife thrown to the ground, his daughter snatched from the street by a madman, a gun pointed at her, a gunshot.

'Did you hear me? How would you feel?' repeated Mr Barlow. Jarrod caught himself, realising he'd been staring at him but not seeing. He blinked and shook off the momentary blackout.

'I know what it's like to have your family threatened.' Jarrod held the man's gaze and there was no response, nothing for long seconds. 'Take your boy home, stay together, just until we find this guy. Call the police immediately if you have any concerns. I will let you know as soon as we have news.'

'Come on, love,' said Mr Barlow to his wife. 'Let's take Jason home.' He stood, pushing his chair out with the back of his legs. He looked at Jarrod. 'Thanks for nothing.'

Jarrod rose from his chair and placed a reassuring hand on Jason's shoulder. 'You'll be okay, mate. I know how hard this must be for you. Listen to what your parents say. Stay home and I'll be in touch. Okay?'

The boy nodded and rose to his feet.

'Can I ask that you just wait for a moment before you leave? I just need to check on my partner. He's been speaking with Seth.'

Jarrod slid out of the room. He knocked on the door of the second interview room. Brad opened it and came out into the hallway, closing the door behind him. They conferred notes. Seth had given the same story, down to the very last detail.

After they cut the two boys loose, Jarrod and Brad debriefed over a coffee in their office.

'It's been one hell of a day,' said Brad, blowing steam off the rim of his mug.

Jarrod chuckled despite himself. 'Been a hell of a week,' he said, staring at his computer screen as he trolled through a mountain of emails. 'Hold up, an email's come in from the lab.' He double clicked and read the email. 'Results came back quicker than I expected. DNA samples found on Lisa Barkley's body don't match Lionel Collins.'

'Well, you did call it.'

'And he's been cooling his heels in a cell all day. He's in the clear. Chasing him was a complete waste of time.'

'We had no way of knowing that,' said Brad. 'You have to admit, he was a red-hot suspect.'

'Yeah, but a complete red herring.'

'What now?'

'We get some sleep, then we track down *pizza face*.'

THIRTY-ONE

EARLY the next morning, Jarrod snuck into Matty's room and kissed him on the cheek as he slept, his teddy strangled in a tight embrace. He didn't have the heart to wake him, so he let him be and then tip-toed into Katie's room. Her sleepy eyes opened as he leaned down to give her a kiss.

'Good morning, Daddy,' she said with a bug-eyed smile.

'Good morning, little girl. Did you have a good sleep?'

She nodded and stretched her arms above her head, yawning.

'I had a dream that I was riding a unicorn,' she said. 'It was white with a pink horn. He was my best friend. I wish you could have seen him.'

Jarrod remembered the unicorn standing guard on Lisa Barkley's bedroom wall. He stared down at his little girl's sweet face, reminded of how much he cherished her. The thought of ever losing her made his heart ache. He ran his fingers through her soft brown hair and kissed her on the forehead.

'I have to head off to work. You have a good day now. I'll see you this afternoon.'

'I know you have an important job, Daddy. But I miss you sometimes. I wish you were home more,' she said with a sad face. 'But it's okay, you help kids, don't you?'

'That's right, sweetheart, at least, I try. I'm sorry I haven't been home much lately. Things will get better, I promise.'

'It's okay,' she said with a reassuring smile, showing the resolve that made him so proud of her. 'Is your arm getting better?' she said with a concerned frown, tapping her finger on the cast on his wrist.

'I think it is, it doesn't hurt as much. You know what, you haven't signed it. Would you write on it for me?'

Her face lit up and she jumped up out of bed, scrambling through her school bag for her pencil case. She directed him to sit on her bed and proceeded to draw on the cast with various coloured felt pens. She used her other hand to cover up what she was drawing, her tongue poking out to one side as she concentrated on her artwork.

'There, it's done,' she said as she removed her hand to unveil her masterpiece.

She had drawn a little picture of a unicorn. Underneath she wrote, *Dear Daddy, I hope you have nice dreams. Love, Katie.*

Jarrod couldn't remember the last time he'd had a pleasant dream. He couldn't remember the last time he'd gotten a good night's sleep. The faces of the dead still haunted him every time he closed his eyes. Last night was no exception.

By 7AM he was back at work, updating his investigation running log in time for the 8AM briefing. Looking up at the clock, he decided he still had time. He headed downstairs and pulled Tammy Heidenreich's laptop out of evidence. Forensic support had arrived from the city, so he commandeered a fingerprint technician to run a print brush and DNA swabs over it. Once cleared, it was released into his custody. The login details provided by the girl's parents would save vital time, a small win. He ran a cursory check of Tammy's web browsing history and emails which showed nothing of interest. It seemed Tammy's use of the laptop was limited to schoolwork only. He'd send it to the Forensic Computer Unit for a deep dive in case he'd missed anything.

Ross Benfield ran the briefing in the CIB office where a large whiteboard, cluttered with crime scene photos and intelligence profiles, formed the focal point of discussions. Murray Long reported on the progress of the grid search back at the pine forest. SES volunteers and police recruits from the academy had been brought in, but there was little to tell. No more evidence had been found at the crime scene. The victim's missing items of clothing hadn't been recovered. The wait continued for the autopsy results and forensics. Both girls had fallen victim to the same killer, that much was certain.

Pressure mounted, as much from within the department as the public, to make an arrest. A sense of dread had swept over the community. Media commentators raised doubts about the competence of the police, another distraction they had to contend with. As expected, Lionel Collins was granted bail that morning. There was no evidence connecting him with the murders. They were back to square one. The real killer was still out there.

Jarrod updated the room of detectives and uniformed officers about the interviews with Seth Francis and Jason Barlow. All energies were now on identifying and locating the man with the scarred face.

The media saturated online news bulletins with the headline *"Small town killing spree"* and the suspect's image was plastered on-screen during live television broadcasts. The fuzzy image of the scarred face appeared on the front page of every newspaper for the second day running. A steady flow of information from the public kept Crime Stoppers' call-takers busy and every lead had to be followed up. So far, there was nothing but dead ends.

Investigation logs were divided up and allocated to teams for follow up. Even the most seemingly insignificant tip had to be chased up. Today they would pound the pavement, door-knocking the neighbourhood near the park where the teenagers had seen the man. They had to work through a long list of child sex offenders registered as living in the local area. The man loitering near a playground was a significant red flag.

Police teams converged onto the surrounding streets to commence the door knock. Details of every occupant at every home were taken down for later profiling by intelligence officers. People were complacent by nature, reluctant to call the police to volunteer information for various reasons. They didn't want to get involved, or they dismissed things as insignificant, or they just didn't trust the police. A witness could be out there who held a vital piece of information that could blow the case wide open. They had to apply pressure, to squeeze hard until the streets gave up their secrets.

Hours later, Jarrod and Brad plodded along the pavement in Brighton Street. They had already spoken to numerous residents. One elderly woman welcomed the unexpected company and invited them in for tea and cake. They politely declined and moved onto the next address. They made a note of addresses where no one was home, for later follow up.

Other residents weren't so happy to see the police due to their questionable history with the law, evading questions by instinctive default. Their names were noted for background checks. Still no sign of *Scar Face*, the nickname the media had given the suspect.

Jarrod's bruised ribs ached, and his broken arm throbbed from all the walking. Ross Benfield had offered him an administrative role collating investigation logs, but he insisted he should be out in the field. Benfield hadn't objected. 'It's your call, O'Connor. Just don't give me grief later about me busting your balls,' he'd said.

They walked past the Barkley residence. The front windows and doors were closed, no sign of life. Jarrod suspected Eric Barkley was inside, hiding from the outside world, drinking himself into oblivion. Daniel hadn't been sighted for days.

At the end of the street, they came across the park where the exchange occurred between *Scar Face* and the teenagers. Jarrod wondered what the man had been doing there that day. What had he been waiting for?

He sat on the park bench where Jason said the man had been sitting that day.

Brad joined him. 'Man, it's good to get the weight off my feet. These shoes are killing me.'

Jarrod looked over at the United Fuels service station across the street. An attendant went about his duties, filling up cars and cleaning windscreens. Real old school, the only servo he knew of that still offered service at the bowser, a nod to the retro days. A sign mounted high on a pole read: *Cheap fuel – cheap cigs. Open 24 hrs.*

'What's your theory?' said Jarrod. 'Why do you think our guy was sitting here in the park? I mean, of all places. Why sit here in a kids' play area?'

'He's probably a paedophile,' Brad offered. 'What better place to target kids?'

Jarrod gave it some thought. 'I don't know. Maybe you're right.'

He looked around and was about to get up when he noticed something poking out of the grass at his feet. He bent down for a closer look. It was a small photograph, folded in half. He picked it up by the edges and held it up to his eyes. It was in colour but looked old, faded. It depicted a bare-footed boy, about twelve years old, face side-on to the camera. His hands were dug into the pockets of baggy shorts, a yellow T-shirt tucked in. Flashing a timid smile, he seemed embarrassed to have his photo taken.

In the background stood an old farmhouse in early stages of disrepair, the front porch enclosed by fly screen panels. At the top of the stairs sat a man in a white singlet, jeans and work boots. He was wiry and weather-beaten, with leathery skin like a man accustomed to manual labour. A tally-ho paper was stuck to his bottom lip. He seemed to be rolling tobacco and stared towards the camera, squinting in the sun. A tall bottle of beer stood on the step beside him.

Jarrod stared at the photo. It captured his gaze. The faces of the boy and the man were frozen in time. For the briefest of moments, he became immersed in their lives. He wondered who had taken the photo. Maybe the boy's mother? What had the boy's life been like? He looked vulnerable. He stared at the photo, willing it to reveal more of the boy's life story, to expose its secrets.

'What is it?' said Brad. Jarrod blinked as though he'd woken from a daydream.

'An old photo. Looks like it fell out of someone's wallet. It might be nothing, but could you grab a plastic exhibit bag from the car? We'll hang onto it.'

'Your spider senses tingling?'

'Maybe.'

The car was parked at the end of the street. Brad soon returned and Jarrod placed the photograph into the bag and sealed it, sliding it into the breast pocket of his shirt.

'Come on,' said Jarrod, getting to his feet. 'Let's go chat to old mate at the servo.'

They crossed over and spoke with a portly middle-aged man who waddled about in a pair of mechanic's overalls and steel capped boots. He introduced himself as Bill Mortlock, service station owner. A red bandana hung from his back pocket, which he pulled out to wipe his brow. His blackened fingernails were stained with grease from a lifetime of working under a hood. His young assistant, a boy no older than fifteen, stared at them as he poured fuel into a customer's car.

'What's this about, detectives?' asked Bill after Jarrod and Brad introduced themselves.

'Just some routine questions, Mr Mortlock,' said Jarrod. 'Have you seen anyone hanging around the neighbourhood lately? Anyone that seemed out of place?'

Bill tilted his cap and scratched his head. 'No, not that I recall. Although I spend most of my day out the back in the workshop. Maybe you could ask some of my other staff. I have people working different shifts. We're open twenty-four hours.'

'We'd like to have a list of your staff members if you wouldn't mind, so that we can contact them.'

'Sure, anything to help. Can I ask if this is about those poor young girls, the ones who were murdered?'

Jarrod and Brad exchanged a sideways glance. 'What makes you think it's about that?' said Jarrod.

'What else would it be about? There's coppers crawling around the entire neighbourhood. It's the biggest news in town.'

Jarrod smiled. 'Fair enough. Yeah, you're on the money. Any information would be appreciated.' He held up a public appeal flier showing the still image of *Scar Face*. 'This man, have you seen him before?'

Bill studied the photo and then felt for his glasses hanging from a cord around his neck. He slid on his specs and scrunched up his nose as he studied the image. 'I've seen this picture in the papers, but I can't help ya. I've never seen him. As I said, maybe one of my staff did. I'll get you that staff list from the office.'

While they waited, Jarrod approached the kid pumping fuel. The boy gave him a cagey look. Jarrod then recognised him as a little pothead he'd officially cautioned for possession. He came from a dysfunctional home, usual story. Jarrod couldn't remember his name.

'Hey mate, remember me?'

'Yeah, you busted me.'

'Don't worry, we're not here for you.'

'Why would I be worried? I haven't done nothin'.'

'I'm glad to hear it.' Jarrod held up the flier. 'Have you seen this man before?'

The boy gave it a cursory glance. 'Nup. Never seen him before.'

'Have a closer look.' Jarrod held it up to his face.

The boy rolled his eyes and gave it a second look. He shook his head, convinced. 'Like I said, I never seen him before.'

'Well, do me a favour. Tell your boss if you see him around. Okay?'

The boy nodded. 'Anything else? I'm busy.'

'No mate, that's all. I'll let you get back to work.'

Bill Mortlock came back out with a hand-written list. He'd circled the names of the staff who would start the afternoon shift, as well as the night shift. Jarrod read the list of names, but none were familiar.

'Thanks for your help, Bill. We'll come back later to speak to the other staff.'

Bill held up his finger, as though a new thought had popped into his head. 'Oh, while you're here. I'm worried about Mrs Bishop. She hasn't been in today. It's out of character. Without fail, she comes in first thing every morning to buy the paper. She'd have to be well in her eighties, but sprightly. Real creature of habit. Do you think you could check up on her? She lives just around the corner.'

'When did you last see her?' asked Jarrod.

'Yesterday morning. Came in to buy the paper as usual.'

Brad folded his arms and sighed. 'I'm sure she's fine. It's hardly a reason to be too concerned. Maybe she's gone away.'

Mortlock chuckled, a hearty, phlegmy chortle. 'You don't know Mrs Bishop. She loves a chat. If she had plans to go away, she would have told me yesterday.'

Brad gave Jarrod a look on the sly, subtly shaking his head, his eyes saying *Don't you dare.*

'Sure, Bill,' said Jarrod, smirking at Brad. 'Which house?'

Bill drew a map in the air. 'Down the street, first left. It's the second house on the right, past the intersection. Old house with no fence. You can't miss it.'

***

'This is just great,' said Brad as they crossed the road. 'Do we have time for this? I'm sure the old bird is fine.'

'Come on,' said Jarrod with a shrug. 'What's the harm? We should door knock that street anyway. Let's go check up on Mrs Bishop.'

They left the car and went on foot. Soon they were out front of a high-set post-war colonial. The front yard was well tended, edges trimmed and lawn recently mowed. A cottage garden of lavender and daisies bordered the front path in carpets of purple, white and yellow.

They climbed the stairs leading to the front door. Jarrod rapped his knuckles on the window. Brad looked around, impatient. No movement inside. Jarrod cupped his hands on the glass and peered in, trying to see past the lace curtains. His stomach dropped when he saw a pair of feet in women's shoes poking out in the hallway. 'Ah, Jesus. She's in there,' he muttered.

He banged on the door, much louder this time. 'Mrs Bishop, are you okay?'

No response.

He tried the doorknob. Locked.

'Here, step aside,' said Brad, annoyed. 'You're not in any condition to be kicking in doors.' He braced himself and then slammed his shoulder against the door. The aging doorjamb was no match for his body weight and timber splintered as the door flung open.

They were hit with stale air as they made their way inside. The old lady was sprawled on the floor on her back, her upper body in the kitchen, her legs in the hallway. As they drew closer, adrenalin surged through Jarrod's body and his heartrate accelerated. He took one look at her and knew she was dead. He crouched beside her. This was no death from natural causes.

The old woman lay in a pool of congealed blood, the handle of a carving knife protruding from her chest.

THIRTY-TWO

JARROD and Brad withdrew from the house and called it in. A uniformed crew attended, securing the crime scene until forensics arrived. The elderly woman from next door sticky-beaked, enticed out of her house by the spectacle of the police car out front. Armed with a hose, she pretended to water her petunias along the side fence, covertly diverting her eyes for a gander at all the excitement. Her blue rinse set dazzled in the sun and enormous hoops dangled from her earlobes. She was a dead ringer for Mrs Betty Slocombe from *Are You Being Served.*

'Oh, here we go,' said Brad under his breath, giving Jarrod a nudge. 'Mrs Mangle's on the prowl.'

'I'll go have a word with her. She might have seen something.'

Jarrod walked over to the fence, holding up his badge. 'Hello there. I'm detective O'Connor from the local police.'

'Oh, my goodness. What on earth has happened?' she said, as if only just noticing the police. She twisted off the hose nozzle and met Jarrod at the fence.

Up close, Jarrod noticed her hand-drawn eyebrows, which gave her face a perpetual look of surprise. Rouged cheeks and bright red lipstick complemented her fiery satin robe and matching slippers.

Jarrod deflected her question. 'How well do you know Mrs Bishop?'

'We've been neighbours for over thirty years. Has something happened to her?'

Jarrod glanced over at Mrs Bishop's front door. 'Yes, I'm afraid something has. She…' he paused, choosing his words. 'She—passed away.'

The old woman covered her mouth with a palm. 'Oh, my,' she gasped.

'Can I have your name please, Ma'am?'

'Oh, I'm Beryl. Mrs Beryl Bainbridge.'

'Mrs Bainbridge, when did you last see Mrs Bishop?'

'Edna. Her name is Edna. Let me think.' She didn't seem to know where to look, her gaze wandering as shock set in. 'Wednesday afternoon, I think.'

'Does she have family?'

'No, none that I know of.'

'No children?'

'No, sadly. She wasn't able to have children.'

'How did she seem when you last saw her?'

'She seemed in good spirits when I last saw her. Perfectly well, for a woman her age.'

A mental picture of the bloodied knife handle wedged in the poor woman's ribcage distracted Jarrod for a few seconds. He found himself staring absently at Mrs Bainbridge.

He blinked away the momentary daze. 'Does she receive visitors?'

'Meals-on-Wheels come once a week. The Blue Nurses also check up on her occasionally. Oh, and the mower man comes every three weeks.'

'How often do you see Mrs. Bishop?'

'Most days. She pokes her head out through her kitchen window when I'm watering my garden, or I might see her when she's checking her mailbox or gardening. She's always on for a chat.'

'Yes, so I've heard.'

Her fake eyebrows raised like the McDonald's golden arches. 'You have?'

'Yeah, Bill at the servo was worried about her. Said she didn't come in yesterday to get her paper.'

'Oh, yes, that is unlike her.' She raised her hand to her mouth again. 'Oh, my. I was away yesterday, went on the bus day trip with the ladies from my church. Poor Edna, she must have been in the house all day. If only I were home, I would have checked in on her.'

The image of the knife flashed in Jarrod's mind again. 'There's nothing you could have done.'

'I hope the poor dear didn't suffer.'

Jarrod didn't respond. 'Does she live alone?'

'Yes, ever since her hubbie, Charlie, died a few years ago. Oh, but there is a man staying downstairs.'

Jarrod jerked his head back. 'What man?'

'I never actually saw him, mind you, but I know he was there.'

'I'm sorry, I don't understand. What man?'

'She has a spare room downstairs, a self-contained granny flat. Before Charlie died, he renovated it himself. He even installed a toilet and bathroom. Handy like that, was poor old Charlie. Anyway, Edna told me one day that she advertised in the local paper. She said she wanted to rent the room out. A few days later she told me a man had answered her ad and would be moving in within the week.'

'When was that, Mrs Bainbridge?'

'Oh, let me think. A few weeks ago, I suppose.'

'You say you never actually saw him?'

'That's right, never laid eyes on him. Edna told me he was a very private person, kept to himself. Rarely left the house. I heard them talking occasionally, just muffled voices. I couldn't hear what they were saying. Edna didn't seem to know much about him, it all sounded a bit mysterious.'

'Did he have a car?'

'No, I've never seen another car there. Although a few times I saw Edna's car come and go. She must have let him borrow it. She doesn't drive it much herself anymore, lost her confidence behind the wheel, you see. Happens to all of us.'

'What sort of car does she own?' Jarrod pressed.

'Oh, it's a little yellow car. I think it's a Toyota Corolla. She's had it for years.'

'Where is the car now?'

'I don't know. I assume it's in the garage.'

'Thank you so much for your time, Mrs Bainbridge. I'll be in touch.'

Jarrod turned and hurried over to Brad.

'What's up? Did Mrs Jessup put the hard word on you?'

Jarrod ignored the quip. 'We need to get inside the garage.'

THIRTY-THREE

ALL Jarrod could do was watch on, his bruised ribs and broken wrist rendering him useless. He was restless, breathing heavy with anticipation. He repeatedly glanced at his watch as Brad wrestled with the stubborn roller door. Metal on metal screeched as he heaved it open, disturbing the stagnant air. A plume of dust particles reflected the sunrays like swirling glitter.

The car was gone.

Tyre tracks and boot smudges were all that remained in the dust on the surface of the concrete floor.

'Call the station,' said Jarrod, still gazing into the empty garage. 'Run a rego check and get a BOLO out on that car. I'll stay here. You hit the road with as many crews as you can and start looking for that car.'

'On it,' said Brad, setting off with his phone to his ear as Larry Carson pulled into the driveway. The senior constable guarding the front of the house untied the barrier of police tape to allow the scenes of crime van to enter.

Larry hauled himself out of the vehicle. 'What am I dealing with this time, O'Connor?' he said, unimpressed.

'Old woman up in the house, stabbed.'

'Who else has been in my crime scene?'

'Just me and Harding. We got out of there and called it in.'

Larry slid open the van door to retrieve his equipment box.

'I still need to search the house,' said Jarrod. 'Mind if I tag along?'

Larry tossed him a set of booties. 'You know the drill.'

After suiting up, Jarrod escorted Larry to the base of the front stairs where another uniformed officer guarded the crime scene.

They climbed the stairs and went inside.

'Looks like a single stab wound to the heart,' said Larry after considering the body for a long while. 'Poor old dear didn't stand a chance.'

'What's your best guess as to time of death?'

'The pathologist will give you a more accurate indication.' He took out a digital temperature gauge and held the button until it beeped. 'Room temperature is twenty-six degrees, fairly warm, which could speed up decomposition. The marbleised discolouring of the skin means the blood's been pooling.'

Larry crouched and prodded the skin on the inside of the woman's forearm. 'There's no blanching.'

He tried to bend the elbows. 'Rigor mortis hasn't yet dissipated. She's been here twenty-four to thirty-six hours, that's my best guess.'

'She was last seen early yesterday morning. It must have happened not long after she got home.'

'Yeah, that timeline fits,' said Larry, following the same thought process. He rotated her hands to inspect the palms. 'No defensive wounds.'

Jarrod held up his gloved hands. 'Am I clear to look around?'

Larry unlatched the clips to his camera case. 'You stay out of my hair, I'll stay out of yours.' The *ka-chick* of Larry's camera shutter echoed off the tongue-in-groove walls.

Old floorboards creaked as Jarrod stepped around the woman's body, taking mental snapshots as he entered the kitchen. It was dated but functional, and spotless. A time piece from the fifties. The lino flooring curled at the edges where it met wooden cupboards, painted light green with matching drawers. Tiled bench tops were wiped clean and a dishcloth was neatly folded over the sink tap. The tubular, aluminum framed table and chairs set with red vinyl coverings reminded him of the one his family had when he was a kid. He'd donated it to Vinnies when his mother died.

A clock tick-tocked above the gas-top stove. A folded newspaper and reading glasses rested on the tabletop. He imagined Mrs Bishop sitting at her table, catching up on the day's news with a fresh pot of tea. He went over to it and used his pen to unfold the newspaper. The eyes of *Scar Face* looked back at him from the front page of yesterday's paper. A fridge from a bygone era, with rounded corners and pull handle, hummed in the corner and convulsed to silence with a shudder as the thermostat kicked in. A clean bowl, spoon and cup had been left to dry in the drainer. A wooden block with slits held matching black-handled knives. One was missing, now lodged in Mrs Bishop's chest.

A hand-crafted, wooden key rack, paint dulled by years of fingermarks, hung on the wall near the kitchen's back door. Jarrod leaned in to inspect it. Spare house keys hung from hooks, but one was empty. Probably the missing car keys.

His eyes scanned around the kitchen to get a broader perspective. He almost missed it at first, but there it was, now plain to see. A rotary dial telephone hung on the wall. The cord had been pulled from the wall, the plug broken. A fine mist of blood had splattered on the handset, fat droplets leaving a bloody trail across the floor to where the dead woman now lay.

'Hey Larry, can you come in here a minute?' he called.

Larry appeared in the doorway. 'Yeah? What is it?'

Jarrod pointed at the blood on the phone. 'What does this say to you?'

Larry came and stood alongside him, squinting through his glasses. 'Well, the old lady has blood on her lips. Her lung might have been punctured. From the splatter pattern, I'd say she spat that blood out. Like she was…'

Jarrod cut in, 'on the phone when she was stabbed.'

'Exactly.'

Jarrod looked over at the newspaper and then back at the bloodied phone. 'The killer stopped her from making a call.'

'That'd be my guess. Anyway, I'm done in the hallway for now. I'll start working in here.'

Jarrod left the kitchen, stepping around the body as he continued down the hallway. In the main bedroom, a double bed was neatly made, the covers pulled up and tucked in at the sides. On a dressing table, beside an antique looking jewelry box, stood a statue of Jesus, a set of rosary beads draped over his outstretched arms. Jarrod could smell a mix of musk perfume and moth balls. It reminded him of his grandmother's room.

The two spare rooms seemed untouched, single beds made up with old fashioned covers with lace edging. Teddy bears sat between pillows on each bed. Jarrod wondered if these were meant for the children she never had.

The lounge room was furnished with a floral couch and matching single chairs, the arm rests protected with knitted doilies. An old, wood-panelled television stood in the corner. Lush, shagpile carpet with brown and tan swirling patterns complemented the fifties décor of the entire house. Everything was neat and tidy, everything in its place.

In the far corner of the lounge room, an internal staircase with polished timber handrails led to an almost hidden downstairs area. Jarrod stood at the top of the staircase and peered down towards the darkness. He flicked a switch and a low hanging light bulb threw light towards the base of the stairs. He guessed the staircase was part of Charlie's renovations, a new addition giving internal access to the enclosed area under the house. He negotiated the stairs until he came to a closed door at the bottom. Turning the knob, he pushed the door open with a creak. Cool musty air flowed out from the dark room. He waited in the doorway for his eyes to adjust. His eyes scanned, making out a bed, chest of draws and a cupboard through filtered light sneaking past closed curtains.

He ran his fingers along the wall until they met another switch. A fluorescent light flickered to life, illuminating the cramped room. He pulled open the curtains and the room filled with sunlight. The cupboard doors sagged open and empty clothes hangers dangled from a railing. Empty dresser drawers were left open, as if the place had been ransacked. The bed was unmade and the impression of someone's head was still molded into the pillow.

The room had its own ensuite. He poked his head inside. The basin had been wiped over and a towel was draped over the glass partition of the shower. A used disposable razor and a half empty tube of toothpaste had been discarded in a waste bin.

Back in the room, he gazed out the window towards the front yard and street. Out on the footpath some high school kids walked by, bags slung over their shoulders, a boy bouncing a basketball and two girls trailing behind. They disappeared down the street.

The window offered a clear view of anyone walking by. The house wasn't far from the Barkley's, on the route Lisa Barkley would have taken to and from school.

He bent down to take a closer look at the bedding. A single hair was nestled in the pillow indentation. He pinched it between his gloved index finger and thumb and held it up to the window light, squinting to focus.

The hair had a distinct auburn tinge.

THIRTY-FOUR

THE one they were calling *Scar Face* lay on a blanket, gazing up at the stars. It was where he felt most at ease, out in the bush away from humanity. People made him sick to the core, more toxic the longer he spent with them. He'd gone back into hiding to calm his mind, to seek guidance from the universe.

Flames of a crackling campfire toasted his face and sent orange sparks dancing into the breeze. Silver-blue smoke twirled heavenward, charming a spell over him. The fire glowed with bitter memories of years past, inviting them to resurface and enter the present, as vivid as the sparks that leaped. He inhaled the tang of charred firewood and embraced his inner fire, fueled by hatred and the hunger for revenge. He now had blood on his hands, the doer of evil deeds. With each kill he grew stronger, liberated, free.

In each hand he caressed the silky texture of human hair, the long strands gliding through his fingers. He raised the scalps of the two dead girls to his nose and inhaled their scent, reliving the moment he squeezed the life out of their eyes. His body tingled as he remembered the invigoration of the hunt, the ultimate power of taking a life. Fate had brought them to him, to test his resolve. They had poked the beast, and the beast bit back. They had unleashed its fury.

Unlike the girls, he took no pleasure in killing the old woman. She had opened her home to him, had been kind. There had been no judgment in her eyes, no ridicule. There was a goodness in her soul that penetrated a soft spot in his hardened heart. In a moment of weakness, he let himself grow fond of her. She saw past the horrible scars, looked into his eyes like no one before. Maybe that's what terrified her in the end, when she caught a glimpse of the evil, the ugliness harbouring inside.

Regrettably, her death was inevitable. She'd uncovered his secret, learned who he was. She was about to hand him over to the wolves. He couldn't allow that to happen, not when he was so close. No, she had to go. He took solace knowing he'd ended her life in one swift blow. No suffering, merciful. It was the least he could do to repay her kindness. She'd served her purpose, given him a place to hide while he planned his next move.

He sat up and poked a stick into the flames, stoking the hot coals. He smiled to himself. *Scar Face.* He liked it. He embraced it as a badge of honour, recognition for his deadly deeds. There was a time when such taunts would have pierced his heart like a rusted edged knife. Not anymore. He had evolved. He'd achieved what he set out to do, to induce fear in the hearts and minds of the people. He was the boogeyman, the thing that went bump in the night, the monster hiding under the bed.

He stood and gathered his things, kicking dirt on the fire. Most of his adult life he'd spent living out of a swag, a ghost always on the move, off the grid, on the run. He'd been running from himself, from his past. But those days were over. He was emerging from the shadows. The demons inside him had awoken. It was time.

He was coming for them.

THIRTY-FIVE

FRANKIE Arnold hated his job, but at least it kept him out of prison. He worked the late shift, pumping fuel for arrogant arseholes who wouldn't bother to piss on him if he was on fire.

'Fill her up, champ,' said the wanker behind the wheel of a Jeep Cherokee Sports. The four-wheel drive clearly had never been off road since it left the showroom. No doubt he was overcompensating to impress the blonde bimbo checking her makeup in the sun visor mirror. The bloke was punching well over his weight.

The driver, a silver fox in his fifties with slicked back hair and muttonchop sideburns, poked his head out the window. He looked like a used car salesman. 'Be a sport and clean the windscreen for me.'

Frankie smiled, a crooked thing, out of kilter. 'Sure thing, *pal*.'

'And your girlfriend can suck my cock,' Frankie mumbled under his breath as he moved to the bowser side. Patronising prick. The automatic petrol hatch popped open.

He unscrewed the cap and inserted the fuel nozzle, looking over his shoulder to cop a perv at the woman's sumptuous cans as she leaned forward to apply more lipstick. She wanted him to look, didn't she? Why else would she dress like that, tits hanging out of a skimpy top for all to see? They must have cost old mate a fortune. Bloody tease. Just like all women, good for only one thing.

Frankie pressed the nozzle trigger and flicked the catch, allowing it to fill on auto. He slid around to the front of the vehicle and dipped the window cleaner into a bucket of stagnant water with dead bugs floating on the surface. Old Bill would have had a cow if he knew he hadn't refreshed the bucket with extra water and detergent. Frankie could never understand why his boss was so passionate about customer service. The old fool took so much pride in being a shitkicker. Embarrassing.

As Frankie scrubbed the windscreen, he peered through the watery smears at the driver talking into his smartphone in defiance of the hazard sign. Who the hell would he be calling at this time of night, anyway? The arrogant son-of-a-bitch basked in his own self-importance, putting on a show for his whore.

Frankie spun the handle of the windscreen cleaner and slid the rubber squeegee across the glass, giving the woman a wink as he leaned over her side. She looked up at him, distaste evident on her face. The fuel nozzle clicked. He moved to the bowser and removed the nozzle, making sure he scraped the metal handle against the vehicle's paintwork. He savoured the grating sound it made as he gouged grooves into the shiny metallic paint. So much for the showroom shine, he chuckled to himself. He returned the nozzle to its slot and moved around to the driver's window. Silver fox dangled a credit card out the window without making eye contact, still talking shit into his phone. The young blonde impatiently chewed gum.

Frankie held up the portable card reader for the driver to tap. 'All good, you have a good night now,' he sneered through clenched teeth.

The driver ignored him and closed the electronic window.

The pained smile slid from Frankie's face and his eyes narrowed as the Jeep pulled away.

He was left alone with the silence of the night and the electric hum of the neon sign flashing the latest petrol prices. He looked around and waited. Not another soul in sight. He stood behind a bowser, out of the security camera's view, and took a piss in the window cleaning bucket. He laughed out loud, a brittle sound. He headed back inside, away from the mozzies and moths.

This was his "stay out of jail card", a job that assured his parole officer would keep off his back. He just had to hold down this job, do the bare minimum to keep the pay cheque coming in. His previous boss was an arsehole, the building site foreman who worked him into the ground. The blisters on Frankie's hands bled after being forced to dig trenches in rock hard clay using only a mattock. A bobcat with a trench digger could have been used, but the foreman took pleasure in belittling him, making him suffer. Enough was enough. He knocked that smartarse prick on his backside. One punch to the nose did the trick. The problem was, it landed him back in prison.

Frankie had never held down any kind of decent job for more than a couple of months. Either his bad temper got the better of him or he fell back off the wagon, hitting the bottle hard. He'd spiral back into his old habits, getting plastered every night and starting pub brawls. He'd end up sleeping in the gutter or getting locked up.

His parole officer arranged for him to stay at a men's hostel in this shithole of a town. The dormitory accommodation was full of washed-out old drunks who sat around pissing their pants and smoking used cigarette butts they'd scavenged. He wondered if he was better off back in the joint.

So here he was, well after midnight, alone and pondering what his life had amounted to. He was fifty years old and broke. His belongings fit into a duffel bag and he called a men's shelter home. Frankie convinced himself he was a victim of circumstance, destined for failure from the day he was born. He'd suffered hardships as a child, never afforded the opportunity of a normal life, whatever that meant. Screw this, he deserved more.

He'd blown last week's pay at the TAB. He only needed one big win, the windfall that would get him out of this dump for good. A good tip on the horses was all he needed to dig himself out of the hole he'd dug for himself.

He leaned against the rim of the open doorway to the servo shopfront and lit a smoke. His eyes focused on the red glow as he inhaled, the burning tobacco crackling. It was balmy and still. A gecko scampered overhead and chirped, making a clicking noise that echoed in the empty night. He blew smoke into the air, watching the cloud disperse into thin wisps, and then inhaled the lingering scent.

He could hear the distant hum of traffic on the highway that bypassed the town to the West. Crickets chirped and bugs swarmed around the glow of the streetlight. It was eerily quiet, the streets deserted.

A muffled noise broke the silence, like the shuffling of feet. It came from the shadows behind the storage shed. He listened for long seconds. Nothing but silence, even the gecko went quiet. Another noise made him jump, despite himself. He stared into the darkness towards the shed. The silence of the night called back.

After a while, he turned and headed back inside, shaking his head with a bemused smile. The nightwork had gotten to him, the solitude playing tricks in his head. He told himself he was just hearing things. Not normally frazzled so easily, he was determined not to let it get the better of him.

A loud shrill pierced the silence, a man's scream. Frankie's skin crawled and goose bumps prickled the base of his neck.

He stepped out into the driveway. 'Who's there?' he called. 'Come on out, you've had your fun!'

Silence followed. He waited. Something moved, a figure running from behind the shed and circling behind the main building. A loud clanking, metal on metal, became a rhythmic '*clang…clang… clang…clang.*' Frankie swivelled on the spot, following the sound as it moved from right to left and grew louder, the rhythm intensifying. It stopped. Silence followed.

Frankie froze. 'What… what do you want, you bloody mongrel?' He tried to shout, but his throat betrayed him, his words stifled by his growing anxiety.

Another scream, taunting.

'Piss off, or I'll call the cops!'

'Frankie,' came a low, guttural voice. 'I've come for you!'

Frankie grabbed a wrench from a toolbox, clenching it above his head, ready to strike. He stepped outside, forcing his legs to move, one foot in front of the other, slowly moving out into the driveway. He was bathed in an oasis of fluorescent light, surrounded by an ocean of darkness. He stopped, hesitant to leave the false security of the petrol bowsers bathed in artificial light.

'Who's there?' he called, trepidation in his voice.

He caught a movement in the corner of his eye as a figure lunged at him, overwhelming him with the element of surprise. He reacted too slow, the wrench useless as a blow to his temple rattled his brain inside his skull. Vision blurring, his ears rung in his head. He could no longer feel his legs and his knees buckled. Falling to the ground, his vision fogged. He felt the warmth of his own blood gushing down his face and neck.

He lay on his back, arms flailing, vaguely aware he was being dragged by his feet. Strong hands propped him to a sitting position against a petrol bowser, his legs outstretched.

A grotesque, smiling face pressed against his. Frankie could feel the man's warm breath.

'Remember me, Frankie?' the man whispered.

Frankie blinked, trying to place the voice.

The man leaned back so Frankie could see into his eyes. For a moment, Frankie had no reaction. His eyes widened, his fear intensifying as distant memories emerged through the confusion. One fused itself to his thoughts, a single image occupying his mind. He knew this face, a ghastly reminder of his past.

The man squatted on his haunches in front of Frankie, balancing his knuckles on the ground like an ape, a metal bar in his hand. 'Ah, you remember now, don't you? I'm glad you could spare a thought for me, after all this time. I don't want you to ever forget about me, my old friend.'

Frankie was numb. Demons of his past had tracked him down. This was his moment of truth, the final showdown. He knew it was inevitable, had always known this moment would come. He opened his mouth, but his voice betrayed him once again. A pitiful groan escaped his lips.

'What's the matter, Frankie old boy? Suddenly you've got nothing to say? You always had the answers. You were always *the man.* Come on, where's the old Frankie I once knew? The one I despised with all my heart, the one I feared. Come on Frankie, aren't you gonna raise your fist to me? I suppose it just doesn't feel the same to hit a grown man. Bashing kids and women is so much more your style. Hey, Frankie?'

The man hissed like a serpent, his rage intensifying with every word he spat in Frankie's face.

'What's the matter, Frankie? You look scared. You scared of me? Who would have thought? The irony is hilarious, don't you think so? How the tables have turned.'

With a sudden surge of rage, the man jumped to his feet and booted Frankie in the stomach. Frankie reeled over in pain, bloody spittle frothing from his lips.

'Look at you now. Pitiful!' The man said, towering over him. 'A pathetic maggot.'

He knelt beside Frankie and grabbed his hand. He traced Frankie's fingers down his scarred face. 'Feel these scars, Frankie. They're real, so very real.' A knowing grin formed on the man's distorted lips. 'You have no idea what it feels like to smell your own flesh melting off your face. The pain has never stopped. Did you know that? No, of course not. You see, now we're getting to the point of why I'm here. I've been waiting a long time for this moment. I'm going to show you exactly how that feels. You get to share my pain. How does that sound?'

The man laughed, a strange and hollow sound.

Frankie gathered up his last remaining strength to speak. 'No, Kaleb. Please, no! I'm so sorry for what I did to you.'

The man lowered his voice, filling it with menace. 'Oh, you will be.'

THIRTY-SIX

JARROD lay in bed in the darkness, staring up at the ceiling. His arm throbbed inside the cast, propped on a pillow to reduce the swelling in his fingers. He soon became uncomfortable and rolled over, trying not to disturb Jayne. She slept soundly, laying on her side facing him. Her breath purred against his face as she exhaled.

He felt the presence of another person in the room, someone watching him. He turned and saw his little boy, blurry-eyed and holding his teddy with one hand, rubbing his eye with the other.

'I'se scared, Daddy,' Matty whimpered.

Jarrod sat up and the pain in his ribs gave a nasty bite. He stifled a moan and swung his feet out of the bed.

'Come on, little man. Let's get you back to bed.' They padded down the hallway towards Matty's bedroom.

Jarrod followed him with his hand on his head for reassurance, guiding him through the darkness. A single lamp in the lounge room provided enough light for nighttime roaming.

The legs of Matty's pyjama pants dragged along the floor, his bare feet pattering as he walked in a dreamlike state.

They arrived at his bedroom and he climbed back into his bed, cuddling his teddy. He fell back to sleep before Jarrod had pulled the covers over him. Jarrod kissed the side of his face and tiptoed out. He checked on Katie, buried in her bed covers and fast asleep.

Jarrod sat in the lounge room in his old recliner and stared at the fish tank shrouded in dull lamp light. The fish went about their business, oblivious to the outside world. Too tired to sleep, he became mesmerised by their hypnotic movements.

His hyperactive brain took over and the events of the last week flashed to the forefront of his mind. He couldn't shake the image of Karl Mundy's dead body, the fatal gunshot. His own near death. He tried to convince himself that he had no choice, kill or be killed. Self-doubt gnawed away at him. His thoughts returned to Karl Mundy's baby, Zalia. He would never forget that name. He'd killed her father. Knowing she was now safe brought him some solace.

The town had become a killing field. Karl Mundy, Lisa Barkley, Tammy Heidenreich and Edna Bishop. So much bloodshed and chaos. Too much sadness.

He shared the fear of all parents, of harm coming to his children. The fear of not being able to protect them from the evils of this world. Loving them so much it hurts. Struggling to control that ever-present fear of losing them. Learning to let go, letting them discover the world on their own, in all its beauty, in all its dangers. Guiding them, watching over them and preparing them for life.

But how does a parent deal with the sudden loss of a child? He'd come so close to knowing that loss. He'd looked evil in the eyes, teetered on the edge as Vincent Miles threatened to kill Katie. He'd been offered a lifeline, a second chance. He'd been spared the grief of losing a child.

He wondered what Lisa and Tammy's parents were doing right now. Would they be able to sleep? Their world had caved in around them, their children taken from them so violently. Needlessly. How does a parent cope with that? That was Jarrod's greatest fear in life, and he prayed he would never know that kind of grief. He prayed he would never have to bury his own child, that death would come for him first.

He got up and checked on Katie and Matty one last time. Giving in to exhaustion, he headed back to bed. He closed his eyes.

His mobile phone buzzed on the nightstand. He sat up in

confusion, unsure if he'd been asleep. The glowing red digits of his digital alarm clock showed 1:07AM. He grabbed the phone and rushed out to the kitchen. What could it be now? He answered it with dread.

It was Murray Long, his voice frantic. 'O'Connor, you've got to get out here right now.'

'Where? What is it?'

'All hell's broken loose! We've got a hostage situation.'

'What? Why do you need me?'

'Your man, *Scar Face*. He's here!'

THIRTY-SEVEN

FLASHING blue and red lights strobed in the distance beyond the apex of the rise. As Jarrod's old Forerunner rumbled closer, the United Fuels neon sign came into view. Three police cars, two fire trucks and an ambulance formed a semi-circle out front. The illuminated scene was in stark contrast to the surrounding dark streets.

The Forerunner picked up speed as it descended towards the chaos. Jarrod's senses came alive as if a bucket of icy water had been thrown over him. As he pulled up behind the ring of emergency vehicles, he peered through his windscreen towards two figures. One man was propped on his backside against a petrol bowser, his head slumped forward. Another man stood over him, pacing up and down with erratic hand gestures.

Police officers took cover behind open car doors, firearms aimed at the two men. A mix of anxiety and frustration on their faces, the officers watched and waited, gun barrels covering the men's every movement. There was an unusual stillness in the air. No one spoke, everyone on a razor's edge. A few of the guys glanced at Jarrod and gave him a nod as he approached. He moved as close as he dared without breaching the perimeter.

Murray Long appeared, looking just as sleep deprived and dishevelled. His eyes darted, furtive as a back-alley cat. He spoke in a low voice. 'O'Connor. Good, you're here. About time.'

'So, what are we dealing with?' Jarrod asked, ignoring the jibe.

'Like I said on the phone, our mate from the security footage, with the disfigured face. That's him.' Long pointed at the man strutting around a bowser with jerky movements. 'He's taken a hostage, wants an audience. The bastard was waiting for us.'

Jarrod turned his gaze to the man who was now out from behind the bowser, making no attempt to conceal his identity under the glow of the fluorescent lights. He opened his arms, like a stage performer acknowledging his audience. In one hand, he held a cigarette lighter, one of those old Zippo types with a flip top lid. In the other hand, he gripped a hunting knife, the sharp tip of the curved blade catching a glint of light. The weapon looked like it would slice the head off a wild boar. With extended arms, chest puffed and chin raised, he flicked the lighter lid open and closed, taunting his onlookers.

At first glance, he looked like he was wearing a novelty Freddie Krueger mask. Jarrod studied the face. It was no mask. A fringe of auburn hair fell over his eyes, his face pale and pasty, disfigured by leathery, grey scar tissue which sagged like hot wax. His left eye and surrounding skin had been spared, a real-life phantom of the opera. There was no doubt, it *was* their suspect from the security footage.

He looked young, maybe early twenties. The legs of military style camo trousers were tucked into combat boots. A tight-fitting black T-shirt enhanced his toned frame. He stood tall and confident, his muscles coiled springs. He seemed to be getting his kicks; the centre of attention.

He lowered his arms and studied the faces gazing back at him, his eyes moving from one to the next. His eyes found Jarrod's and his expression changed, as though he'd seen someone he recognised. He held his gaze, tilting his head with a puzzled look. Interest sparked in his eyes. Jarrod resisted the urge to break eye contact, trying to read his thoughts, to get inside his head. His eyes radiated nothing but hatred, a deeply troubled individual. Seeing him in the flesh was unnerving.

'He's looking straight at you,' said Long.

Jarrod didn't answer, caught under the man's spell.

'Do you know him?'

Jarrod drew a breath and shook his head, his eyes held in the man's gaze. 'No. I don't know him.'

'Well, he seems to know you.'

The man broke eye contact and stared past Jarrod into an imagined distance, as if considering something of great importance. He spun around, distracted by something, and continued pacing. The man on the ground still hadn't moved.

Jarrod cleared his throat, his mouth dry. 'What does he want? What's he waiting for?'

'Don't know. He hasn't said.' Long looked around, a nervous gesture. 'He's threatening to slice the other guy's throat and set the place on fire if we come any closer. I've tried to negotiate, but he refuses to talk.'

'Stalemate,' Jarrod muttered.

'Yeah, stalemate. We need to shut off those fuel pumps. We're waiting for the owner to get here.'

'Who's the guy sitting on the ground?'

'Servo attendant. Poor bastard was at the wrong place at the wrong time.'

The man was bound to the bowser by a rope coiled around his waist, hands tied behind his back. He sat limp, shoulders forward.

'Maybe, maybe not,' said Jarrod.

Long shot Jarrod a look, one eyebrow raised. 'What do you mean?'

'I don't think this is random.'

The idea hung in the air.

Car tyres crunched on loose bitumen stones as an old ute pulled up, mounting the curb. Bill Mortlock was behind the wheel. The suspension springs groaned with relief as he hauled himself out.

'That's the owner of this place.' Jarrod told Long. 'I met him here earlier today, um, yesterday. I don't know what fucking day it is anymore.'

'Get him over here, now.'

Bill's eyes searched until they met Jarrod's, looking relieved to see a familiar face. Jarrod waved him over.

'What the hell is going on, detective?' said Bill, wheezing through a smoker's cough.

'Some lunatic is threatening to burn down your servo,' interrupted Long, holding up his badge. 'How do we shut off the fuel pumps?'

'Well, um, there's a kill switch inside, behind the counter.'

Long crossed his arms. 'Yeah, no. Front door's not an option. We can't get anywhere near it.'

'Is there a back door?' asked Jarrod, hopeful.

'Yes, but it's a fire safety door with a push panic bar. Internal exit only. Can't be opened from the outside.'

Long tilted his head and looked skyward. 'Shit. There must be another way. Can we get the electricity company to come and kill the power?'

'Oh, no need for that. There's a power box on the outside. I can manually activate the circuit breaker.'

'Okay, now we're talking. That's what we'll do,' said Long, decisive.

'It's locked, but I have the key.' Bill produced a set of keys jingling on a large hoop. 'Here it is, this one,' he said, sliding a key from the ring.

'So, where's this power box?' said Long, impatient.

Bill pointed. 'On the wall, down the left side of the building. I'll need to show you.'

'I'll go with him,' said Jarrod. 'You need to stay here, Murray. Keep the guy distracted.'

Long stared at Jarrod, his mind working. 'Okay, I'll distract him with the loudhailer while you make your move. Don't screw this up.'

Jarrod looked at Bill. 'You right to do this?'

Bill wet his lips, apprehensive. 'If it means stopping this lunatic from torching my servo, then yeah, let's do this.'

Jarrod was impressed with Bill's doggedness.

'Come on, let's go, while he's not looking this way,' said Jarrod. He and Bill backed away, inconspicuous, slipping into the darkness behind the emergency vehicles. They hunkered behind Jarrod's truck, waiting for Long's signal. Jarrod hoped the flashing red and blue lights would obscure *Scar Face's* line of sight when they made their dash.

'The guy sitting beside the bowser,' Jarrod said to Bill, 'what's his name?'

Bill squinted as he studied the two men at the bowser. He nodded, certain. 'That's Frankie… Frankie Arnold. He's working the night shift tonight. What the hell has the good-for-nothing bastard done now?'

'We don't know.' Jarrod placed his hands on Bill's shoulders so they faced each other. 'Listen to me. It's important to think hard. Do you know why anyone would come after Frankie?'

Bill shook his head, wearing a blank look. 'No, I don't know. God knows who Frankie pissed off this time. The man is an arsehole.'

Bill did a double take. 'Wait, who is that guy? Is that the guy in the flier you showed me? It's him, isn't it?'

Jarrod nodded. 'Yeah, he's the one we've been looking for. Maybe connected to the murders of those girls. We need to know why he's here now.'

A loudhailer squelched. Long stepped forward of the perimeter. 'You in the service station,' his voice echoed, sounding tinny through the speaker. 'This is Detective Murray Long again. We need to talk.'

'Fuck you pig!' the man yelled back.

'That's our cue,' said Jarrod, grabbing Bill's elbow. 'Let's go.'

They scampered through the shadows, hugging the fenceline. They tucked in behind a portable cold room with "Party Ice" signage. Bill pointed to the power box on the side wall of the service station about fifteen metres away. Jarrod peeked around the corner of the cold room. They had circled around so the man's back was to them. He gave Bill a nod and they made their last dash, throwing their backs against the brickwork. They shimmied out of sight along the narrow corridor of shadow until they came to the power box. Jarrod held up his phone light so Bill could see what he was doing. Bill inserted the key and pulled the handle, hinges creaking as the door opened.

'Shit,' Jarrod whispered.

They froze and waited.

Murray Long spoke again in the loudhailer and the man replied with a spray of obscenities.

'Keep going,' said Jarrod. 'I don't think he heard it.'

Bill nodded and wiped sweat from his brow. He flicked a latch and opened a plastic box containing a row of safety switches. There was a hum of electricity. 'Here, shine the light.'

Bill read out the labels. 'Front sign, driveway fluros, front office, cold room, circuit one, circuit two, fuel pumps. It's this one.' He pressed the switch and the panel beeped. 'That should do it. Pumps are off. There'll be residual fuel in the lines at the bowser but once that's drained, no more fuel will come out.'

'Good work. Let's get back.'

They retraced their steps and snuck back out to their position behind the vehicles, the strobing lights blinding Jarrod as his vision adjusted.

'Pumps are dead,' Jarrod told Long.

Long lifted his eyes towards the bowser. 'Just in a nick of time. Negotiations didn't go well.'

Scar Face reached for a fuel dispenser, pulling the nozzle from its housing. Dancing like a kid in the rain, he showboated with the hose. He pressed the trigger and petrol gushed out onto the concrete, encircling Frankie. He doused Frankie's head and upper body for good measure. Frankie spat and gagged, shaking the fluid off his face as it dripped from his hair. His tormentor looked down at the nozzle as the flow ran dry. He squeezed the handle trigger on and off, shaking it in frustration. He looked up with a bemused expression and threw the nozzle onto the ground.

Long offered a flash of a smile. 'Look out, gigs up.'

'Ha, ha!' the man yelled. His outburst of laughter, high pitched and demented, gave Jarrod the chills. 'This won't stop me.' He held the knife's blade under Frankie's chin. 'This man is already dead!'

Heads turned as a Channel 8 van screeched to a stop across the road. The cameraman rolled out like a paratrooper, camera and tripod slung over his shoulder. He scaled the ladder and climbed up onto the roof of the van.

The stalemate broke when the scar-faced man shrieked, a high-pitched shrill straight out of a horror movie. It drew every set of eyes and the camera lens towards him.

'Media parasites! What took you so long?' he bellowed, hand cupped to his mouth. 'You've come for your breaking news, haven't you? Well, here it is!'

The camera rolled and police guns were trained squarely at him, trigger fingers twitching. The risk of taking pot shots was too high. The hostage would be burned alive if things went south. One flick of the lighter and it was over. Only an instant kill shot would do. Handgun accuracy at twenty-five metres was questionable at best, and there were no snipers amongst them. The man knew he was in control, calling the shots.

Containment and negotiation were the go-to strategies, police protocol. Tried and tested. Most sieges ended without loss of life if they waited it out. But now the Channel 8 camera had a front-row seat, filming every move they made. They had to do this right, by the book. If they didn't, it would be trial by media. Jarrod had an awful feeling the man was calculating every move, not as unhinged as he made out. He worked to a plan, the whole thing choreographed. He already knew how this would end, a foregone conclusion. There would be no negotiations.

The man bent down, grabbed a fistful of Frankie Arnold's hair and yanked his head back.

Frankie whimpered, terror in his eyes. 'Don't you coppers leave me here! Don't let him kill me.'

The man grabbed Frankie by the jaw and pushed his face from side to side, his mouth gaping like a sideshow clown.

'Look at this face and never forget it,' the man yelled. 'Come on, zoom that camera right in. This face represents sin. This is a man who must be punished. But revenge takes time, and you will all have your turn,' he sneered. 'All of you!'

He let Frankie's head drop and rose to his feet. Pointing a menacing finger at the camera, he lit the lighter, an orange flame dancing. 'I'm coming after all of you. You will *all* pay! The whole world will burn!'

THIRTY-EIGHT

'THAT'S it! We have to take him down,' Long yelled. 'We've got no choice.' He drew his firearm and moved forward of the line. The uniformed officers responded, moving forward with guns out. Their training kicked in. Heel toe, heel toe. Knees bent, maintaining balance, arms scanning with stable shooting platforms like the rotating turrets of military tanks.

Jarrod drew his Glock with his good hand, fashioning an unorthodox two-handed grip with the fingers of his cast arm. 'You stay here, Bill.'

Bill nodded, mouth gaping.

Jarrod moved forward, wheeling to the left of the petrol bowsers for a clearer view of *Scar Face*. The line of police officers emerged from the concealment of flashing lights, now exposed under the bright fluorescent bulbs.

'Armed police! Drop the knife!' shouted Long. 'Turn the lighter off and toss it towards me. Back away from him, now! Fail to comply and we will have no choice but to shoot.'

Scar Face feigned a sad face. 'What, this?' He waved the burning lighter and held Long's gaze, daring him to do something.

'Do as I say!' barked Long.

Scar Face ignored Long and swivelled his head to face Jarrod. 'I knew it was you hiding back there. We finally meet, *Jarrod O'Connor*.' His face contorted, Jarrod's name bitter as bile in his mouth.

'How do you know me?' said Jarrod, one eye closed, the other aimed through the gun's sights.

'Vincent told me all about *you.*'

'Vincent? Vincent Miles?'

'He's not gone, you know. Not really. His spirit is all around, guiding me.'

Sweat dripped down Jarrod's forehead, stinging his eyes. 'How do you know Vincent Miles? What's this really about?'

'You want to know, do you?'

'Yes. Why are you doing this?'

'Well ask Frankie,' he said, like it was obvious. 'He'll tell you.'

'No, you tell me,' Jarrod responded.

'Where's the fun in that?'

Frankie squirmed against his bindings. 'He's fucking nuts, he's gonna kill me. Shoot him!'

'Shut it!' snapped Long. 'Stay calm and be quiet!'

Jarrod took a punt, acting on a hunch. He saw the opportunity to change tact. 'Those girls. Why did you kill them?'

Scar Face kept his eyes locked on Jarrod, not averting his gaze for a second. Then something changed, a chink in his armour. His good eye twitched, and he jammed the butt of the knife against his temple, grimacing as though a sharp pain had torn through his skull.

'Those… witches,' he said, voice guttural. 'They… got… what… was coming to them!'

'What did they do to deserve that?'

He shook his head, refocusing. 'In time, you'll understand. You'll have to join the dots.'

'And the old lady?'

His scowl softened, replaced by a look of regret. 'She knew too much.'

'It's over. Drop the knife!' Long commanded.

The man returned his gaze to Long. He backed away, one slow step after the next, knife by his side, the flame of the lighter flickering in the breeze.

He turned his attention back to Jarrod. 'Have you ever smelt burning human flesh?'

Jarrod didn't answer.

'That smell. There's nothing like it. The skin sizzles and peels and drips like pork fat.'

He backed away, closing the gap between himself and the front door of the service station. Behind him, in front of the plate-glass window, stood a cage filled with swap-and-go gas bottles.

'I want you to smell it, right up close,' he said.

'Easy now,' said Long, gripping his gun with one hand, the other hand out in a calming gesture. 'Let's take this slow. That lighter is making us very nervous. How about you kill the flame, toss the lighter to me and drop the knife?'

Scar Face giggled, a maniacal sound like a hyena. He kept moving backwards, almost at the door. 'The past has caught up with Frankie, and the rest of them. But I am the future. Vincent told me so.'

He froze, his eyes fixed on Jarrod's, ignoring the guns trained on him. He spoke in a slow drawl. 'What will be, will be. And so it shall be.'

What happened next played out in slow motion. He tossed the lighter. It tumbled in the air, end on end, the flame fluttering. All eyes followed the lighter as it floated in an arc.

'Noooo!!!' someone yelled.

Two gunshots, *boom boom*. The ping of metal cylinders puncturing, escaping gas hissing. More gunshots reverberated in Jarrod's ears as *Scar Face* dived to his right, rolled in a tight ball and disappeared into the service station doorway.

Heads turned in unison, following the trajectory of the lighter as gravity tugged it towards the ground. It hit the concrete with a clatter, bounced and toppled onto its side. The flame danced.

Whoosh! Blue flames erupted on the concrete, a burst of hot air stinging Jarrod's eyes. He threw his arms up to cover his face.

'Get back!' screamed Long.

The flames raced along the ground towards the petrol bowsers like a lit fuse, heading straight for Frankie Arnold. He stomped his shoes as his trousers caught fire. The flames took hold of his shirt and bit at his throat. He wriggled against the ropes, thrashing his head from side to side. In an instant, his whole body was engulfed in flames. He writhed, his screams blood curdling.

The smell of gas was overpowering. Orange flames went airborne. A firestorm consumed oxygen with a sucking sound, the heat stifling. A boom shook the ground, throwing Jarrod off his feet. He thought he was on fire. He rolled and rolled until he felt grass against his face. His ears rung and his head pounded. He checked himself. No flames. He looked up to see police officers scattering, diving for cover.

Flames leapt in the air towards the gas cylinders. For a moment, all sound was sucked towards the fire, an enormous vacuum. Then a god almighty explosion ripped through the front of the service station, glass and debris shattering in the fireball. A pulse of searing air threw a fist of energy outwards, swallowing everything within its radius.

Frankie's screams grew louder, but as flames consumed his flesh, his cries gurgled and fell silent. The fire had taken hold of the petrol bowsers, the ceiling of the overhead roof already burning. The service station building was well ablaze, popping and crackling as flammable items inside exploded. A mushroom of smoke ballooned into the sky. Jarrod struggled to his feet, watching the roaring flames and devastation.

'Around the back!' yelled Long. 'Don't let him get away.'

Jarrod sprinted down the side of the building, following the foresight of his Glock. Sharp pains stabbed at his ribs with every stride. When he reached the back corner, he rolled out his upper body, barricading against the wall. He paused and inhaled through his nose to calm his heart rate. He looked past his gun and found the rear emergency door. Closed. The silhouette of a person moved towards him from the opposite corner. Jarrod aimed his gun. The person moved closer, hugging the back wall.

He recognised Murray Long's imposing profile and lowered his gun. Jarrod stepped out from cover. Long gestured with two fingers in a V, pointing at his own eyes and then the door. Jarrod nodded. They covered the door from opposite sides. The bricks of the back wall were hot against Jarrod's shoulder, like leaning against an oven door. A burst of hot air and flames blew the door off its hinges. They cowered, covering their mouths from the smoke billowing from overhead windows.

The heat drove them back. They took a wide berth, circling towards each other until they came together. Through the open door, they could see flames licking the walls and ceiling, the fire's tentacles burning everything it touched. No one could have survived that inferno.

Jarrod turned and surveyed the rear of the service station and neighbouring yards. 'Do you reckon he made it out?'

'Dunno,' said Long, dazed. 'If he's still inside, he's rooted.' He turned in a circle, shining his torch around. 'If he made it out, he could be anywhere. Let's get some patrols happening in these back streets and see if we can get a dog unit out here.'

They made their way back out front, the blistering heat keeping the firies at bay. Both trucks had launched into action, already connected to the hydrant and battling the towering flames with heavy hoses. It wasn't long before the roof of the building caved in on itself, throwing up a ball of smoke and ash. The detached roof over the petrol bowsers buckled and collapsed under its own weight with a thunderous crash. Somewhere in the burning rubble lay Frankie Arnold's charred corpse. It was a scene of devastation, an absolute calamity.

There were only minor injuries among the officers, abrasions from flying debris and smoke inhalation. As the firies fought the inferno, more police units were called in on overtime to keep civilians back, while other units patrolled the streets. By now, it seemed half the town had emerged in the early hours of the morning to watch the disaster unfold. Mobile phone camera lenses peered out from the darkness, like the eyes of nocturnal animals.

Word came back a police dog had been deployed from the city. If *Scar Face* had escaped, the scent may grow cold or be contaminated by all the looky-loos.

They had no idea if the murderous lunatic was dead or alive.

THIRTY-NINE

BY sunrise, Ross Benfield had taken charge of the forward command post. The entire block had been evacuated and an exclusion zone declared while the cleanup of hazardous materials got underway. The service station was a scene of total annihilation, ground zero. By mid-morning, the firies had the blaze under control. It would be days before the search and recovery of bodies could begin. Every off-duty blue shirt and detective in the district had been called in. All efforts were on securing the scene, locating the suspect and interviewing potential witnesses.

The canine unit attended, but the result was inconclusive. The dog detected a scent leading away from the rear of the service station, but the trail went cold. So far, there had been no sightings of *Scar Face*. Jarrod hoped he'd met his doom inside the inferno, although he feared the man had the survival instincts of a cockroach. There was something unhuman about him.

Brad was one of many officers drawn into the manhunt. He checked in with Jarrod at the scene before being sent out into the field. Benfield ordered Jarrod back to the station, tasked with pulling files on Arnold. He knew it was Benfield's way of looking out for him, given what he'd been through in the last few days. He was physically and mentally near breaking point.

On the way, he called home. Jayne's voice was laced with worry. He assured her he was fine but wouldn't be home anytime soon. He knew she was sick and tired of the near misses and long hours. He'd make it up to her, he promised. The line went silent and she put the kids on the phone.

When he got back to the station, he focused his energy on learning more about Frankie Arnold. Steam curled from an instant coffee as he tapped away on the police computer, his clothes smelling of smoke and petrol. It didn't take long to pull up the history. Franklin Charles Arnold was raised in the streets of Sydney's Western Suburbs. He had an impressive criminal history spanning over thirty-five years, with arrest records in just about every state and territory in the country. Break and entering, stealing, fraud, willful damage, assault, drugs and vagrancy offences featured on his rap sheet. He'd spent most of his adult life in and out of prison. Jarrod compiled a chronological profile including criminal history, prison and court records and intelligence reports. The man was a lowlife, a career petty criminal.

Arnold had been released from prison four months earlier after serving a twelve-month stint for breaching a domestic and family violence order. The parole office had found work for him and temporary lodgings in Lockyer, most likely to get him out of Sydney and away from the woman he'd beaten. Jarrod thought back to the Vincent Miles case and the bond Miles had formed with Edward Ryan in prison. He wondered if *Scar Face* and Arnold were linked through the prison system. Perhaps a vendetta. Maybe he crossed the wrong person in the joint. He made a note to follow this up as a lead.

Everything changed when a particular record caught Jarrod's eye. Twelve years ago, Arnold had been charged with grievous bodily harm and stood trial in the District Court. Jarrod copied the criminal offence report number and opened the digital file. He read the summary of facts. Arnold had been in a relationship with a woman named Caroline Carmichael. There was extensive history of domestic violence, with a pattern of withdrawn complaints. Caroline had a twelve-year-old son, father unknown. His name was Kaleb.

According to the court report, during one of his drunken outbursts, Arnold assaulted Caroline in their kitchen. Kaleb, trying to defend his mother, put himself between them. In a rage, Arnold threw Kaleb against the stove where a pot of boiling water with potatoes was simmering. The pot upended, scolding Kaleb and leaving him with horrific burns to his face and upper body. The file contained evidence photos of the boy's injuries. Only his left eye had been spared, the rest of his face unrecognisable. He clicked to a before image, a smiling Kaleb in his school uniform. Jarrod couldn't believe he was looking at the same boy, the two images bearing no similarity. His smiling face had been erased, the flesh peeled off like wet tissue paper. He couldn't fathom the agony. He clenched his jaw, his throat tightening, and blinked away the moisture in his eyes. That poor kid.

Jarrod turned away from the computer and stared at a spot on the wall. He remembered what Scar Face had told him. *Join the dots.*

Jarrod returned to the computer screen and read on. At the end of the trial, Arnold was acquitted of the charge. The report ended there, no clues as to what became of Kaleb and his mother after the trial. He ran more computer checks, but Kaleb Carmichael had completely dropped off all systems. His name appeared in no further records, no driver's license, no registered vehicles or addresses. Nothing. He'd become a ghost.

He leaned back in his chair and rubbed his eyes. Stretching his back, he sipped the coffee as he assembled the pieces in his mind. He remembered the old photograph he'd found in the grass opposite the service station and rummaged through his files until he found it. He studied the image of the boy in the foreground and compared it to Kaleb Carmichael's photo. It was the same boy. He then focused on the man in the background. His gut dropped as though he'd jumped off a cliff. He brought up a mug shot of Frankie Arnold and maximised it on the screen. His eyes flitted from the old photo to the mug shot. The man in the photo was Frankie. It was an incidental moment in time, before the horrific events that changed Kaleb's life forever.

A rush of disconnected thoughts flooded Jarrod's mind. He

pulled out his notebook and read through the notes of his interview with Jason Barlow. He had described a man sitting in the park with facial scarring. Lisa and Tammy had laughed at him.

Join the dots.

Jarrod reviewed the facts, joining the dots. Kaleb Carmichael was *Scar Face*, that much was clear. The park was a perfect vantage point to case out the service station, to study the movements of Frankie Arnold. He must have dropped the photo or discarded it. For whatever reason that only he knew, Kaleb had returned from the shadows after all these years. Lisa and Tammy were not his intended targets. He'd come for Frankie. The girls were victims of circumstance, dumb luck. They had crossed his path by sheer coincidence, a random event that led to deadly retribution. He remembered Kaleb Carmichael's words. *They got what was coming to them.*

He remembered what Carmichael had said when he confronted him about the old lady. *She knew too much.* He took his mind back to the newspaper in Edna Bishop's house, the suspect's image plastered on the front page. He'd been hiding in plain sight, using the old lady's basement as a base while he plotted his revenge against Frankie Arnold. She became expendable when she learned he was wanted in connection to a girl's murder. He killed her out of necessity, clean and quick.

He mulled it all over, assembling the jigsaw puzzles in his head. His mobile phone vibrated in his pocket.

'We found the old lady's car,' Brad said. 'Burnt out in a secluded section of the pine forest. Walking distance from town. Oh, and get this.'

'What?'

'As the crow flies, it wasn't far from the Heidenreich property.'

'Makes sense,' said Jarrod, thinking out loud.

'How?'

'I'll explain it all later once I've pieced it all together. Any sightings of the suspect?'

'Nope, nothing. If he made it out of the servo alive, then he's well and truly gone to ground.'

'Okay, thanks for the update. If you see Benfield, let him know I'll have some new info for him soon.'

'Okay, mate, shall do. I'll let you go. Oh, how you holding up?'

'I'm running on fumes, but I guess we can all get some sleep when this shitshow is over.'

Brad chuckled. 'Yeah, I guess. Speak soon.'

After the call, Jarrod phoned the Department of Children's Services for a copy of any records relating to Kaleb Carmichael. While he waited for them to get back to him, he called an old academy friend, Karen Jackson. She'd also made detective sergeant and formerly worked in the Child Abuse Unit but had since transferred to the Drug Squad. According to the file, she was the arresting officer in the grievous bodily harm case.

'Man, that was an awful case,' she explained on the phone. 'One of the reasons why I ended up leaving Child Abuse. I cried for days after I interviewed that kid.'

'I can only imagine,' said Jarrod. 'What happened in the court case? Why did Arnold walk?'

'Mother refused to give evidence, skipped town before the trial. Bloody hopeless bitch—' She clipped her sentence short. 'Sorry, Jarrod. I know I shouldn't say that about the woman, but it made me so angry at the time, still does.'

'Why did she clam up?'

'Oh, I don't know. Arnold got to her I suppose, as usual. Makes me sick to the core, these women who don't have the fortitude to do what's right to protect their own kids. She took the easy option and went running back to the arsehole after the trial.'

'Did the boy give evidence?'

'Yeah, poor kid. It was over a year later by the time the case made it to trial, kid had spent most of that time in hospital. He fronted court, his face still bandaged, and looked Arnold right in the eye and told the court what happened.' Karen paused, lost in her memories. 'I've seen nothing like it, a hell of a thing. The kid was so brave in the witness box, so determined. He hardly broke eye contact with Arnold while he gave his testimony. Arnold, on the other hand, fucking coward, looked down at his feet the whole time.'

'So, what happened?'

'Defense barrister badgers the poor kid, making out he was confused and couldn't remember what really happened. The kid stayed firm but some doubt crept in. You know how these defense barristers work. They drive the wedge in, open big holes in the tiniest cracks. Loaded questions, confusing the witness, rapid fire cross examination. Well, Arnold ends up in the box and tells a bullshit story about it being an accident, that Kaleb was playing and knocked the pot onto himself. The kid was twelve, for Christ's sake, not a toddler. I don't know how he expected anyone would buy that crock of shit. Of course, the little missus wasn't there to corroborate the kid's version. She'd gone AWOL by this time. In the judge's summing up, he said the child's uncorroborated evidence was unreliable and there was no evidence to convict Arnold. He dismissed the jury before they even got a chance to deliberate. He let him walk. Fucking mockery of our justice system.'

Jarrod sighed. 'Shit. God, that must have been hard to take.'

'Yeah, I put in a report recommending that DPP lodge an appeal, but you know what they're like, weak as piss. Same old story, understaffed, too many cases backing up. In the end, the whole thing was swept under the carpet.'

'What became of the kid?'

'Got lost in the system, foster care. You know how that goes.'

'Yep. Did you ever hear from him again?'

'No, nothing. I moved on and I lost touch with his case manager at Children's Services.'

Karen hesitated. 'You think Kaleb is your killer, that he's come back for retribution?'

'Yeah, looks that way. Still waiting on DNA confirmation that hair samples found at each murder scene are from the same person. As Carmichael's a cleanskin, we have no evidence samples to compare them to. This will be the first thing we do if we ever find him. That's if he's even alive.'

'You think he's alive?'

Jarrod considered his answer. 'Yeah, I do. He had time to slip out the back door.'

'Scary, you know. To think what trauma can do to a child, what it can turn them into.'

They wrapped up the call, promising to catch up on old times over a coffee next time Jarrod was at Police Headquarters.

A case worker from the Department of Children's Services called back after locating the case files on Kaleb Carmichael. He bounced around from foster home to foster home, in and out of hospital, ongoing counselling. The mother stayed with Arnold until he wound back in prison for more domestic violence order breaches. Kaleb had supervised visits with his mother, but she died when he was fourteen. Drank herself to death. Arnold was back out but long gone by this time. When Kaleb turned eighteen, he dropped out of the child protection system and was never heard of again. He was never reported missing. No one seemed to care. No one looked for him.

Jarrod spent the afternoon sending emails to various government departments. Every inquiry came back with nothing. Carmichael had left no digital footprints, no unemployment benefits, no health or bank records of any kind. He had vanished. How he'd spent the last six years and why he waited so long to resurface were complete mysteries. Yet somehow, Carmichael had tracked down Frankie Arnold to the town of Lockyer. Jarrod wondered how long he'd been hunting him. He then remembered what Carmichael had said about Vincent Miles.

His spirit is all around me, guiding me.

What was the connection between Miles and Carmichael?

Miles was taunting Jarrod from the grave.

FORTY

FOR days, arson investigators scoured the twisted rubble of what remained of the service station. It looked like the scene of a terrorist attack. Frankie Arnold's remains were found, a charred mass of flesh and intestines and bones turned to ash. A second body was not located. The operation had scaled up with a Homicide Squad taskforce taking over. All available resources were poured into the investigation, the net widening beyond state borders. The biggest manhunt in recent Australian history was now underway. Despite the media saturation, there had still been no sightings. Carmichael had blended into his environment, a human chameleon. He clearly had a fallback plan.

Days turned to weeks. The local community was still on edge. DNA results confirmed what Jarrod already knew, that the same killer was responsible for the murders of Lisa Barkley, Tammy Heidenreich and Edna Bishop. Circumstantial evidence linked Carmichael to all three. He was still at large and could strike again, if one was to believe the media speculation.

The state opposition leader held his own press conference, demanding the police minister resign. He called for a board of inquiry into the police investigation that allowed a killer to roam free. He promised funding for more police and tough new penalties for criminals if his party was to be voted into power at the next state election. Jarrod had heard it all before, the usual political rhetoric and self-serving bullshit. In response, the government defaulted to arse-covering and finger pointing, citing "*those responsible will be held accountable*". There were even rumours of a Netflix docuseries to delve into the sordid life of Kaleb Carmichael. Details of his life story had leaked and he became somewhat of an enigma, the poster boy for extremists.

The victims of Carmichael's killing spree were all laid to rest, the community grieved and tried to heal. An inquest into their deaths was put on hold, subject to the ongoing police investigation. People wanted to feel safe in their own homes again, to send their kids off to school without fear. The Carmichael case only compounded the festering wounds left by Vincent Miles' rampage. The reputation of Lockyer had been stained in blood.

Christmas came and went. A new year had begun. Jarrod's injuries had healed, and a date set in April for the coronial inquest into the Karl Mundy shooting. The police commissioner and union president had offered their full backing of Jarrod's actions in what were "very difficult circumstances". It gave him some peace of mind, but it wasn't enough to quell the ongoing nightmares and recurring self-doubt. He busied himself with routine and the mundane, anything to distract him from his internal demons.

As months passed, new headlines reclaimed the front pages and the Carmichael case slipped into obscurity. Police resources were scaled back, the official line being that, while less overt, the investigation remained a priority for the police department. It had been taken out of the hands of the local detectives, but it didn't stop Jarrod from continuing his own covert investigations. He followed up on the weakest of leads, only to hit a dead end every time. Carmichael could be anywhere in the country by now, and there was no apparent reason for him to return to Lockyer. He'd found what he was looking for, taken his revenge and moved on, back into the shadows from which he emerged. People in town just wanted to forget the whole ordeal.

Jarrod learned that Tammy Heidenreich's mother, Marcia, had died. His heart sank when he read the funeral notice in the local paper.

He attended the funeral, hoping not to be noticed in the back row. As Tom Heidenreich followed his wife's coffin out of the church, his eyes sought Jarrod out in the congregation. He held his breath, every muscle tensing as Tom threw him a look, cold and accusing.

Outside, it was a bright cloudless day. In the broad daylight was a sense of serenity, a peace that invited itself into the soul and made itself at home. Jarrod slid on his sunglasses, keeping his eyes low to remain inconspicuous. Out on the church lawns, he tucked in behind a row of mourners, watching in silent reverence as the coffin was lifted into the back of the hearse. Tom Heidenreich whispered a private farewell and placed a bouquet on the coffin, inconsolable as it slid forward on rollers. Jarrod waited, anonymous, and jostled against bodies as he planned his exit strategy. He saw a break in the crowd and turned to leave. A hand gripped his shoulder. Tom had cut a path straight to him, ignoring well-wishers to intercept him before he made good his escape.

Jarrod felt a sudden heat in his cheeks. At that moment, he wished the ground would swallow him. He extended his hand, an awkward gesture. 'Mr Heidenreich, I'm so sorry for your—'

Tom interjected, waving away Jarrod's words. 'Don't patronise me.' He gritted his teeth. Heads turned, nearby whispering fell silent. All eyes were on them.

'Any leads on my daughter's killer yet?' said Tom. 'Or are you mob still sitting on your hands?'

'We're doing all we can, I promise.' Jarrod's voice trailed off.

'Don't give me any more of your empty promises.' Tom's words were coarse as sandpaper. 'You find that piece of shit and hand him to me. Marcia was all I had in this world, and now she's gone. *He* took it all from me, that evil…' He searched for the right word. 'That pathetic coward. Save your kind words, detective, and give me the one last thing I have to live for. Give me my revenge!' His chin tremored, desperation on his face. 'Go do your job.'

He strode off, nudging his shoulder against Jarrod's. His words were like a sucker punch to the gut. Water rushed to Jarrod's mouth and he fought against the urge to vomit where he stood. His hands were shaking.

He lowered his head and skulked away through the crowd of mourners, laden with shame and guilt. He vowed to keep his promise to a grieving man, to hunt down his daughter's killer.

Tom Heidenreich's last words rang in his ears. *Go do your job.*

FORTY-ONE

BARRISTER Winston Sheffield descended the grand staircase of the Police Law Court building in Sydney's central business district. As he crossed the terraced outdoor area facing Liverpool Street, an insolent wind gust caught his black robe, the fabric swirling and catching the rough surface of the sandstone balustrade. One hand anchored his curled wig from the threat of going airborne while his other clutched a briefcase full of law books and evidence briefs. Despite the impracticality of wearing his courtroom attire out in public, it bolstered his ego and sense of self-importance. Taking long strides onto the busy sidewalk, he disregarded the commoners who crossed his path. He carried himself with an air of superiority, a man who graced the lavish halls of the upper echelon and indulged in the extravagance of high society.

He gloated and smiled to himself. He'd just notched up another courtroom win, reaffirming his status as a lawyer who could name his price. Specialising in defending criminal cases, he milked the Legal Aid system for every penny it had. He thrived on the courtroom drama, sparring with inept public prosecutors and hoodwinking crusty old judges. It was all a game to him, and he was a pro.

Today's case was an indecent dealing matter. His client, a wealthy land developer, had been accused of sexually assaulting his twelve-year-old stepdaughter. Sheffield had broken the girl down in the witness box, played his role in testing her evidence. Had he gone too hard on her? Been too heavy-handed with his cross-examination?

Maybe. But that was all just part of the game. The girl's evidence was thrown out, deemed by the judge as inconsistent, and his client walked. Sheffield now considered whether he should put the foot on the jugular and sue the Department of Public Prosecution for costs. The idea made him smile. He felt no empathy for the complainant. He'd already forgotten her name.

Too absorbed in his own affairs, he didn't notice the figure falling in behind him. Sheffield rounded the corner into the deserted laneway towards his private parking space. The soles of his Italian suedes made the sound of tap shoes on the cobblestones, echoing between the brick walls of the adjacent buildings.

He then heard footfalls behind him, heavy thuds like boots. They quickened, growing closer, louder. Sheffield looked over his shoulder. His eyes traced the outline of a man, hands in the pockets of a jacket, head low, his face a blurred silhouette under the shadow of a hood. The man was now just metres behind, closing in fast. Sheffield looked ahead. The car park wasn't far. He hurried with a nervous flutter in his stomach.

'Where are you going, *Winston*?' the man called, his voice edged with gravel.

Sheffield stopped and spun on his heel at the sound of his own name. He faced the man, who now stood at arm's length, eyeballing him. The man removed his hood to reveal a hideous face. The edges of his thin lips pinched upwards to form a contorted smile.

'Hello, *Winston*. Remember me?'

'Who are you?' snapped Sheffield, self-assured. He pursed his mouth and raised his chin, looking down his nose. 'What do you want?'

The man tilted his head like an insect. 'You don't remember me?'

Sheffield stared back, studying the man's horrid face. He raised his eyebrows in a question. 'Should I know you?'

'You should. But it's been a while. I've changed,' the man said, his words slow and deliberate.

'Well, I'm a busy man. If you think you can afford my time, then call my office and make an appointment. Good day to you.'

The man reached behind his back and his hand dropped to his side. Sheffield's eyes widened when he saw the long blade protruding from the man's jacket sleeve.

'Do you want money?' Sheffield dropped his brief case and fished around under his gown for his back pocket. He produced his Gucci leather wallet and held it out in front of him. 'Here, take it. There's about five hundred in cash.'

'You disappoint me, *Winston.* Do you think you can talk yourself out of this? Your smart words won't help you today.'

Sheffield searched his trouser pocket and produced a car key. 'My Mercedes, it's just over there in the car park. It's yours. Take it and leave me alone.'

He tossed the key at the man, who let it hit him in the chest and fall to the ground.

The man raised the knife, a terrifying instrument of death. Sheffield froze, his limbs numb. He craned his head back as the man stepped into his personal space, his breathing loud with excitement. The man lifted the blade and hooked a curl of Sheffield's wig. He lifted it off his head and tossed it aside like a clump of snagged seaweed.

Sheffield willed his legs to move, terrified. Move or die, he told himself. He backed away, one foot after the other. He turned and ran, but his shoes slipped on the cobblestones, unable to gain traction.

The man was on him in a flash, grunting like an animal. He grabbed Sheffield by the collar of his gown and yanked him to the ground. Sheffield yelped, a high-pitched sound that sounded strange in his own ears. The man rolled him onto his back and straddled his chest, pinning his shoulders with his knees. Sheffield thrashed his arms and legs, but his body went limp when he felt the tip of the blade under his chin. The warmth of blood trickling down his Adam's apple followed a stinging sensation.

'What do you want from me?' Sheffield whimpered.

The man lowered his head and whispered in his ear. 'Revenge.'

'Revenge for what? I don't even know you.' He had to talk himself out of this. It was his only chance. He was physically no match for this brute. 'Listen to me, take it all. The money, my car. It's yours. I won't even report this to the police if you let me go.'

'Now that's just another lie, *Winston*. You can't help yourself, can you?'

'No, no. I promise. I won't call the police. Just let me go,' Sheffield cried. 'Let me go. I don't want to die.' Wetness warmed his groin as his bladder let go.

'Lies!' the man shouted. 'Nothing but lies. That's all you ever do, isn't it? You stand in that courtroom and spin lies. You torture the victims, helping guilty people walk free. You're nothing but vermin, a scourge on society.'

'Wait, no,' said Sheffield, desperate now. He mustered his courage and his wits. 'No, that's where you're wrong. It's my job to ensure the integrity of the justice system, to test the evidence to ensure a fair trial.'

'Justice!' the man spat with a sneer. 'What justice? No, that's not justice. I'll show you real justice.' He pushed the blade harder against his chin. Sheffield could feel his skin slicing open.

He looked into the man's eyes, hope fading. 'Who are you?'

'I'm your worst nightmare. I was just a child when you defended the man who did this to me,' he said, pointing at his own face. 'That man is dead. He suffered just as I have suffered. Now *that* was justice, fair and decisive. You still don't remember, do you? Frankie Arnold? A little boy with a burnt face. Ringing any bells?'

Images flashed in Sheffield's mind. He closed his eyes and tried to remember. His eyes snapped open. 'I remember. You're that boy?'

'Say my name.'

'Um, I don't… I don't remember the boy's, um, your name.'

'Of course you don't. Why would you? That little boy meant nothing to you.'

'Why have you come after me? I don't deserve this. I was just doing my job.'

'Your job? No, you take far too much pleasure in the misery of others for it to be just a job. Because of you, I was robbed of justice. Well, I'm here to make things right. I'm here to claim my justice.'

'No!' Sheffield screamed. 'Help, someone help me!'

The man put his fingers to his lips. 'Sshhhh.'

He raised his fist and punched Sheffield in the nose, the back of his head slamming into the ground with a loud crack. A second punch to the side of his head turned the world on its axis. His brain throbbed inside his skull and his thoughts became mush. His vision strobed and his head lolled to one side. He couldn't feel his body, his thoughts consumed by the pounding in his head.

He had the sensation he was moving, that he was being dragged. Yes, he was moving, the backs of his legs were scraping along the ground. A beeping sound. Where was it coming from? The *bip-bip* of a remote car lock, yes, that's it. Where was he? The opening of a car door. His body being lifted. Had someone come to help him? His scrambled brain assembled fragments of information. Something tugged at his feet, moving them into position. He was now sitting up. Something tight on his wrists, a zipping sound. The crunching of boots on gravel. A lid being unscrewed from a tin. The smell of petrol fumes. A sloshing sound. He willed his eyes to open. He blinked and looked around. He was sitting in the passenger seat of his own car. Liquid splashing on him, stinging his eyes. Petrol vapours burned his throat. His wrists were bound with a zip tie.

A man's face leaned in. An ugly, evil face. The face of a demon.

'Kaleb Carmichael. That's my name. Say it!'

Sheffield felt woozy. He opened his mouth to speak, but no words came out.

The man grabbed Sheffield's mouth, prising his jaw open. He squeezed Sheffield's cheeks, forcing his lips to pout.

'Kaleb Carmichael,' he repeated. 'Say it!'

'Kaleb… Carmichael,' Sheffield sputtered

The man let go of his face. 'And so it shall be. Your final words. Remember my name forever in hell. I find you guilty. Justice is served.'

Sheffield's eyes opened wide. He gasped as a match was struck, a little flame flickering orange and bright. Then a sudden *whoosh* and heat all around. Everything around him burned, blinding him by flames. His eyes burned first, then his face. He tried to scream, but he gagged on scorching fumes clawing at his throat. The sheer terror, the horror. He was burning alive. He writhed in agony, choking on smoke. His skin was on fire, melting.

The man's laughter faded, and everything went black.

FORTY-TWO

THE murder of Winston Sheffield was big news. "Barrister burned alive" shouted one headline. "Lawyer slain in car fire" read another. There was media speculation of Sheffield's rumoured links to the underworld, all baseless innuendo and sensationalism. Jarrod remembered back to when he last saw Sheffield sauntering from the courtroom after the Daniel Barkley trial. Jarrod had despised the man and his conniving tactics, but even Sheffield didn't deserve such brutality. His mind drifted to potential motives. He figured a man like Sheffield would have made a long list of enemies over the years, but it was the sheer violence and premeditation of the murder that made Jarrod on edge. The killer or killers were making a statement. It had all the hallmarks of a vendetta, a revenge killing. His attacker must have known Sheffield's movements, known when to strike. The similarity to Frankie Arnold's death wasn't lost on Jarrod.

A thought tugged in the back of his mind, something he'd read but not taken any notice of as being important. He needed to be sure and clicked open the Kaleb Carmichael case notes on his computer. He scrolled through the transcript of the court proceedings until he found the name he was looking for. Winston Sheffield had been Frankie Arnold's defense lawyer. Sheffield had cross-examined Kaleb Carmichael, badgering the boy in the witness box until his evidence was deemed unreliable and thrown out by the judge. Jarrod's stomach clenched at the gravity of the discovery, the obvious link to Kaleb Carmichael. He closed his eyes, flashbacks of Carmichael's threats replaying in slow-mo. He remembered the night of the service station fire. What was it he'd said? *I'm coming after all of you. You will all pay! The whole world will burn!*

Jarrod pulled up the internal bulletin the Homicide Squad had circulated regarding the Sheffield investigation. A taskforce had been stood up with a hotline number listed. He reached for the handset of his desk phone and dialed the number. After waiting in cue for twenty minutes, a call taker finally answered. He relayed the information about the link to Kaleb Carmichael. The operator sounded overwhelmed, flustered. They were inundated with calls. Various motives were being explored. He instructed Jarrod to write up an intelligence report and send it through to the taskforce email address for collation and prioritisation. Jarrod sighed but understood the process. The investigation team wasn't going to drop everything to follow a hunch from a country hick detective. After the call, he typed up the report and marked it as PRIORITY before hitting send. The ball was now in their court.

He stared at the pile of files on his desk, his mind wandering. He opened the folder containing the clip seal bag with the old photo he'd found in the playground. It was smeared with fingerprint dust. A partial thumbprint was found on the back of the photo but had not been matched to any on the fingerprint database. Just like the DNA samples collected at the scenes of the three murders, Jarrod suspected the print belonged to Carmichael. Only time would tell.

He stared at the images of Carmichael as a boy standing in front of an old house and a younger Frankie Arnold sitting at the top of the stairs. He examined every detail, looking for something he may have missed. The house. Where was it? He needed to know more about where the photo was taken. He dialed Karen Jackson's office phone. The ring tone almost rang out.

'Drug Squad. Detective Jackson speaking,' she answered as Jarrod was about to hang up. Her manner was abrupt, like she'd just caught the phone in time.

'Hey Karen, Jarrod O'Connor. Hope I haven't called you at a bad time.'

'Hey, mate,' she said, short of breath. 'No, you're all good. I was just on my way out. What's up?'

'Have you heard about the murder of Winston Sheffield?'

'Yeah, of course, it's all anyone can talk about.'

'I think it might be connected to Kaleb Carmichael.'

'Shit, Jarrod. Have you let the taskforce know?'

'Yeah, yeah. I rang 'em. Had to submit an intel report.'

'Poor buggers must be run off their feet. So, what makes you think it's linked to your cases?'

'The general MO. You know, victims being burned alive. Sheffield was the defense barrister who crossed examined Carmichael as a boy.'

'Of course! Holy shit, Jarrod. I should have remembered that. You think Carmichael is coming after anyone connected with the case?'

'That's my gut feeling.'

Karen hesitated. 'Do you think… this might sound silly… but do you think I should be worried? Could I be on his hitlist?'

'I don't know. What do your instincts tell you?'

'He seemed like a sweet kid. A battler. I always felt we had a connection, you know, a rapport. I'd like to think he has no reason to hold me accountable for the failed court case. I did everything I could to build a strong case. It all turned to shit in the courtroom. That was out of my control.'

'Then there's your answer. Look, you probably have nothing to worry about, but don't be complacent. Take precautions. We have no idea what warped frame of mind Carmichael is in right now.'

'Yeah, well thanks for the heads up. Is that why you were calling?'

'Actually, I was hoping to pick your brains about that case.'

'Okay,' she said, questioning. 'What do you need to know?'

'I've got an old photo. Can you take a look at it?'

'Yeah sure.'

Jarrod took a photo with his phone and texted it to Karen.

'Okay, got it. What am I looking at?' she said.

'Carmichael dropped this pic when he was casing out the service station. Recognise the people in the photo?'

'That's Kaleb. Before his injury. And Frankie Arnold, that's him on the stairs.'

'Right. What can you tell me about that house? Is that where they were living at the time of the incident?'

'Hang on, just zooming in.' There was a pause at the end of the line as Karen studied the photo. 'Yeah, that's the house where it happened. I went there myself to examine the scene. I'll never forget it.'

'Where is it?'

'It's on a property, out near the Blue Mountains. Not far from Katoomba.'

'Who owned the house? Were they just renting out there?'

'No, the house belonged to Kaleb's grandparents. The property had been in the family for generations. Kaleb and his mother moved in with her father not long before he died. The grandmother had been dead for years. Kaleb told me he and his grandfather were close, that he was lonely after the old man died. Not long after that, his mother hooked up with Frankie Arnold and he moved into the house with them.'

'What became of the house?'

'Don't really know. Last I heard, the place was abandoned.'

There was a long pause as they both pondered.

Karen spoke again. 'I just remembered something. I didn't think much of it at the time.' Her voice trailed off, as if lost in an old memory.

'What is it?'

'It was a throw away comment that Kaleb made one day when I was interviewing him at his bedside in hospital. I didn't give it much credence. He said that his grandfather had left him a stash of money in a secret hiding spot. That it was their secret.'

'So, if it was a secret, why did he tell you about it?'

'Who knows? The kid was in a lot of pain, delirious on painkillers. I dismissed it as ramblings.'

'Well, if he had access to a large amount of cash, that would explain how he's been able to stay off the grid for so long.'

'Hmm, maybe.' Karen became lost in her thoughts again. 'Hey, one other thing I remember. There's a family burial plot on the property. Just a handful of graves.'

'Really? Who's buried out there?'

'Not sure exactly. The grandparents, I think, and descendants from earlier generations.'

'Interesting. Do you know if there are any other family members around who have a claim to the property?'

Karen exhaled, thinking. 'No, as far as I know, Kaleb is the last in the family line. The property would legally be his.'

'Can you send me the address? I have a hunch.'

FORTY-THREE

JARROD steered one-handed, resting his elbow on the car door window ledge. Nerve pain shot through his other arm and clunky shoulder. He shook his hand and wiggled his fingers to get the circulation going. He nudged Brad. 'Oi, wake up.'

Brad's face scrunched as he prised his eyes open. He yawned and stretched his back, adjusting his seatbelt as he shimmied upright in his seat.

'You've been catching flies ever since we left the Lockyer town limits,' said Jarrod, without taking his eyes off the road. Truth be told, he hadn't minded the two hours of solitude behind the wheel to mull things over in his head.

Brad gave Jarrod a furtive side glance, wiping drool from the corner of his mouth as he peered out the window. 'We're here? I can't see anything.'

Jarrod glanced at the GPS map on his phone. 'We're just coming up to it.' He pointed to a spot beyond the windscreen.

He slowed and steered into a property entrance swallowed by a weeping willow tree, its dangling branches grazing the ground with fluttering, silver-tinged leaves. The grassy strip between gravel wheel tracks scraped the car's undercarriage. No one had driven on it in a long time.

Brad shot Jarrod a questioning look. 'You sure you know where you're going?'

Jarrod didn't answer as he negotiated the overgrown track,

threading the car through a corridor of overhanging branches forming a shadowy tunnel of thick scrub. He squinted behind sunglasses as they burst into a clearing, the morning sunlight bright and stark.

'There!' Jarrod pointed. In the distance, a rusty, corrugated iron roof came into view behind a falling slope. A rickety looking barbed wire fence and steel gate cut across the track up ahead.

'Shit!' said Brad. 'Looks like we're walking from here.'

Jarrod pulled up and sighed. He killed the ignition. The coolness of the air conditioning dissipated. Heat from outside seeped through the window glass. The ticking of the settling engine broke the silence.

'Place looks deserted,' said Brad. 'What are we doing here again?'

'Chasing ghosts. But truthfully? Buggered if I know, mate.'

'Still got that hunch?'

Jarrod twisted in his seat to face Brad. 'You got any better ideas?'

Brad raised one eyebrow and shrugged.

'Didn't think so,' said Jarrod. 'This place is the last known link to Carmichael. It's worth a look.'

Brad did one of his half-smiles. 'If you say so.'

'Come on. Let's get this over with.'

Hot, dry air invaded the car as they opened the doors. Gravel crunched under their shoes as they trudged towards the gate. A padlock was fastened to a heavy chain, welded closed with rust. Jarrod propped his elbows on the gate and listened. Not a sound. Spindly scrub grass caught a whisper of breeze and swayed, moving in steady waves between gentle lulls. Threadbare paddocks were a patchwork of earthy browns and reds. Discarded farm machinery and tractor carcasses were scattered around the sprawling property. A dilapidated hay shed leaned as though it could topple on itself with the slightest nudge. In the far paddock, a livestock loading ramp stood alone, defiant against the elements.

They hoisted themselves over the gate and followed the tracks towards the two-storey farmhouse hunched at the base of the hill, a sun-bleached log fence forming a perimeter around the lonely structure. Overgrown creeper vines twisted and curled up the walls and staircase railings. A loose sheet of roofing iron clanged and creaked as its edges flapped in the breeze. A wind chime dangled from the veranda ceiling, its tinkling tunes echoing across the barren fields.

White paint flaked off the weatherboard walls like dead skin. The windows on the ground level were boarded over with plywood sheeting. Fly screen that had once enclosed the veranda was torn and tousled by the wind. Tufts of weeds filled cracks in the cement path. Timber staircase treads were bowed.

Jarrod stopped and gazed at the house, shielding his eyes from the sun.

'What is it?' said Brad, standing alongside.

'This is the house.'

'You sure?'

'Just there,' said Jarrod, pointing. 'That's where he was standing.'

'Who?'

'Carmichael. In that photo. When he was a boy.' He shifted his gaze to the house. 'And up there, top of the staircase. That's where Frankie Arnold was sitting.'

Brad looked up at the house. Tattered lace curtains hung limp inside the upper windows. 'Feels like the house is watching us,' said Brad. His upper body shuddered. 'Bugger me. I just got the chills… like someone walked over my grave. Place gives me the creeps.'

Jarrod said nothing. He didn't tell Brad that his legs grew heavier with each step towards the house. He kept to himself the rising feeling of dread in his gut.

He tested the bottom step with his foot to see if it would bear his weight. It groaned but held firm. The staircase railing wobbled. He took the next step, and the next. Brad followed. At the top, a fly screen door sagged from rusted hinges. Jarrod pushed and it creaked open with little resistance. He crossed worn veranda floorboards and stopped in front of a heavy looking door. An old-fashioned barrel key was seated in the keyhole.

'Strange,' said Brad. 'Windows are boarded up, but the key's been left in the door.'

Jarrod met his gaze. 'Everything about this place is strange.' He reached for the doorknob, the brass cool in his hand. The latch clunked as he turned the knob. He pushed the door open, and the old house exhaled musty air as though breathing for the first time in years. They waited for the dust to settle before gingerly stepping inside.

Jarrod blinked as his pupils adjusted to the gloom. The front sitting room was spacious and bare. Their footfalls echoed as they moved about the house, poking their heads into adjoining rooms. Shoe prints trailed behind them on dusty floorboards. Through pinprick holes in the edges of boarded windows, chinks of sunlight angled towards the floor. Jarrod and Brad split up, clearing each room on ground level. Plumbing in the kitchen and bathroom had been gutted, leaving gaping holes in internal walls and floorboards. All fixtures and furnishings were gone. The house was a hollow shell.

They met at the base of the internal stairs and headed up, scaling two flights to the upstairs landing. The bedrooms were empty. Sunlight rippled through lace curtains, casting grey shadows across the unvarnished floors. Jarrod entered what would have been the master bedroom and moved to a window. He pushed a curtain aside so he could peer out over the backyard and paddocks beyond. A thin track meandered through long grass and around trees towards a grassy knoll. He couldn't tell if the track was manmade, or a route used by kangaroos. His eyes followed the track as it wormed its way up the slope towards a cluster of headstones behind a picketed wrought-iron fence. He remembered what Karen Jackson had told him about the family burial plot. *Bang!* A slamming door downstairs shook the walls. Jarrod jumped.

Brad scuttled into the doorway. 'Shit! Scared the crap out of me. The wind?' His voice echoed off the walls.

'Probably,' Jarrod replied. He looked around the empty room and sighed. 'I've seen enough. There's nothing here. Let's get out of this place.'

'No arguments from me.'

They negotiated the creaky staircase and headed towards the front door, now closed.

Brad turned the knob, but the door wouldn't budge. He twisted the knob in the opposite direction and tugged harder, but it didn't give. 'Bloody great, it's locked.' He bent down and peeked through the keyhole with one eye closed. 'Weird. The key's gone.'

'Fell out when the door slammed, I'd say,' said Jarrod. 'The lock's probably jammed. Come on, let's see if there's another way out.'

Their eyes snapped back towards the front door at the sudden *thump thump thump* of boots stomping along the veranda outside.

'Hey! Who's out there?' Jarrod yelled.

No response. Everything went silent.

'Can you smell that?' Brad whispered.

Jarrod sniffed. His nostrils burned as petrol fumes permeated from under the door. 'Get back!'

Whoosh!

An explosion of flames ignited outside the door. The orange light of fire flickered through hairline gaps in the wall panels. Flames licked the edges of the door and around the plywood covering the veranda windows. Jarrod and Brad backed away from the radiating heat. Flames engulfed the walls outside. Fire crawled inside and leapt up the walls towards the ceiling. Black smoke filled the room. The place was a tinder box.

'The back door!' Jarrod yelled over the roar of the flames. He gagged as fumes and smoke choked him. Brad covered his face with the crook of his elbow. Through the smokey haze, they made their way to the back of the house. The door was locked, its window boarded over. Planks were nailed across the door on the inside. They'd need a crowbar.

Brad yanked at the knob and threw his shoulder against the solid door. Panting, he moved back a few paces and ran at the door, hurling his bodyweight against it. The wall shuddered but the door didn't budge. It was hopeless.

More heavy footsteps outside, this time at the back door.

'Hey! Let us out, you mongrel!' yelled Brad, thumping the door with his fists. 'We're trapped in here!'

No one answered.

A sudden whoosh and then flames exploded outside the back door.

Brad recoiled. 'Aargh! Lunatic's trying to kill us.' His face was a look of desperation, the whites of his eyes prominent. 'He's dousing the whole place!'

Jarrod and Brad moved to the base of the internal staircase, the most central point in the house. They pressed their backs against each other.

'What now?' said Brad. 'We have to find a way out before the whole place comes down on us.'

Jarrod dropped to one knee, coughing as his lungs filled with toxic smoke. His throat burned and his vision strobed. 'The smoke will… kill us first.' His eyes stung and scorching heat stroked his face.

Brad stood over him and squeezed his shoulders. 'Just hold on. I'm gonna find a way out.' He darted away.

Smoke churned inside the house like a tornado. Window glass imploded. Flames raged, hot and violent, with no care for the destruction it left behind, consuming everything it pleased. Floorboards vibrated beneath Jarrod's feet. The walls and ceiling were engulfed in flames, rising upwards towards the upper level. He dropped to his hands and knees and crawled along the floor, gulping for air. He'd lost sight of Brad. Disorientation set in. He was groggy, like he'd been drugged. 'Keep moving! Keep breathing!' he ordered himself. 'Brad! Where are you?' He coughed and gagged.

No response. Jarrod dropped to his belly and dragged himself to the base of the staircase, clambering with his hands and elbows. He drove with his feet, but his shoes slid on the dusty floorboards. 'Stay low,' he told himself. He lay with his face pressed against the bottom stair.

Beyond the roar of the flames, the air outside vibrated with a whining buzz, faint at first but then louder. Jarrod's scattered thoughts imagined a giant mosquito coming for his blood. In a moment of clarity, he recognised the tinny purr of a two-stroke trail bike engine revving as it circled the house. A tyre slid in dirt and the engine died. A shrill voice from outside seethed with bitterness. It shouted with violence, polluting the air with rage. It was a voice he'd heard before. 'You're not welcome here! Pray for redemption or burn in hell!' The engine fired and revved. A wheel spun and the motorbike engine faded away.

Jarrod's arms and legs trembled. He grew weaker. He tried to push himself up, but his elbows buckled under his weight. Every moment cost more energy than it should, like someone had just turned gravity way up. Laying helpless, he gasped for air, eyelids heavy as lead. A horrid face flashed in his mind. Snarling. Menacing. Sneering.

He couldn't feel his arms and legs anymore, like he was outside his body. His eyes closed and for a blissful moment everything went dark. He no longer felt anything. Kaleb Carmichael's words replayed in his head. *Pray for redemption or burn in hell.*

FORTY-FOUR

JARROD had a vague awareness that he was moving, sliding across the floor through an orange glow and smoky haze. His conscious brain processed fragmented images, replaying the last few scenes. His senses were numb, a cloud of confusion fogging his thoughts. He needed to gain a greater perspective, to rise above himself and see a wide-angled version of his surroundings. His limp body was being dragged. That much became clear. His throat burned as he gasped for air. He remembered where he was, trapped and about to be incinerated alive.

Strong hands released their grip. He tried to get up but lost his balance, stumbling to the floor as a wave of dizziness took hold. He looked up. The outline of a figure moved with purpose. Jarrod rubbed his eyes. Brad's form took shape in the smoke, launching himself against a side door. *Thud. Thud. Thud.*

'Fuck this!' Brad yelled. 'Cover your face!' Gun in hand, he fired towards a boarded-up window. *Boom! Boom! Boom!* Glass shattered. Brad kicked and plywood splintered. Sunlight burst into the room, followed by a glorious gust of fresh air. Smoke sucked out through the opening.

Jarrod felt his body being lifted from under his armpits. Arms wrapped around his chest.

'Come on, Jarrod. Move your legs!' Brad wheezed. 'You need to help me. I can't do this on my own.'

Broken glass crunched under Jarrod's shoes. He could feel his legs again and willed himself to his feet. Brad helped him to the opening and kicked away shards of glass clinging to the window frame. Jarrod inhaled. Cool air entered his lungs, and with it came more clarity. He looked around. The walls of the sunroom were alive with flames.

Brad heaved their bodies out the window, like a pair of tandem skydivers rolling out of a plane. They were falling, toppling as gravity yanked them hard. Flame fingers clawed and snatched after them. *Oof!* The air was knocked out of Jarrod's lungs. His ribcage crunched as his body hit the ground in a tangle of arms and legs. He rolled free of Brad's grip. Cuts stung his face and hands. His shirt sleeve was soaked with blood, but he was alive. They lay on their backs, gasping and gagging. Jarrod opened his eyes, his vision clearing. Brad got to his feet, dragging Jarrod away from the house before he collapsed onto the dirt, his breathing short and raspy.

Flames blasted out through windows like blowtorches and crawled up the walls. The house groaned as the intense heat weakened its foundations. Smoke rose high and swelled outwards, smearing the blue sky with a sooty smudge.

Fresh air soothed Jarrod's throat and lungs, his breathing more controlled. He sat up and faced Brad. 'Thanks mate. You saved my arse in there.'

Brad lay on his back, his chest heaving, arms outstretched. He held up a bloodied hand and gave a thumbs up and a grimace.

A new realisation hit Jarrod, an icy fear. *Carmichael! Where was he?* He looked around in panic but saw no one. He found his legs and stood. 'We can't stay out here in the open.'

Brad sat up and coughed. 'Carmichael? It was him, wasn't it?'

'You heard him too?'

Brad nodded. 'I also heard a motorbike.'

Jarrod drew the Glock from his ankle holster. 'Come on. I'll go right, you take the left. We'll circle around to the front.'

Brad drew his gun from his hip holster and staggered to his feet. They limped off in opposite directions, scanning their line of sight with their guns. Brad disappeared around the corner of the house.

Jarrod followed the foresight of his Glock, index finger prepped outside the trigger guard. He moved towards the front, pulsating heat forcing him further away from the cover of the burning building. He willed himself forward until he arrived at the side of the front veranda. Brad emerged from the far corner. They moved to the front yard, where they met at the foot of the staircase. A jerry can lay on its side in the dirt, fuel dripping from a nozzle.

Jarrod slid his phone from his trouser pocket. No reception. 'Shit! You got a signal?'

Brad squinted at his phone and shook his head.

There was no sign of Carmichael. Jarrod's eyes scanned the line of scrub hugging the open paddocks. He imagined the killer lying in wait, face pressed against the dirt, hiding in the long grass. Watching. He wondered if the fire was just a warning, part of Carmichael's grand plan.

'You better run, you gutless mongrel!' Jarrod yelled, turning on the spot as he peered out, eyes searching. 'Do you hear me—*Kaleb*?' The man's name was acidic on his tongue. He spat and wiped his mouth with his shirt sleeve. He expected to hear maniacal laughter, taunting. Tree branches swayed in the breeze. Crows cawed and jeered. Burning wood crackled, twisted iron clanged. Kaleb Carmichael stayed silent.

The house groaned and flames roared behind them. Jarrod and Brad spun around and, sensing imminent danger, their legs carried them away from the house. Cautious at first, but quicker and more deliberate, they retreated up the driveway. Jarrod's attention was drawn back towards the burning house as a loud crash echoed from within. The roof collapsed on itself, sending ash and sparks into the air. The walls caved in. A dazzling ball of flames leapt high into the air.

They hobbled up the hill to the gate, still chained. The car was intact, untouched. They helped each other climb over.

'Where do ya reckon he went on that trail-bike?' said Brad,

grimacing at the blood seeping from his sliced hand.

Jarrod rifled through his pockets for the car keys. 'Must be another way off the property. He didn't come this way.' He unlocked the car with the remote and they flung the doors open. It seemed like an eternity since they had left the protection of the vehicle. It was like coming home. Jarrod checked his phone again, hands shaking. A single bar offered the slimmest hope of network reception. He dialed triple zero, relieved to hear the dial tone and the operator's voice, calm and reassuring. He identified himself and called in backup. Crews were on their way.

Jarrod popped the boot and they moved to the rear of the car. Brad unclipped the first aid kit and they field-dressed their cuts.

'Let's vest up,' said Jarrod. 'Just in case he turns up again. We can't just wait here, we're too exposed. He could be watching us now for all we know.'

They slid into their ballistic Kevlar vests and inserted the ceramic plates in the chest compartments.

Jarrod noticed Brad's laboured breathing as he fastened the vest straps. 'You up to it?'

Brad checked his gun's magazine and rammed it back into the handle. He winked. 'What could possibly go wrong?'

They scaled the gate again and dragged their feet towards the inferno. Jarrod's thoughts returned to Carmichael. It was as though he expected them to discover the farmhouse sooner or later. Had he been waiting for them to make the next move? A thought occurred to him, and he prodded a hand on Brad's chest. They stopped. 'He knew we were coming. Watch out for any sign of traps, or…' Jarrod remembered the Vincent Miles manhunt.

'Or bunkers,' Brad cut in. 'Yeah, I know. I was thinking the same thing.'

'Come on, let's take a look at that family burial plot up on the hill. It'll give us a better viewpoint.'

They wheeled around to the rear of the burning house until they came to the narrow track that cut its way through knee-length, brown grass. They trudged single file up the hill, wheezing from the aftereffects of smoke inhalation. A tiredness and lethargy weighed down Jarrod's body. He worked hard to draw in breath, his lungs pulling for all their worth, gulping as if he was drowning in the air.

They reached the summit, where two rows of headstones in various states of decay and neglect, eight in total, stood watch over a panoramic view of the abandoned farm. The oldest graves dated back to the early nineteen-hundreds; headstone edges weathered smooth. According to the faded inscriptions, various members of the Carmichael family, including two infant boys, lay beneath the dirt on that hilltop. One grave stood out among the drab granite stone and concrete. This one looked the most recent, polished black marble etched with a simple white cross. Jarrod opened a creaking picket gate and leant in closer to inspect. He read out the inscription. 'Frederick Cecil Carmichael. In God's care. Much loved husband, father and grandfather. Dearly missed. Watch over us 'Pop'.'

A fresh bunch of wild daisies were arranged in a vase at the foot of the grave. It had recently been tended to, freed of weeds and wiped clean.

'This is why he's here,' said Jarrod. 'It's his grandfather's grave. It's his home, his family. He's bound to this place.'

'Has anyone thought to search this place before? How did this get missed?'

'I guess it just got overlooked in the hype of the manhunt and false sightings. This place had been forgotten about.'

Brad looked around, his gaze fixing on something. 'Hey, look.' He pointed to a worn trail disappearing down the far side of the hill towards the old hay shed.

'It's worth a look,' said Jarrod.

They followed the track down the hill and across a paddock. As they approached the shed, they crouched in the long grass, eyes searching for any movement. There was no sign of a motorbike. The shed had an annex with no side walls, designed for storing hay bales and machinery. The main door to the shed was closed. Newspaper was taped to the inside of the window glass.

'Fan out,' Jarrod whispered, gesturing with hand signals. 'I'll go down this side. You take the other.'

Brad nodded and peeled off towards the side of the shed, crouching as he moved. Jarrod hurried across to the opposite side, his gun drawn. They positioned themselves on either side of the door with backs pressed against the wall. The heat of the sunbaked tin penetrated the back of Jarrod's shirt, biting at his skin. He tried to control his breathing and listened for any sign of movement inside. The corrugated iron roof creaked as the sun rose higher in the sky and the wooden frame groaned, stressed from supporting its own weight. No shuffling of feet or sounds of movement inside.

They made eye contact. Brad furrowed his brow and nodded. Jarrod knew that look. His partner was ready. Jarrod took a deep breath, his heart pounding. He reached over and grabbed the door handle. When he applied downward pressure, the handle obeyed and the latch clicked. He mouthed, 'On me.' He pulled the door open. 'Go!'

They moved as one. Brad rolled in and went right. Jarrod followed and took the left. They went bold, storming the room with firearms scanning.

'Armed police! Don't move!' Jarrod announced, crouching behind an oil drum. Brad slid along a wall until he reached a cupboard in the corner, pressing against it for cover. Jarrod blinked to adjust his vision to the dusty gloom. A corridor of sunlight burst through the door behind them.

The shed smelled of oily rags and lucerne hay. At one end, hand tools hung on a wall rack above a cluttered workbench. Wooden crates and cardboard boxes were stacked beneath. A pair of gumboots, coated with red dust, were cast aside as if someone had just stepped out of them. The far end of the shed had been converted to makeshift living quarters where a large square of carpet covered the concrete floor space. The living area was surprisingly clean and consisted of a canvas camping swag, table and chair and a battered recliner propped in front of a portable television on milk crates, coat hanger wire fashioned into an aerial.

They moved again, clearing the tight space. 'Clear!' said Brad.

'Clear!' Jarrod responded.

The ramshackle hideout was empty, no sign of Carmichael.

'Go outside and keep watch, will ya? In case he comes back on foot,' said Jarrod. 'I'll look around in here.'

Brad nodded. 'Righto. I'm not in the mood for being trapped in another burning building. I'll sing out if there's any movement. Backup should be here soon.' He moved to the open doorway, peered out and slid into the daylight.

Jarrod holstered and swivelled on the spot, taking mental snapshots. Men's clothing was draped over rope, strung between low ceiling beams. In the middle of the table stood a kerosene lantern. On a bench top, canned food and long-life milk had been organised, stacked alongside cooking utensils, pots and pans. A portable gas grill had been used for cooking and a pipe from a tank outside fed water to a stainless-steel sink. A washed plate, bowl and cup were laid out for drying. In the corner, a small refrigerator hummed, powered by a solar panel outside and backed up by a diesel generator. It was a doomsday prepper's haven.

Jarrod needed to find some answers, to delve further into Carmichael's depraved mind. He looked for clues as to where Carmichael might run. He searched drawers and cupboards. Nothing. He looked around the room again, taking in the bigger picture. He still had no idea what he was looking for.

Something caught his eye. The corner of a brown bundle poked out from beneath the swag mattress. He bent down and slid out an old leather pouch. He unwound the leather ties and opened the pouch. Inside was something soft and black. A clump of hair attached to something dry and leathery. A scalp – human skin. His stomach lurched as a flashback of Lisa Barkley's dead body came to him. He remembered the bloody wound where the sick memento had been sliced from her hairline. Jarrod stood there, frozen. He gazed at the disturbing find, his body numb.

His senses returned and he closed the pouch, tying the leather straps. They'd uncovered Carmichael's hidden lair. But what now? Where would he resurface? Who was next on his kill list? Had they now forced his hand? One thing was certain. He'd kill again, soon. On the run, he had nothing to lose. He remembered what Carmichael had said before he burned Frankie Arnold alive. *Revenge takes time.*

Sirens broke the silence and grew louder, echoing through the hills. It was difficult to tell what direction they were coming from.

Brad poked his head in the door, relief evident on his face. 'Cavalry is coming.'

FORTY-FIVE

THE sirens amplified into a muffled chorus, trumpeting the arrival of police and fire crews. Next came the crunch of tyres on gravel, the slamming of car doors, frantic voices bellowing, instructions being ordered. Brad took the car keys and went to meet them. Jarrod remained alone in the shed, immersed in Kaleb Carmichael's world – a dead girl's scalp in his pocket.

He sat at the table, relieved to take the weight off his aching legs. He felt giddy. Cuts on his hands and forearms felt as though they'd been flash-burned with acid from the inside. His muscles felt like they'd been replaced by aging rubber bands, thick and twisted. An innocuous Sydney Morning Bulletin on the table caught his eye. He slid the newspaper over and unfolded it. A blue biro pen fell out and clattered on the tabletop. He checked the date. Yesterday's edition. He flicked through the pages absentmindedly and stopped when he came to a page in the classifieds. A random ad in the miscellaneous section was circled in blue ink. The heading read "Death Notice". Strange, thought Jarrod. He wondered why it wasn't listed in the official obituary notice section. Curious, he read the block of text, crammed in a narrow column amid adverts for escort and erotic massage services. "Announcing the sudden death of Henry Atkins, in life you plundered, in death you suffered. You've been delivered into eternity. Be free of your sins."

For some reason, the grim obituary notice had significance for Kaleb Carmichael. Why had he circled it? Jarrod read it again. *Henry*

Atkins. A niggle in the back of his mind told him he should know the name, but he couldn't place it. Shuffling feet approaching the door caught his attention. Hairs on the back of his neck bristled and he reached down to his ankle holster and gripped the handle of his Glock, unclipping the strap with his thumb. The tension in his shoulders eased when Brad appeared in the doorway, followed by a stern-faced uniformed sergeant he didn't know. Brad introduced him as the shift supervisor from the local station.

'Firies cut the gate padlock with bolt cutters,' said Brad. 'They're dealing with what's left of the fire. Pissing in the wind. It's so far gone they may as well sit back and roast marshmallows.'

Jarrod nodded but barely registered, instead staring at a spot on the wall, the name Henry Atkins still bouncing around his brain.

Brad waved a hand in front of Jarrod's face. 'You still with us, mate?'

Jarrod shook his head. 'Yeah, yeah. I'm good.'

'Anyway,' Brad continued. 'I've given the brass a sit-rep. The Patrol Inspector's here already. He's setting up a forward command post. SERT is on their way. He reckons they'll try to flush Carmichael out. But if you ask me, he's long gone.'

'Local CIB guys are on their way,' said the sergeant. 'They'll take up with you for a handover as soon as they get here.'

Brad looked at the newspaper Jarrod held. 'So… just been catching up on the news, have we?' He turned and spoke to the sergeant. 'He blacked out from the smoke. Might still be a bit out of it.'

The sergeant gave a knowing nod.

Jarrod glared at Brad. 'I *am* just here, ya know. And yes, I'm fine.'

Brad put out his hands, surrendering. 'Whatever you say, mate.' He shot the sergeant a conspiring look which said, 'yeah, right'.

'If you must know,' said Jarrod, pointing to the circled classified ad, 'Carmichael seemed to be interested in a dead guy named Henry Atkins.'

'What?' the sergeant said, deadpan. 'As in *Judge* Henry Atkins.'

Jarrod's face felt flushed as the blood in his cheeks drained. He stared at the sergeant. 'Say that again.'

'Henry Atkins. That's the name of a Supreme Court judge in the city.' He stroked his chin. 'Nah,' he said, dismissing his suggestion with a wave as if swatting a fly. 'Old Judge Atkins is alive and well as far as I know. A dead judge would be big news.'

The penny dropped. Jarrod remembered where he'd seen the name. Judge Henry Atkins had presided over Frankie Arnold's trial. It was in the old case notes. Atkins had dismissed Carmichael's evidence as a boy, deeming him an unreliable witness. His ruling had allowed Arnold to walk free.

'Listen to this.' Jarrod read the strange obituary notice out loud.

Brad and the sergeant just stared at him, puzzled. They exchanged glances.

'Maybe a coincidence?' said Brad. 'Could be some other old codger named Henry Atkins who carked it.'

'So why would Carmichael circle the name? And look how it's worded.'

'Dunno.' Brad shrugged. 'He might have just recognised the name.'

Jarrod returned his attention to the circled advertisement. 'No. I don't buy it.'

He glanced down at two newspapers on the floor and picked the top one up. It was dated 14th March.

'What are you looking for?' asked Brad.

'I don't know. Just give me a second,' Jarrod told him. He flicked through the pages until he found another circled advert. His stomach churned when he recognised the name. 'Listen to this.' He read the notice out loud. 'Announcing the death of Winston Sheffield, esteemed man of law. May you stand in awe of God's presence and repent your sins. In his eyes we are all equal.' He looked up at Brad. 'Winston Sheffield. Oh, shit. What date was he murdered?'

Brad pulled out his phone and searched online. 'Fifteenth of March.'

'The day *after* the ad was published.'

'So, what exactly are you suggesting? That Carmichael placed a bullshit advert telling the world he was going to kill Sheffield the following day?'

'He's playing with us,' Jarrod said, thinking out loud.

He picked up the last newspaper lying on the floor, fumbling through the pages until he came to the classifieds. Another bogus obituary notice had been circled.

Brad looked over his shoulder and read it out. 'Announcing the untimely death of Frankie Arnold, long have you endured your unfortunate life. Your sins have been cast away by the flames, into God's hand you will be delivered, then you will suffer the final judgement.'

Jarrod looked at the paper's date. 16th November. The date of Frankie Arnold's murder had been seared into his memory. Arnold died on 17th November.

Jarrod threw the newspaper down and sprung to his feet. 'Judge Atkins! He's in danger. If Carmichael is sticking to his pattern, then he might already be on his way to the city.'

'What? To kill Judge Atkins?'

Jarrod didn't answer. He turned to the sergeant. 'Can you get an urgent message to the State Government Security Service? If Atkins is in court today, they need to find him and get him out of there. He's the next intended victim!'

'I'm on it!' The sergeant pulled out his phone and strode out the door. His hurried footfalls faded away.

Jarrod took a deep breath and exhaled slowly to control his heartrate. He ran his eyes over the shed's features, noting details, searching through fresh eyes for anything he might have missed. He noticed something below the workbench, hidden beneath a canvas tarpaulin. Moving to it, he uncovered two bulky chemical containers with handles and screw top lids. He leant down to read the labels. One read “Ammonium Nitrate” and the other “Hydrogen Peroxide”. Hazardous chemical warning labels shouted from each.

Brad looked over Jarrod’s shoulder. ‘Um, I hope I’m wrong. But aren’t those used to make explosives?’

FORTY-SIX

THUMP! Judge Atkins slammed a beefy fist on his desk. 'I will not be intimidated by some deranged lunatic! Do you understand?'

The head of court security stood rigid, arms crossed, hands clutching tattooed biceps. 'But Your Honour…' he began, his tone conciliatory.

'No, Malcolm. I won't have it,' the judge cut in. 'You're telling me this, *person*, is coming after me because of a bogus obituary notice in a newspaper? Don't be absurd.'

'Well, that's the police theory. They've requested a lockdown of the courthouse.'

'Nonsense! I am in the middle of a trial. I'm due back in court in ten minutes.' He shook his head, resolute. 'No. Absolutely not. Do what you must. Put in place whatever security you see fit, but the trial will continue, nonetheless. I do not want any disruptions. Am I clear?'

'Yes, Your Honour. I'll see to it immediately.' The security chief about-faced and left the judge alone in his chambers.

***

Downstairs in the foyer of the Supreme Court building, a contingent of uniformed police and State Government Security personnel took up positions at various checkpoints. Floor by floor, police dog units swept the building for explosives. Anyone entering the building was propped and searched, their identification checked. Police field commanders barked orders. Security officers stood guard at elevators, stairwells and all entry and exit points.

In the mayhem, the vagrant went unnoticed as he stepped inside the crowded foyer and padded towards a security turnstile.

A security officer pounced on him. 'Hey old man, you can't come in here. Out you go.'

Gnarled hands in fingerless gloves reached out from the sleeves of a tattered trench coat. 'He said to give this to you.' The vagrant produced a shoebox and presented it to the officer.

'Whoa! Step back with that.' The officer splayed his hands and angled his body. 'Who told you that?' He looked past the vagrant towards the front entrance. 'Who gave this to you?' he demanded when the vagrant didn't respond.

'Him.' The vagrant stretched a bent finger to the glass doors. 'That strange fella at the bus stop. He paid me a hundred bucks to give it to you. Must be somethin' important.'

The officer scanned the busy sidewalk outside. A gaggle of businessmen and women set off across the street as the pedestrian light went green. Gesticulating into mobile phones, the herd of suits passed. Through the clearing of bodies, the officer spotted a man leaning against the bus stop across the street. Arms folded, the man's face was shrouded inside the hood of a pullover, a cap tilted down over his eyes. The man gave him a wave.

The officer pointed an index finger at the vagrant and raised his voice. 'Don't you move!' He spoke into his radio handset. 'Urgent! Urgent! Suspicious package! Main foyer.'

'What?' said the vagrant, tilting his head to the side with a confused frown. 'Don't you want to see what it is?' He lifted the lid and peeked inside.

'No!' the officer yelled. 'Don't open it!'

Boom! The explosion ripped through the foyer. *Whoomph!* Searing air sucked into a vacuum, exploding windows from the shockwave. Shrapnel and glass shards tore flesh and shattered bones. The entire building shook. A shrieking alarm drowned out the screams and cries of anguish. Water spurted from sprinklers.

People scattered. Some crawled, others ran, slipping on debris and water. Others writhed in agony, covered in blood, clothes shredded. Bodies lay motionless. The vagrant and security officer were both dead.

Through a smoky haze, Kaleb Carmichael sauntered past the carnage. He entered unnoticed, unchallenged in the confusion.

***

Up in courtroom number two, a shudder vibrated the bar table and furniture. The Coat of Arms plaque came free of its wall mounting and slid down the wall behind Judge Atkins. A glass of water toppled from the witness stand and bounced, then shattered. Everyone in the courtroom stampeded to the door, creating a bottleneck of bodies squeezing to escape out into the corridor. The head of security pushed his way against the surging crowd and ushered Judge Atkins out the back door.

'Stay here, Your Honour.' The security officer spoke with authority, now in command. 'You'll be safe. I need to go downstairs and see what the hell is going on. It's important you don't move. Do you understand?'

'Yes, yes. I'm not going anywhere,' said Judge Atkins, shaken but still dignified. As the door slammed behind the security officer, he tossed his wig on his desk and waited alone in his private chambers. Muffled alarms rose through the carpeted floor. He paced up and down, wringing his hands together. *Was it a terrorist attack? Maybe a plane crash?* Being cooped up in his chambers while chaos unfolded downstairs was more than he could bear. He reached for the hip flask hidden in the top drawer of his mahogany desk and took a swig of whiskey.

He gazed out the window at flashing blue and red lights and people scampering back and forth. Behind his back, the door to his chambers opened. 'Ah, good. You're back, Malcolm,' he said without turning around. 'What the hell is going on down there?'

No answer. He turned and shot a hand to his mouth. The stranger's muscular frame filled the doorway, his face disfigured. One edge of his mouth rose to a menacing half grin, as if his top lip had been caught on a fishing hook. The other side of his face drooped as though he'd suffered a stroke. He was holding a bloodied knife by his side.

Judge Atkins froze. 'Who… who are you?' His voice tremored. 'What do you want?'

The man stared at him.

'Malcolm!' cried Judge Atkins, his voice high pitched. 'Malcolm! I need your help now!'

The man stepped inside the judge's chambers, lavishly furnished with ornate trimmings. Judge Atkins pressed his back against the polished oak cabinet crammed with leather-bound law books.

The man closed the door behind him, easing the latch until it clicked. 'Malcolm isn't coming.' He moved to the judge's desk and picked up the wig, inspecting it like it was roadkill. He wiped the blood from the blade with it.

Judge Atkins' eyes bulged, his mouth gaping.

'We meet again, *Judge*.'

'Do I know you?' the judge whimpered.

The man's eyes narrowed. 'Oh, you know me.' His eyes studied the judge from head to toe. 'That's a fancy gown you're wearing. Does it have wings? Can you fly, *Judge*?'

Amid the confusion and noise down on the street, no one heard the smashing window above, or the screams of Judge Atkins as his arms and legs flailed. No one looked up when he hurtled to the ground. He slammed headfirst into the concrete pavement, his head exploding like a dropped watermelon. His broken body bounced and tumbled down the stairs, coming to rest in a bloodied heap.

FORTY-SEVEN

JARROD and Brad were en route to the city when the urgent broadcast came over the police radio.

'All units, all units! Proceed priority code 1, priority code 1, to the Supreme Court building, Phillip Street, City. Confirmed job code ten-eighty. Standby for more information.'

The radio crackled to life with a barrage of transmissions as units responded with their locations and ETAs.

Brad's head snapped around to face Jarrod. 'What's a ten-eighty?'

Jarrod swallowed and forced out the word. 'Explosion.'

'Ah shit! Do you think it could be… him?'

'Has to be. Hold on.' Jarrod flicked a switch and the hi-lo siren bleated. The dash-mounted lights strobed, reflecting a blue and red glow against the windscreen. He planted his foot and the engine whined as he weaved through traffic. Jarrod lost all sense of time, tunnel vision setting in as he negotiated the twists and turns of the city streets. The roads were a mess, jammed bumper to bumper at every turn. Traffic couldn't get into the city and those trying to get out were wedged tight, inching their way into tight spaces. By some miracle, cars reacted to the flashing lights and siren of their police vehicle, mounting curbs to create a narrow corridor for them to carve their way into the city.

The courts precinct came into view as Jarrod crawled the car through a blockade of vehicles and scattering of people spilling out onto the streets. Police vehicles formed a makeshift exclusion zone outside the Supreme Court building. He pulled into a gap between two marked police cars and they got out. Jarrod prodded his ear canals and opened his jaw to quell the high-pitched ringing from the siren, but the din outside was just as bad. The air was heavy and pulsated with a hum of fire engine pumps, honking horns, sirens and voices yelling and screaming. Jarrod and Brad held up their badges and were waved through by uniformed officers who kept onlookers at bay behind the perimeter.

Jarrod approached a constable, raising his voice over the hubbub. 'Who's in charge here?'

Her eyes bounced between Jarrod and Brad, studying their bandaged hands, sooty faces and blood-stained shirts. She shrugged, seeming to decide it was none of her business and all part of the shit show unfolding around her. She pointed towards a huddle of police and fire commanders. 'The brass are all over there. Good luck getting anywhere near them, though. Their arses are hanging out of their pants.'

Jarrod and Brad entered the fray, tussling their way through the mayhem, dodging panic-stricken people covered in dust, their clothes charred. Paramedics corralled bloodied survivors who wandered dazed and confused amid the smoke and debris. Water leaked onto the pavement from heavy hoses, like a tangle of fat earthworms, feeding water to firefighters battling flames inside the building's foyer.

A woman appeared out of nowhere, her face covered in blood. She bumped into Brad, clutching at his shirt. 'Help me! He's still in inside. Please, no one will help me!'

'Where? Who's still inside?' he said, holding the woman by her arms as her knees buckled.

'My husband. He was with me when… when it happened. I can't find him anywhere.'

'Stay calm,' said Brad. 'We're the police. We'll help you.' He lowered her to the ground and she sobbed, her body dissolving into his. 'We'll find him.' He looked at Jarrod with a pained expression, his eyebrows drawn in. He shook his head and shrugged, his eyes saying he didn't like her chances.

People streamed out of the building, some uninjured, some limping and others being helped to walk. Lifeless bodies were carried out, arms dangling over the sides of stretchers. Paramedics triaged the wounded as more firefighters filed into the building.

Jarrod caught the movement of a skulking figure in the corner of his eye. Something about the way the man moved seemed at odds with the situation. Head bowed and hooded, hands buried in the pockets of his pullover, the man sauntered out of the building with a spring in his step, purposeful. Jarrod's eyes followed him. The way the man moved, shoulders hunched, was familiar. The man looked back over his shoulder as he peeled away from a group of people hurrying from the building. For a split-second, Jarrod saw his face and his breaths quickened. In that moment, the realisation, the certainty, his gut wrenched. Through the smoke and sea of faces, amid the noise and chaos, he glimpsed Kaleb Carmichael just as he turned onto the street and disappeared.

Jarrod ran, barging through the crowd, jostling against bodies towards the street.

'Hey! Where are you going?' Brad yelled.

Jarrod only had eyes for Carmichael. Nothing else mattered. There was no time to hesitate, to explain what he had seen. He pushed on. Brad called after him until his voice was drowned out in the mayhem.

Through a gap in the crowd, the back of Carmichael reappeared but, in another instant, he was gone. Jarrod squeezed through onto the street where he had a clear line of sight. As though sensing he was being followed, Carmichael turned and cocked his head to one side. Their eyes met. Time froze as they faced off in the middle of the street. Distracted by the pandemonium, no one seemed to notice them. They were inside their own bubble, invisible to the outside world.

Carmichael's expression was devoid of emotion, a rigid thousand-yard stare. His eyes squinted and he raised his hand to form a gun with his thumb and forefinger, aiming it at Jarrod. He pressed the imaginary trigger and blew the smoke from the finger muzzle. His face contorted into a half grin. Side-stepping, he disappeared into a side alley.

Jarrod drew his Glock from his ankle holster and willed his legs to move. Their response was slow at first, but he ignored the pain biting at his ribs and drove one leg in front of the other until he was sprinting. His shoes skidded as he turned into the laneway. Up ahead, Carmichael was streaking away.

'Stop! Armed police!' Jarrod yelled. 'Stop or I'll shoot!'

Carmichael ignored him and surged ahead. He was too far away for Jarrod to take a shot. Jarrod ran after him, his lungs burning. He willed himself forward, following Carmichael, who turned into an underground car park. When Jarrod reached the entrance, he threw his back against a concrete pillar and sucked in air to calm his breathing. He took three deep breaths and spun into the open driveway, gun trained ahead. His heart thumped in his chest as he drew in air with short gasps.

A figure darted into the shadows beyond the boom gate and disappeared into a maze of parked cars and pillars. Jarrod steadied himself and followed, fixing his sights straight ahead. When he reached the unmanned toll booth, he ducked under the boom gate. His hands were shaking, the gun heavy in his sweaty grip. The ringing in his ears grew louder in the hollowness of the vast concrete bunker. The air was cool and stale, the light dim under the artificial glow of fluorescent bulbs. One flickered overhead, *tink-tink, tink-tink*. A halo of strobing light obscured his peripheral vision. He blinked and continued deeper into the car park.

A silhouette weaved in and out of cars, cloaked within the shadows. Jarrod followed the echoing footfalls leading to the far end of the car park. He caught his first clear glimpse of Carmichael as he zigzagged behind concrete columns before making a dash towards the basement ramp. Jarrod aimed his gun, prepping the trigger. Stabilising his stance, he balanced his shooting platform, just as he'd been trained. He inhaled and exhaled slowly, closing one eye as he aligned the gun's sights on Carmichael's centre of mass. He hesitated. Carmichael was still in his sights, within range. Jarrod lowered his gun. He couldn't shoot the man in the back.

Carmichael disappeared down the ramp. Jarrod sprinted after him and rounded the corner just as Carmichael reached the basement. He glanced back at Jarrod over his shoulder and bolted out of sight. Jarrod ran down the slope, sensing he was gaining ground. He turned into the basement, this time not bothering to take cover. His legs burned and his arms were heavy. He scanned the gun. It was much darker down there, no natural sunlight. A neon exit sign glowed in the gloom above a fire door, but Carmichael hadn't headed towards the exit. He was hiding somewhere in the grid of parked cars.

Jarrod flinched as a lightbulb shattered up ahead. Glass tinkled to the floor. He pivoted as another bulb smashed, this time further to his right. Then another. Carmichael was circling around him, taking out the lights as he went. Section by section the car park descended into darkness. Jarrod slowed, clearing each row of cars as he moved from a lit area towards a dark corner of the car park. He took cover behind a pillar. Everything fell silent. A shuffling of feet broke the eerie stillness and it went quiet again. The space around Jarrod felt more confined as the walls closed in on him. A wave of vertigo brought on a bout of dizziness. He squinted to regain focus in the gloom.

Through the ringing of his ears, his own breathing reverberated inside his head. He flattened his body against the pillar, closed his eyes and listened. Seconds slipped by. In the silence, the ceiling above vibrated from the movement of the world above. Gusts of wind shuddered elevator shafts and the heavy bustling of traffic echoed from the streets. It occurred to Jarrod that in the chaos, no one would have seen where he ran off to. It all happened so fast. No one knew where he was. He was alone with a cold-blooded killer.

He jumped when a shrill voice broke the silence.

'*Detective O'Connor*!' Carmichael giggled. Playful. Mischievous. 'Did you enjoy the show, watching Frankie burn to death?'

Jarrod held his breath, not wanting to give away his location. He crouched into a kneeling position, making himself smaller.

'And you tracked me down to the farm. Good for you,' continued Carmichael, condescending. 'Took you long enough. Thought you dumb arse coppers would never work it out. I have to say, though, I enjoyed watching that shit box burn to the ground. Some bad memories in that place. Of all the days, my *big* day, along came you and your mate, like two good little piggies. It was meant to be. A greater force was at play. And you made it so easy.' He chuckled, humourless and callous. 'I see you made it out. Well done on that, by the way. You got some balls. I'll give you that. But that's how the game's played, you see. The universe decides the outcome, makes the rules. I place my faith in it, always. As much as I was hoping you and your mate would be turned into crispy pork, it just wasn't your time. Not yet anyway. Besides, it brought us together – right here, right now. Just you and me.' He let the silence draw out.

Jarrod clenched his jaw to stifle his rapid breathing. He remained still, clutching the gun's handle in a single-handed grip. Every part of his body ached and burned. Fresh cuts, burning throat and lungs, bruised ribs, jelly legs – the day had claimed him, chewed him up and spat him out.

'Cat got your tongue, copper?' Carmichael jeered, his words bouncing off the walls.

Movement circled around. A lightbulb smashed and another pocket of light snuffed out. The darkness deepened.

'Do you think you can end this all by yourself?' Carmichael shouted, this time from a location Jarrod couldn't pinpoint. 'You have no idea what you're up against.'

'So, tell me, *Kaleb*,' Jarrod blurted, fed up with the games.

'Oh, it speaks. Very good.'

An uncomfortable silence lingered.

'Well, if you must know,' Carmichael's voice sounded closer. 'There's a greater plan, but I doubt the likes of you would understand.'

Jarrod laughed out loud. He couldn't help himself. It wasn't funny, it was pathetic. 'I've heard this self-righteous bullshit before. Okay, I get it. You had step-daddy issues. You wanted your revenge. But those two girls, the old woman. That's just sick.'

No reply. The slightest hint of movement, drawing closer.

Jarrod changed position, crouching as he slid behind another pillar. 'Come on, got nothing to say?'

'He told me about you,' said Carmichael from the shadows. He seemed close.

'Who did? Vincent? How did you know him?' Jarrod moved again and slid behind a four-wheel drive.

'Ah, all in good time, my friend. I'll tell you all about it someday, I promise.'

Jarrod moved around the vehicle and aimed his gun across the bonnet towards Carmichael's voice. He slowed his breathing and waited.

A figure emerged from behind the pillar, where only moments earlier, Jarrod had been hiding. 'Aarrghh!' Carmichael flailed a hunting knife, the blade swishing the air and striking the pillar with a metallic clang. The blow would have taken Jarrod's head off.

Jarrod whistled, a cheeky two-toned tune.

Carmichael's eyes followed the sound, his face a twisted scowl. Their gazes met.

Jarrod aimed, prepped and squeezed the trigger. *Boom! Boom! Boom!* Three shots in quick succession, deafening. The explosions were amplified in the cavernous space, echoing like the cracks of a stockman's whip. Orange sparks of ignited gunpowder spat from the gun's muzzle.

Jarrod couldn't tell where all three shots had landed, but one clipped Carmichael in the shoulder and he spun like a twirling ice skater. Somehow, he found the will to stay upright. Jarrod moved out from behind the vehicle, following the sights of his gun.

'Motherfucker!' Carmichael screamed, clutching the bloody wound with his free hand. He still clung to the knife with the other. He grunted like a wild animal. Spittle drooled from the corner of his mouth. He gritted his teeth, his evil face contorted. Bloodlust in his eyes, he ran at Jarrod, knife extended like a warrior charging into battle. His broad shoulders heaved, his bulky frame casting a long shadow across the floor. He drew nearer.

Jarrod fired again. The shot missed, the bullet whizzing past Carmichael's ear. He kept coming. Jarrod stepped backwards, his grip loosening. He fired again, the recoiling gun almost jumping out of his hand. The shot struck Carmichael in the thigh and his leg crumpled under his weight. The knife fell from his grip and clattered to the floor. He leaned on his knuckles like a gorilla, groaning. He looked up at Jarrod and screamed, a determined cry of defiance. Retrieving the knife, he clambered to his feet. He took one step, then another, zombie-like. He waved the knife like he was swatting flies.

His expression changed and he let out a chuckle. 'Do you think this is it? Huh? Do you really think you've stopped me?'

'Drop the knife and get on the ground or you'll be leaving here in a body bag!'

'Ha, ha! You arrogant son of a bitch, you know nothing!'

'What don't I know?'

Carmichael stood still, blood spurting from his wounds. He lowered the knife, too weak to hold it. It slipped from his hand. 'The killing has only just begun. You can't stand in my way, no one can.' His words slurred. 'I've seen my own destiny. Only I know how this will play out.'

'How can you be so sure?'

'Oh, I'm sure. Every man creates his own fate, most just don't know it. You won't stand in my way, no matter how this ends today. I've seen my destiny.'

His stance wobbled and he staggered. He arched forwards and his body slumped onto the concrete floor. 'Revenge will be mine… you'll see,' he whispered as blood pooled around him.

Jarrod stepped over him and kicked the knife away. 'Yeah, we'll see about that.'

FORTY-EIGHT

Six months later

JARROD couldn't remember where he'd first heard the quote, but it had stuck with him. *'Before you embark on a journey of revenge, dig two graves.''*

Kaleb Carmichael's distorted concept of retribution had twisted his mind. As far as Jarrod was concerned, he was nothing more than a psychopath, albeit the product of an abusive childhood, but a brutal killer just the same.

Carmichael had survived the gunshot wounds. Dressed in prison browns, he stood in the dock to face judgement before the court of the people, his head shaved and face expressionless. Onlookers spilled out onto the veranda and the Lockyer courthouse lawns. The Supreme Court trial had lasted over a month but was finally over. It had been a harrowing ordeal for the witnesses and, of course, it had been a media circus. The evidence was overwhelming. Jarrod sat in the second row, behind Eric and Daniel Barkley.

The jury foreman rose to his feet, eyes glued to a piece of paper clutched in his shaking hands. A hush came over the crowded courtroom. He cleared his throat and spoke. 'The jury finds the defendant guilty on all charges.'

The courtroom erupted in cheers and applause. Carmichael was rigid as a statue, a permanent scowl chiselled into his face. Wrists cuffed to the front, fists clenched, the tensing sinew in his forearms was the only sign he was still a living, breathing human.

His head turned, his eyes seeking Jarrod's until they locked in a haunting gaze. A smile formed on his scarred lips as he raised his hands to his mouth. The index and middle fingers in one hand formed a V. He pointed to his own eyes and extended the V towards Jarrod. '*I'll be watching you,*' he mouthed.

When the courtroom rabble came to order, the judge announced the sentence. Life imprisonment with no option for parole.

A man's yelling cut through the crowd from the back of the room. All heads turned. People jostled as the man pushed his way through the crowd towards the dock.

'As God is my witness, I'll kill you!' yelled Tom Heidenreich. 'You took my little girl, you bastard! Life in prison is too good for you!' He lunged forward but was intercepted by two uniformed police officers who grabbed his arms. He struggled, twisting his body to break free. 'An eye for an eye!' he yelled. He spat toward Carmichael before he was led away.

Kaleb Carmichael held Jarrod's gaze and smiled.

FORTY-EIGHT

THE bailiff stood to attention as the judge shuffled from his seat behind the bench to the door to his chambers. The convicted killer was ushered by two Corrections officers out the side exit and downstairs to the awaiting prison van. Journalists pressed forward in the gallery, waving microphones and voice recorders. Jarrod could only sit and watch, his limbs numb.

As the courtroom emptied, the crowd filed downstairs and spilled onto the courthouse lawns, chanting '*rot in hell*' and '*bring back the death penalty*'. The crown prosecutor and defense barrister shook hands and chatted like old chums, lamenting over their performances. The curtain had dropped with no calls for an encore. The show was over. Their assistants shuffled papers and crammed law books into briefcases, checking their phones and discussing lunch options. When they all left, Jarrod sat alone with his thoughts. He closed his eyes and sighed, rubbing his temples.

A shrill scream erupted from outside. Jarrod's eyes snapped open. He jumped to his feet, bounding out of the courtroom to the veranda. Down on the lawns, the crowd scattered. People darted, ducking their heads as they ran.

Amid the confusion, two figures remained steadfast. Kaleb Carmichael and Tom Heidenreich. As Jarrod watched on, the next few seconds played out in slow motion. The barrel of a rifle was aimed at Carmichael's chest. Tom Heidenreich held the weapon up to his shoulder in readiness to fire. His arms trembled. Carmichael stared Tom down, stony-faced and unflinching.

The Corrections officers reacted. One fumbled for his sidearm as the other released his grip of Carmichael's arm and launched himself at Tom. The officer grabbed the barrel and jostled with Tom to gain control of the rifle. A deafening crack echoed across the grounds as the rifle discharged. People screamed and dropped to the ground, arms shielding their heads.

Just metres away, Eric Barkley stood rigid as a statue, clutching his abdomen. A crimson circle expanded on his shirt like an inkblot. He shot Tom Heidenreich a bewildered look. His eyes lowered to his bloodied hands. Sinking to his knees, he collapsed headfirst onto the grass. Daniel threw himself to his dying father's side. 'No!' he screamed. 'Dad, no!'

The first Corrections officer wrestled the gun from Tom's grip and tackled him to the ground. Carmichael swung his handcuffed fists, crunching them against the other officer's jaw. The officer stumbled and dropped his handgun. A police officer ran at Carmichael who reacted with a headbutt. Jarrod heard the crack of the officer's nose from up on the veranda.

Carmichael bent down and clutched the handgun with his cuffed hands, firing it towards more approaching officers. One officer took a hit to the leg and dropped, yelping in agony. Carmichael unclipped the unconscious officer's keys from his utility belt and fired another shot towards the police. The bullet zipped past them, smashing a first-floor window of the courthouse. Carmichael turned and ran down the sloping lawns towards a line of maple trees ahead of a burst of returning police gunfire. He dived, rolled and sprung to his feet, sprinting away.

Jarrod bounded down two flights of stairs. Out on the lawns, he pushed through the dispersing crowd and joined the foot chase. As Carmichael reached the line of trees, he turned and rapid-fired three more shots. Officers dived for cover. Jarrod pressed his body against the trunk of a fat tree. Carmichael set off again, disappearing down the slope of a grassy embankment, heading straight for the river.

Ahead of Jarrod, other officers rose to their feet and trudged onwards, guns trained in front. Glock in hand, Jarrod followed.

A splash.

'He's in the river!' an officer yelled.

'After him!' said another.

They fanned out and hurried over the crest of the slope towards the river. By the time Jarrod arrived, the other officers had been swallowed by a thick canopy of mangroves. He went in after them, not knowing the path Carmichael had taken. His shoes sunk in the mud as he entered a tangle of branches that clawed at the sleeves of his suit jacket. Mosquitos buzzed in his ears and he imagined leaches latching onto his flesh through his soggy socks. Inside the labyrinth of roots and creeping vines, the air stunk of stagnant sludge.

'He's ditched the handcuffs!' an officer called from somewhere in the quagmire to Jarrod's right.

The mud made a sucking noise as Jarrod's shoes sunk deeper. He grabbed an overhanging branch to steady himself. There was no getting through. He backed out of the mud, looking for an opening. It was no use. The mangroves were too thick. Carmichael hadn't come this way. He backtracked along the grassy embankment towards the excited voices of other officers. Standing in a narrow clearing on the water's edge, they pointed towards bubbles breaking the river's surface in the centre of expanding ringlets. The muddy water eddied as if it were hand-stirred hot chocolate. About fifty metres wide, the tidal river snaked its way through town. After a recent deluge, logs and debris bobbed to the surface, crashing into each other as they raced downstream.

'I saw him swimming out, but he was swept away,' said one officer. 'He went under and hasn't resurfaced.'

'Going in after him is suicide,' said another.

Jarrod pointed to where the river curled in a hairpin bend. 'The current will take him across to the far bank. We've got to get some guys over there.'

'It's a bloody sugar cane paddock.'

Jarrod pulled out his phone and called for backup. The news had already reached the station. Crews were being scrambled. Shit had already hit the fan.

While waiting for the Polair chopper to be deployed from the city, a Water Police vessel with divers arrived upriver from the coast. A police dog unit and tactical response officers had crossed the river over Nelson's bridge and carved a path through the cane fields in four-wheel drives.

Hours raced by. Afternoon bled into evening. Kaleb Carmichael had slipped away with the setting sun.

EPILOGUE

IN the wake of Kaleb Carmichael's escape, community backlash and media scrutiny were ruthless. The media had whipped themselves into a frenzy. Mobile phone vision of the chaos outside the courthouse did the rounds on social media. News broadcasts flashed mugshots of the wanted man on TV screens and online. Headlines shouted, *'Police Bungle – killer still at large'*. The state opposition leader demanded an inquiry into what he described as failings of the system that led to the debacle, and he made the obligatory calls for the police minister's resignation.

Eric Barkley was dead. Tom Heidenreich was charged with manslaughter and remained in custody. After his father's death, Daniel Barkley went completely off the rails.

A national manhunt was in full swing. Public confidence in the police department was at an all-time low. Weeks rolled by and despite unconfirmed sightings, Kaleb Carmichael had slipped through the net. He'd gone to ground. Jarrod lived with one eye looking over his shoulder, waiting for Carmichael to emerge from the shadows, to come after him. He hadn't resurfaced yet, but Jarrod knew that day would come.

Everyone had a theory about where Carmichael was or where he might emerge next. Speculation was rife that he would strike again soon. The media had joined the dots and made the links between his victims. What had first seemed like a random series of killings now made sense following analysis of Carmichael's past. It was clear he was working towards a plan. He had instilled fear in people's hearts and minds across the country. No one was safe. Jarrod knew he was biding his time; he would strike again.

One morning, about a month after Carmichael's escape, Jarrod had to get out of the office. The walls were closing in. He needed fresh air. His skin absorbed the sunshine, and the warmth of the pavement rose through the soles of his shoes. As he ambled through town, going nowhere in particular, he browsed shop windows. He caught his own reflection and his thoughts returned to Carmichael. He studied the faces in the street, paranoia getting the better of him.

A young couple came towards him, the man pushing a pram. The woman's eyes were drawn to Jarrod, and she held his gaze. She reached for her partner's forearm and her eyes widened. They stopped in front of Jarrod and the woman's expression softened. 'Excuse me, Detective O'Connor.'

Jarrod couldn't place them, yet she knew him. Maybe she'd seen his face in the media reports. The man gave a courteous nod and smiled.

'Yes. Can I help you?'

'Sorry to bother you,' said the woman. 'We've never met in person. I'm Julie, and this is my husband, Darren.'

'G'day,' said Darren, extending his hand.

Jarrod shook his hand, a sense of unease rising in him. 'I'm sorry. Do I know you?'

Julie glanced at Darren and he gave her a reassuring nod. 'It's okay, love. Tell him.'

'Tell me what?'

'Well, you don't know us but… you know this little one.' She pulled the pram's cover back, revealing an infant squishing a gooey teething rusk between her fingers. She kicked her plump legs with excitement and blew bubbles of drool.

'Do you recognize her?' said Julie.

Jarrod bent down and studied the little human. 'She's a cute little thing.' He looked at the couple, who gazed back at him expectantly. 'I'm sorry, I don't understand.'

'This is Zalia,' said Julie. 'She's fattened up since you last saw her.'

Sketchy memories flashed in Jarrod's mind. He remembered the neglected baby in that filthy, cramped van. He remembered her crazed mother and her father, the man who came for him, deranged and driven by revenge. He visualised Karl Mundy's lifeless body lying in a pool of blood in the police station driveway. Jarrod clutched the healing bones of his wrist, a sharp pain biting.

'Zalia? I remember you now. Oh, wow! Haven't you grown.' Jarrod reached down and slimy little fingers wrapped around his index finger.

'She's in our full-time care now,' said Julie, beaming. 'We couldn't have kids of our own, so we registered as foster parents.'

Darren spoke. 'The people at Children's Services told us about her past, and what you did for her. She's changed our life.'

'Just doing my job.'

'No.' Darren shook his head. 'What you guys do is more than just a job. Look at that face. She's safe, she's happy. You did that. You brought her to us. We just wanted you to know that.' He looked at Julie and she smiled. 'We just wanted to say thank you.'

ABOUT THE AUTHOR

Jack Roney is a member of the Queensland Writers Centre, Australian Society of Authors and Australian Crime Writers Association. He lives with his family in Brisbane, Australia. His writing is inspired by over thirty years in law enforcement where he gained experience as an investigator, tactical skills and firearms instructor, police academy instructor, strategic policy writer and media officer. He draws on his experience as a former detective to bring authenticity and realism to his writing. He was a police consultant for the ABC television series Harrow. *The Demons Woke* is book 2 of a three-book series, with the first novel in the series, *The Angels Wept,* reaching the Wattpad Awards shortlist. He has completed writing courses with Curtis Brown Creative and Brisbane Writers Workshop and was selected for the Queensland Writers Centre residency program. His speculative fiction novel, *The Ghost Train and The Scarlet Moon*, was the runner-up in the Hawkeye Publishing Manuscript Development Prize.

www.jackroney.com.au

Book reviews can make or break a book. If you liked what you read today, please do consider posting a review on Goodreads or your favourite forum.

The Demons Woke is available at www.hawkeyebooks.com.au and all good bookstores and libraries.

BOOKS BY JACK RONEY

THE ANGELS WEPT (JARROD O'CONNOR #1)

THE DEMONS WOKE (JARROD O'CONNOR #2)

THE SHADOWS WATCH (JARROD O'CONNOR #3)

THE GHOST TRAIN AND THE SCARLET MOON